WOMEN AND ECONOMICS
AND OTHER WRITINGS

broadview editions
series editor: Martin R. Boyne

Charlotte Perkins Gilman, c. 1900. Photographer unknown. Photograph courtesy of the Library of Congress.

WOMEN AND ECONOMICS AND OTHER WRITINGS

Charlotte Perkins Gilman

edited by Rachel Elin Nolan

broadview editions

BROADVIEW PRESS – www.broadviewpress.com
Peterborough, Ontario, Canada

Founded in 1985, Broadview Press remains a wholly independent publishing house. Broadview's focus is on academic publishing; our titles are accessible to university and college students as well as scholars and general readers. With over 800 titles in print, Broadview has become a leading international publisher in the humanities, with world-wide distribution. Broadview is committed to environmentally responsible publishing and fair business practices.

© 2023 Rachel Elin Nolan

All rights reserved. No part of this book may be reproduced, kept in an information storage and retrieval system, or transmitted in any form or by any means, electronic or mechanical, including photocopying, recording, or otherwise, except as expressly permitted by the applicable copyright laws or through written permission from the publisher.

Library and Archives Canada Cataloguing in Publication

Title: Women and economics and other writings / Charlotte Perkins Gilman ; edited by Rachel Elin Nolan.
Names: Gilman, Charlotte Perkins, 1860-1935, author. | Nolan, Rachel Elin, editor.
Series: Broadview editions.
Description: Series statement: Broadview editions | Includes bibliographical references.
Identifiers: Canadiana (print) 20220441898 | Canadiana (ebook) 20220441936 | ISBN 9781554814978 (softcover) | ISBN 9781460408186 (EPUB) | ISBN 9781770488823 (PDF)
Subjects: LCSH: Women—Economic conditions.
Classification: LCC HQ1426 .G45 2023 | DDC 305.42—dc23

Broadview Editions
The Broadview Editions series is an effort to represent the ever-evolving canon of texts in the disciplines of literary studies, history, philosophy, and political theory. A distinguishing feature of the series is the inclusion of primary source documents contemporaneous with the work.

Advisory editor for this volume: Colleen Humbert

Broadview Press handles its own distribution in North America:
PO Box 1243, Peterborough, Ontario K9J 7H5, Canada
555 Riverwalk Parkway, Tonawanda, NY 14150, USA
Tel: (705) 743-8990; Fax: (705) 743-8353
email: customerservice@broadviewpress.com

For all territories outside of North America, distribution is handled by Eurospan Group.

Broadview Press acknowledges the financial support of the Government of Canada for our publishing activities.

Typesetting and assembly: True to Type Inc., Claremont, Canada
Cover Design: Lisa Brawn

PRINTED IN CANADA

Contents

Acknowledgements • 7
Introduction • 9
Charlotte Perkins Gilman: A Brief Chronology • 35
A Note on the Texts • 39

Women and Economics: A Study of the Economic Relation Between Men and Women as a Factor in Social Evolution • 43

Selected Poems from *In This Our World and Other Poems* • 217
    The Rock and the Sea • 217
    Heaven • 219
    Where Memory Sleeps • 219
    What Then? • 220
    Baby Love • 220
    For Us • 221
    "We, as Women" • 221
    To the Young Wife • 223
    Mother to Child • 224
    The Survival of the Fittest • 226
    An Obstacle • 227
    The Cart before the Horse • 229
    "The Poor Ye Have Always with You" • 229
    Waste • 230
    Nationalism • 231

Selections from *Suffrage Songs and Verses* • 233
    The Socialist and the Suffragist • 233
    The Malingerer • 234
    The Anti-Suffragists • 235
    The "Anti" and the Fly • 236
    Women Do Not Want It • 237
    Song for Equal Suffrage • 239

Something to Vote For • 241

Appendix A: Socialism, Feminism, Humanism • 261
1. Charlotte Perkins Gilman, "Masculine, Feminine, and Human," *Woman's Journal* (9 July 1892) • 262
2. Charlotte Perkins Gilman, "Women as a Class," *Impress* (7 November 1894) • 265
3. Charlotte Perkins Gilman, "When Socialism Began," *American Fabian* (November 1897) • 267
4. Charlotte Perkins Gilman, "Socialism and Patriotism," *American Fabian* (May 1898) • 269

Introduction

Charlotte Perkins Gilman (1860–1935) ranks among the leading American public intellectuals of her generation. At the height of her career, Gilman's ideas concerning women's dependency upon men were known to Americans of all classes and backgrounds. Women's rights activists credited her with "revolutionizing the attitude of mind in the entire country ... as to women's place" ("Charlotte Gilman Dies").

Gilman was also a remarkably prolific writer. She published numerous theoretical works, including *Women and Economics: A Study of the Economic Relation Between Men and Women as a Factor in Social Evolution* (1898), *Concerning Children* (1900), *The Home: Its Work and Influence* (1903), *Human Work* (1904), and *The Man-Made World; or, Our Androcentric Culture* (1911). She also published novels, short stories, poems, book reviews, and hundreds of nonfiction articles. Between 1909 and 1916, she wrote, edited, and self-published *The Forerunner*, a magazine devoted to her two enduring intellectual commitments: socialism and the emancipation of women. Gilman's autobiography, *The Living of Charlotte Perkins Gilman*, was published posthumously in 1935, and it remains an important source of information about the relationship between her personal experiences and professional writing.

The scholarly debate concerning Gilman's body of writing has been thoroughgoing and rigorous, although noticeably skewed toward Gilman's fiction. Today, a reader's likely first encounter with Gilman will be as the author of the 1892 feminist classic "The Yellow Wall-paper." As Gilman scholar Judith A. Allen observes, almost three quarters of the nearly eight hundred scholarly publications concerning Gilman's oeuvre address this short story, which remains one of the most vivid literary representations of nineteenth-century women's physical and mental confinement (7). A substantial amount of scholarship addresses Gilman's novels, including *What Dianthe Did* (1909), *The Crux* (1910), and *Herland* (1915), works of fiction that all explore themes relating to sex, marriage, and the family.

Over the past thirty years, Gilman's position on race and ethnicity has emerged as a topic of particular concern and even controversy. Several important studies published in the 1990s and early 2000s found in Gilman's writing evidence that her ideas were rooted in a preoccupation with white superiority. Charges of racism have been levied against texts by Gilman that deal explicitly with race and race relations—especially her essays "A Suggestion on the Negro Problem" (1908) and "Is America Too Hospitable?" (1923)—although some studies find that Gilman's entire oeuvre betrays an abiding attachment to racist ideas. Gail Bederman and Louise Michele Newman have argued that Gilman elevated white women's status by reducing the sexual difference between white women and white men while widening the gap between whites and nonwhites. Across her works, including in *Women and Economics*, Gilman "was merely proposing to replace one kind of exclusion with another," Bederman writes (168). Alys Eve Weinbaum cautions that scholars who fail to acknowledge the "centrality of racialized reproductive thinking to [Gilman's] feminism" ultimately "mimic ... the problems endemic to her feminism" (273).

Other scholars have argued that reading Gilman's work in relation to historical context offers a more complete picture of her intentions and contributions. Gilman's contemporaries, including some African American progressive intellectuals, regarded Gilman's analysis of women's economic condition as instructive. Educator Anna Julia Cooper regarded Gilman's life as "full of inspiring interest and stimulating encouragement" (Washington 10), while sociologist W.E.B. Du Bois drew upon Gilman's insights in his work highlighting the exploitation of Black women workers (16). Taking such evidence into account, Allen characterises arguments that Gilman was racist as "reductionist" and even "antihistorical." She observes that Gilman did not associate with the many "racist popularizers" of her day, rejected the idea that race is biologically determined, reviled anti-Semitism, and spoke out against the use of literacy testing as a qualification for voting—a position that set her at odds with many leaders and members of the American women's suffrage campaign. Recent scholarship on Gilman has continued in this vein. For instance, Kimberley A. Hamlin, in her study *From Eve to Evolution*, finds that Gilman "helped craft the arguments against biological determinism and biological hierarchies, not just for white women but for everyone" (21).

But it was *Women and Economics* that earned Gilman international recognition as the leading American feminist intellectual of the late nineteenth and early twentieth centuries. This text was translated into seven languages and reached a ninth edition in the author's lifetime. *Women and Economics* contains Gilman's most important and influential analysis, including her signature idea that the relationship between men and women is at core "sexuo-economic." In the nineteenth century, most American women attempted to source personal safety and economic security from individual wage-earning men in the context of marriage. Gilman set out to show that female dependency was not a natural but rather a cultivated phenomenon. To demonstrate this, she analyses marriage and the family as institutions, seeking to make visible their cultural and economic frameworks. It is only by engaging with *Women and Economics*, then, that we can understand Gilman's enduring contribution to diverse fields—including economics, sociology, feminist theory, and political science.

In *Women and Economics*, Gilman is at once a sociologist and a cultural critic, but even as she engages a range of theoretical ideas and specialist studies she speaks as a public intellectual concerned with changing commonsense ideas about the role of women in American society. Readers at the time identified Gilman's work as a particularly lively and accessible treatment of the woman question, as documented in the book reviews collected in Appendix B. As is often the case with nineteenth-century women authors, Gilman's popular success stemmed in part from her astute understanding of her audience, a broad cross-section of reading Americans who would welcome frank analysis and good humour. Her frequent allusions to Shakespeare and popular poets such as Elizabeth Barrett Browning (1806–61) and Alfred Lord Tennyson (1809–92) would have been well received by nineteenth-century readers, who would have easily recognized such references as an appeal to shared culture.

At the same time, Gilman presents her readers with a bold and devastating depiction of the family, middle-class America's most dearly cherished institution. Gilman was hardly the first to cast a critical eye on marriage and motherhood. Numerous American women writers, including Judith Sargent Murray (1751–1820), Margaret Fuller (1810–50), Sara Payson Willis (1811–72), and Kate Chopin (1850–1904), explored the complex dimensions of American women's vulnerability. Additionally, Caroline Wells Healy Dall (1822–1912) and Virginia Penny (1826–1913) were early pioneers in feminist economic thinking. Moreover, well-known male intellectuals of the Progressive Era were interested in uncovering women's perplexing role in the economy. In *Theory of the Leisure Class* (1899), Thorstein Veblen analysed how upper-class women played an essentially consumerist role in the economy, describing their activity as an example of what he termed "conspicuous consumption" (68). But Gilman's analysis offers a much fuller picture of adult women's degradation. Marriage, for Gilman, is a transactional affair in which women exchange sex and maternal services for material resources and protection offered by men, and she elaborates her argument with startling frankness: "The girl must marry: else how live? ... He is the market, the demand. She is the supply." Strikingly, Gilman brings her argument to women themselves, urging women to recognize their role in perpetuating the sexual economy: "with the best intentions the mother serves her child's economic advantage by preparing her for the market.... It is common. It is most evil" (p. 91).

Such indictments of women, which Gilman makes frequently and unsparingly throughout *Women and Economics*, were not lost on Gilman's contemporaries, as the reviews in Appendix B demonstrate, and noting this aspect of the treatise helps us to understand its larger concerns. Gilman was a humanist, and she addressed women directly because she believed that women had an obligation to exercise their physical, intellectual, and moral powers for the betterment of all humankind. The problem, as Gilman saw it, is not that women suffer at the hands of men, painful as that might be. Rather, economic dependence curtails the possibility of growth and leaves women, as a class, in a state of stagnation. The inability of half the population to fulfil its potential, she writes, "acts upon us continually as a retarding influence, hindering the expansion of the spirit of social love and service on which our very lives depend" (p. 214). In some instances, Gilman cautions female readers against even righteous anger. The suffering of centuries past, she writes, "should never be mentioned nor thought of by a womanhood that knows its power" (p. 115). Gilman's criticism of women and her message of forbearance may strike twenty-first-century readers as judgmental or disappointingly restrained. But these features of her writing fit with her larger intellectual project of encouraging more women to overcome cultural impediments to contribute more fully to human progress.

Indeed, Gilman is at her best when she is provoking readers to think more deeply about their unexamined assumptions, which she refers to as "the commonplace conditions of every-day life" (p. 86). Her powerful analytical ability is on display in Chapter 5, where she analyses the underlying tendencies that lead individuals to perpetuate patterns of behaviour that, upon closer examination, are quickly revealed as detrimental to the individual and collective good. Part of the problem has to do with the human tendency toward fixity of habit: "what we are used to we do not notice," Gilman writes (p. 86). A further challenge stems from the difficulty of mapping individual experience onto larger systems of meaning—"it is easier to personalize than generalize" (p. 88). By presenting such concerns as tendencies among people *generally*—as "simple laws of brain action"—rather than personal failings on behalf of any one individual, Gilman encourages critical reflection without provoking defensiveness (p. 86).

And yet Gilman is conscious that merely revealing the spuriousness of society's ideals will not ultimately inspire change but will, more likely, incite fear of the unknown. She writes that "[e]ven if convinced that a change of condition will remove the source of injury, [human beings] ... fear to be disturbed, lest their last state be worse than their first" (p. 151). Gilman argues explicitly that social reform will be successful only if demands that people relinquish their attachments to inherited values be accompanied by a proposal for some other—better— way of living. And Gilman, as I outline below, was not short on ideas.

This volume also includes a selection of Gilman's poetry and reproduces her 1911 one-act play *Something to Vote For*. This necessarily limited sample of additional writing, along with the four Appendices, allows readers to appreciate Gilman's intellectual and stylistic range. This introductory essay will provide an overview of Gilman's life and the intellectual and reform contexts in which she developed her ideas, and it will demonstrate how these contexts inform Gilman's major ideas and arguments. Throughout, I will emphasize how *Women and Economics* intervened in public debates about women's economic roles at a time when Victorian ideals concerning the family as the mainstay of society were undergoing a transformation.

Charlotte Perkins Gilman's Biography

Charlotte Perkins was born in 1860, on the eve of the American Civil War, and she died in 1935, in the middle of the Great Depression. Her life spanned one of the most significant periods of change in American history. In addition to spectacular economic inequality and class conflict, the nation wrestled with social problems concerning race, gender, and immigration. Gilman participated in this culture of unrest. From a young age, she perceived herself to be full of "ideas, percepts ... of wide reach" and possessed of "an enormous sense of responsibility" (*Living* 13).

Gilman was born in the prosperous banking and manufacturing city of Hartford, Connecticut. She was the younger of two children born to Mary Ann Fitch Westcott (1829–93) and Frederick Beecher Perkins (1828–99). Gilman's childhood, which she describes in her autobiography, was not a happy one. The "delicate and beautiful" Mary was a diligent but ineffectual parent. "If unswerving love, tireless service, intense and efficient care, and the concentrated devotion of a lifetime that knew no other purpose make a good mother, mine was one of the best," Gilman would later write in her autobiography (*Living* 6). Gilman criticised this model of childrearing across her writing. Several of her poems, including "To the Young Wife" (p. 223), "Mother to Child" (p. 224), and "Baby Love" (p. 220), invoke an alternative model of motherhood, one in which a woman subordinates maternal care to productive work. In *Women and Economics*, Gilman takes a severe view of women such as her mother, whose affection for their children is not moderated by reason but is "too intensely personal" (p. 192). While Gilman regretted her mother's limitations, she was probably more deeply hurt by her intellectual and harsh-tempered father, who deserted his wife and children when Gilman was still very young. Her experiences of rejection during her early years had a lasting impact, and Gilman suffered from depression and insecurity throughout much of her adult life.

At the same time, Gilman's extended family was a source of tremendous inspiration. Hartford in the 1860s was an important intellectual centre. The city was home to numerous influential authors, including Gilman's paternal great-aunt, Harriet Beecher Stowe (1811–96), whose anti-slavery novel *Uncle Tom's Cabin* (1852) had made Stowe a household name. Gilman was immensely proud of her extended family. The Beechers were among the oldest families in New England, descendants of English settlers who arrived in the 1630s. Lyman Beecher (1775–1863), Gilman's great-grandfather, was a prominent clergyman. He was also a reformer who encouraged his parishioners to see themselves as "members of civil community" with a responsibility to work together to bring about desirable change. "You have heard inculcated," Beecher wrote, "the duty ... of uniting your exertions in accordance with the demands of our country" (143). Across her work, Gilman expresses tremendous optimism about the possibility that national institutions might be improved, and she urges fellow progressives to remain faithful to the promise of America (see, for example, Appendix A4). She shared her family's reformist convictions, and she spent her life arguing, as her great-aunt and great-grandfather had done, for greater social and moral cooperation among Americans. And yet, unlike her Beecher forebears, Gilman was a religious sceptic who grounded her social philosophy in scientific facts rather than the teachings of a church. In the years following the Civil War, many middle-class Americans began to question the authority of religious institutions, and Gilman as a young girl developed her own theory of moral agency. While still in her teens, she struggled to distance herself from what she describes in her autobiography as the "condition of compelled obedience" to external authorities and, instead, embarked upon a period of extensive study: "I set about the imperative task of building my own religion, based on knowledge," she writes (*Living* 38). Understanding rather than faith per se became Gilman's criterion for moral life. As a young girl, she could not have known the extent to which her scepticism was shared by a larger number of her peers, or that later in life she would develop friendships with other intellectuals who shared her critical views about the need for religious institutional reform.

By the time she reached young womanhood, Gilman found herself pulled in two directions. On the one hand, she craved the intimacy and mutual affection that women of her generation expected to find in marriage. On the other hand, she was plagued by an abiding fear that marriage would restrict her intellectual horizons. In May 1884, Gilman married the artist Charles Walter Stetson (1858–1911), and her fears about the incompatibility of marriage and female intellectual activity were, sadly, realized. Stetson's artistic work was immensely important to him, but he took a dim view of Gilman's own creative ambitions, preferring his wife to submit to keeping house. Stetson was also a sensualist who derived great pleasure from his interactions with the models he invited to his studio. In his diaries, Stetson drew a contrast between his wife and the "graceful" and "restful" young women who posed for him. Gilman, he complained, "subdued" such feminine virtues to her "activity" (Stetson 92).

Gilman suffered intensely because of her brief first marriage. Chapter Eight of her autobiography—titled "The Breakdown"—describes the "darkness, feebleness, and gloom" that descended upon her in the period following the birth of her only child, Katharine (1885–1979). Gilman and Stetson agreed to separate in autumn 1887 and eventually divorced. The separation and divorce proceedings became a matter of public record, and

Gilman suffered as her "name became a football for all the papers" (*Living* 143). A journalist for *The San Francisco Examiner* seized on the divorce as an opportunity to rehearse tired arguments about literary women, heaping derision on what the journalist called "sham 'clever' women," whose "posing ... dullness ... scribbling and gushing and vanity and discontent more than suffice to make miserable the best of men who may have the misfortune to be their husband" ("Women"). The divorce, together with the fallout in the press, had a lasting impact, and Gilman considered herself permanently damaged by the experience.

The years following Gilman's separation from Stetson were intellectually generative. She would stay in California until 1894. During these years, she published several important works, including the short story "The Yellow Wall-paper," which appeared in *New England Magazine* in January 1892, and a book of poetry, *In This Our World*, published in 1893. In addition, Gilman wrote numerous poems and plays, usually alone but sometimes in collaboration with her friend Grace Channing (1862–1937). Through her writing and speaking engagements, Gilman deepened her connection with women's movement activism. In her poem "Women of To-day" she entreated American women to reflect on their experiences, declaring, "There is no hope until you dare to know / The thing you are!" (*In This Our World* 38). Here, and elsewhere, Gilman took up themes and arguments that she would examine more fully in *Women and Economics*.

Even as she devoted herself to women's emancipation, Gilman gained notoriety for her work on behalf of Nationalism, a socialist movement that advocated for the nationalization of industry. In the poem "Similar Cases," originally published in the April 1891 issue of *Nationalist* magazine, Gilman engages with evolutionary theory to satirize conservative arguments opposing change. This poem established Gilman's reputation among leading progressive intellectuals, including Lester Frank Ward (1841–1913), who initiated a friendship with Gilman in 1895. Samples of Ward's writing, which influenced Gilman's own, are included in Appendix D2.

But the California years (1888–94) were also marked by ambivalence as Gilman attempted to support herself as a writer while also performing the chores of motherhood. The anxiety and doubts about the compatibility of motherhood and female creativity, which Gilman had initially experienced in the weeks and months immediately following her daughter's birth, did not subside, and "mothering ... often felt closer to smothering," as Cynthia J. Davis writes (133). Gilman delighted in Katharine, took pleasure in her relationship with her daughter, and, as her autobiography indicates, was closely involved in Katharine's emotional and intellectual development. But Katharine's presence was nonetheless a burden, and one that was compounded by Gilman's transient lifestyle and financial insecurity. Gilman's small earnings from writing and speaking were supplemented by donations from friends. She lived first in Pasadena and from there moved to Oakland. On the eve of a third move—this time to a boarding house in San Francisco—Gilman sent Katharine back east, where she was to live with her father and stepmother, Grace Channing. Just as Gilman's divorce was a source of public gossip, so her bold decision regarding her daughter's welfare left her vulnerable to censure.

Gilman's difficult—and frequently painful—life experiences likely deepened her emerging feminist consciousness. Gilman's "heightened awareness of misogyny around her," Allen writes, "led her to seek intellectual reinforcement and deeper knowledge of women's situation" (36). She never regretted her decision to divorce Walter, nor her decision to devote herself more fully to a life of intellectualism and creativity. In Chapter 14 of *Women and Economics*, she strongly defends the right of all women to engage in "close, direct, permanent connection with the needs and uses of society" (p. 197). Gilman, as much as any American writer, converted her personal experiences of trauma into curiosity, and this important feminist treatise is testimony to her resilience.

As Gilman's case demonstrates, by the close of the nineteenth century middle-class American women were no longer condemned to be permanently subsumed by the family but might elect, as Gilman herself had elected, to live a life more attuned to the goal of "true personal expression" (p. 197). Gilman devoted herself to writing and public speaking, embarking upon a lecture tour that took her across the nation (near the end of her life she had visited every state in the country and lectured in all but four). Her travels brought her into contact with people from different walks of life. Exhausting as they sometimes were, the years Gilman spent living out of hotels and guestrooms provided her with ample opportunity for growth. She learned to speak confidently, effectively, and inclusively to diverse audiences, putting into practice the dictum that "a public speaker should address the farthest person in the room" (122). By the time she wrote *Women and Economics*, Gilman was able to speak with understanding about the opportunities that were opening up for American women such as herself, who opted for a less conventional but, as she saw it, more fulfilling social and intellectual life.

Evolutionary Thought in Nineteenth-Century America

The growing interest in evolutionary science in the second half of the nineteenth century is the most important intellectual context for understanding Gilman's approach to analysing marriage and the family. The first American edition of Charles Darwin's pathbreaking work *The Origin of Species by Means of Natural Selection* was published in 1860, the year of Gilman's birth, and during her lifetime she witnessed the intellectual revolution that transformed scientific as well as popular thinking about the origin and nature of life on earth. In *Women and Economics*, Gilman argued that while patriarchy may have served a purpose in the distant past, women's economic dependence on men no longer served society's interests. Drawing upon the basic evolutionary precept that all life on earth undergoes continual change, she set out to show readers that American women can move beyond their present moral and intellectual stagnation and transition into a more advanced stage of human development. Encouragingly, as Gilman saw it, some American women were already transitioning toward a new phase, as evidenced by the rise of the woman's rights movement.

Ideas about the mutability—or changeability—of species were circulating in Europe before Darwin, and historians of science today regard the work of Jean-Baptiste Lamarck (1744–1829) as the first attempt to develop a comprehensive theory of life as an evolving process. The French naturalist outlined his findings in his 1809 book *Philosophy Zoology*, and Lamarck is best remembered today for his belief in the heritability of acquired characteristics, the theory that features acquired during one's lifetime are in turn passed on to one's offspring. According to this (incorrect) theory, for instance, giraffes have long necks because they spend their lives stretching up to reach the leaves of tall trees. The giraffe's neck elongates over the course of its individual lifetime— the result of habit—and this feature is passed on to offspring. Lamarck is also remembered today for his espousal of *progressionism*, the idea that simple forms of life evolve progressively toward a state of perfection. According to this theory, humankind represents the most complex and therefore most perfect form of life, a view to which Gilman subscribed and that persists in the popular imagination even today.[1]

Even during Lamarck's lifetime, attentive readers recognized the cultural implications of evolutionary thought. Such a theory implicitly challenged traditional worldviews that many in the Christian West during this period took for granted. According to Genesis, the first book of the Bible, life on earth resulted from a single divine act of creation. Evolutionary theory presented a rival theory of creation and thus threatened to throw the traditional moral order into disarray. Conscious of this, Lamarck reassured his readers that the findings of natural science were, at least in theory, compatible with the idea of a supreme and infinitely wise God. Lamarck writes, "Could not His infinite power create an *order of things* which gave existence successively to all that we see as well as to all that exists but that we do not see?" (36). Elsewhere in the book, however, he argues for the importance of retaining an open mind in regard to new ideas: "Should we recognize as well founded only those opinions that are most widely accepted?" He concludes, "Authorities in the sphere of knowledge should weigh one another's worth and not count one another's numbers" (6).

Throughout the nineteenth century, the idea that that scientific truth ought to form the basis of good thinking grew increasingly to be considered common sense among both European and American intellectuals. Gilman wrote *Women and Economics* in the spirit of scientific enquiry, urging readers to reassess received opinion that, she says, is too often informed by emotion rather than particular knowledge or understanding about a subject. "Many of our feelings are true, right, legitimate," she acknowledges. But other feelings are "fatuous absurdities, mere dangling relics of outgrown tradition, slowly moulting from us as we grow" (p. 172).

Gilman is sometimes described as "neo-Lamarckian," but her influences included Darwin, whose writing had done more than Lamarck's to erode the basis for the belief in a divine order. In *The Origin of Species* (1859), Darwin presented his readers with a vision of the natural world as a scene of unremitting competition, one in which individuals endowed with divergent traits struggle against unknowable odds to survive and reproduce. Darwin's theory of natural selection emphasized the power of the environment as a key factor in the struggle for life. Organisms possessing

---

1 For analysis of Lamarck's work, see Bowler.

traits best adapted to their environment are selected by nature to live and reproduce, while "less-improved" forms are selected to die. According to Darwinian philosophy, the death of the so-called unfit is neither a tragedy nor the act of an all-knowing God. Rather, it is the necessary condition allowing the production of more evolved forms of life. Darwin's claims about the powerful reach of natural forces were startling. "Nature," he writes, "can act on every internal organ, on every shade of constitutional difference, on the whole machinery of life" (81), a claim he was forced to defend against the accusation that it elevated nature to the position of a deity.

Scholars have long debated the American reception of European ideas, and much has been written about the complicated relationship between evolutionary theory and American social thought in the latter decades of the nineteenth century. While Lamarckian and Darwinian theory would continue to be debated into the twentieth century, the work of English philosopher Herbert Spencer (1820–1903) struck an especially powerful chord with American readers. Spencer was a proponent of *laissez faire*, an economic system based on the principles of a free market and little to no government regulation, and he believed competition among individuals to be the driving force of social progress. As an alternative to Darwin's "natural selection," Spencer famously coined the phrase "survival of the fittest," an expression that was subsequently taken up by American industrialists such as John D. Rockefeller (1839–1937) and James J. Hill (1838–1916) as a means of justifying exploitative business practices (Bowler 302).

In addition to enjoying a popular following, Spencer's particular variety of evolutionism inspired a generation of intellectuals, including some of America's most famous conservatives. Samples of writing by noted conservative William Graham Sumner (1840–1910) are included in Appendix D1. Sumner was America's first professor of sociology, and he subscribed to Spencer's view that that the laws governing biological evolution also applied to society. Sumner makes plain his irritation in his 1883 political essay *What Social Classes Owe to Each Other*, in which he reprimands progressive reformers, who assert the "right to claim and the duty to give one man's effort for another man's satisfaction" (Appendix D1, p. 304). Any attempt to "supervise" society is bound to set things off track; it is impossible to "get a revision of the laws of human life," he insists (Appendix D1, p. 303). In addition, Sumner sneered at the idea that the state might play a central role in orchestrating national reforms. The state, he scoffed, is merely a "little group of men" (Sumner 9).

Whereas conservatives such as Sumner drew upon the ideas of Darwin and Spencer to rationalize the status quo, Gilman, along with feminist contemporaries, drew upon the principles of evolutionary science in order to make the case for social reform. Thirty years before G.P. Putnam's Sons published the first English edition of *Women and Economics*, the company printed Antoinette Brown Blackwell's study of the gendered dimensions of evolutionary theory, *The Sexes Throughout Nature* (1875). Blackwell's analysis revealed that evolutionary science, while a potentially powerful analytical tool, was nonetheless something of a double-edged sword for women who wished to wield it as instrument for change. By calling attention to the operations of natural law, the theories of Darwin and Spencer promised to sweep away religious dogma for good. On the other hand, evolutionary theory was written by men who, in Blackwell's words, "studied nature from the male standpoint" (16–17). The preponderance of male bias meant that evolutionism only imperfectly aligned with the political agenda of late-nineteenth-century feminists.[1]

Women and Economics should be read in the context of this debate over the relationship between natural and divine law. Gilman drew upon Lamarck's theory and critically engaged with Darwin's and Spencer's ideas to offer an account of evolutionary change that was more favourable to women's interests. Indeed, there was much at stake in challenging conventional sexual settlements, as Hamlin's analysis of nineteenth-century feminists' appropriations of evolutionary theory notes. Sexual selection theory, Hamlin writes, "provided the scientific justification to question whether patriarchy, monogamy, and female domesticity were in fact natural when so many alternative domestic and sexual arrangements could be found in the animal kingdom" (15). In *Women and Economics*, Gilman celebrates women's "great position as selector of the best" (p. 94) and in doing so explicitly stakes a claim for women's sexual autonomy and de facto right to choose sexual partners.

---

1 Hamlin's *From Eve to Evolution* provides extensive analysis of American women's engagement with evolutionary theory. Also see Deutscher; Kohlstedt and Jorgensen. For discussion of Darwin's account of the evolution of women see Erskine; Richards.

A Progressive among Progressives

Gilman was at the height of her intellectual powers during the Progressive Era (1890–1920), a crucial period of change in American social, political, and economic history. Theodore Roosevelt (1858–1919)—Republican president and, after 1912, leader of the newly established Progressive Party—described the years surrounding the turn of the century as a time of "fierce discontent" (McGerr 11). Following the Civil War (1861–65), the United States had transformed from a largely agricultural and rural nation to one that was industrial and urban. By the end of the century, any American who cared to look could see manifestations of economic inequality.

Progressivism emerged out of this context of general dissatisfaction. During these years, the middle class launched an epic program of reforms designed to rein in corporate power and ameliorate the suffering of the poorest citizens. While President Roosevelt brought progressivism into the highest echelons of national politics, social worker Jane Addams (1860–1935) devoted herself to finding practical solutions to the nation's manifold problems and philosopher John Dewey (1859–1952) promoted greater understanding of the relationship between democracy and public education. The efforts of these self-identified "progressives" resulted in a set of reforms and policies that would shape the nation for more than a century.

Progressivism comprised a broad spectrum of political positions, but progressives, on the whole, agreed that many of the nation's problems emanated from a culture that rewarded extreme competition and economic self-seeking. Individualism—as a concept and a value—has deep roots in American traditions of self-reliance. Throughout the nineteenth century, the emphasis on individual moral agency made possible many morally laudable and heroic acts. Abolitionists and women's rights activists, for instance, were profoundly inspired by the idea of personal moral consciousness, as were literary lights Henry David Thoreau (1817–62) and Ralph Waldo Emerson (1803–82), the latter arguing that the "great man is he who in the midst of the crowd keeps with perfect sweetness the independence of solitude" (181). Gilman's Beecher heritage taught her to respect the power of individual moral conviction, and we find in her work a similar plea for conscience over conformity.

And yet this characteristically American virtue also provided an ideological basis for self-serving and anti-social behaviour.

The term "individualism" itself was introduced into the Euro-American lexicon in the 1830s by the French travel writer Alexis de Tocqueville (1805–59), who saw that it posed a threat to social cohesion. Individualism, de Tocqueville writes, is a feeling that "persuades each citizen to cut himself off from his fellows and to withdraw into the circle of his family and friends in such a way that he ... willingly abandons society at large to its own devices" (587). He went on to suggest that this aspect of the American way of life "threatens in the end to imprison" individuals "in the isolation of their own hearts" (589). Individualism—as de Tocqueville noted and as progressives including Gilman came to see—had a dark side.

Progressives were particularly concerned about the nation's business and financial elite, whose wealth accumulation was unlike anything seen before in the nation's history. The success of men such as J.P. Morgan (1837–1913), Rockefeller, and Andrew Carnegie (1835–1919)—the so-called captains of industry—ostensibly provided evidence for the popular idea of America as a place of opportunity. These men stood as living proof that the United States would indeed heap material rewards on those willing to work hard. Such men were not blind to inequality. On the contrary, they saw that inequality existed and they even, in the case of Carnegie, argued that inequality was itself a sign of progress. "Much better this great irregularity than universal squalor," Carnegie writes in one of a series of essays expounding the virtues of wealth accumulation. Drawing on the language of social Darwinism popularized by Herbert Spencer, Carnegie argued that rich men were rich because they had successfully competed in the struggle for life. Rich men were not exploiters, as labour leaders claimed, but the rightful guardians of the public good, he reasoned (653). Gilman likely had in mind the spurious claims of such men as Carnegie when she wrote "'The Poor Ye Have Always With You,'" a poem that concludes with the rousing line "Let man to-day / Rise up and put this human shame away— / Let us have poor no more!" (p. 230).

Working- and middle-class Americans recognized that the capitalist elite wielded individualism as a weapon of class warfare, using one of the nation's core values as cover for their "obviously self-serving and often self-deluding" behaviour that "guaranteed social tension and conflict in the new century," as historian Michael McGerr writes in his study of the Progressive Era (10). It wasn't that progressives were opposed to the idea of self-culture—or the work of building "character," as Theodore Roosevelt put it—but, rather, that they judged as morally objectionable the idea that one must bear the burden of succeeding or failing on an individual basis.

While capitalists framed free economic competition as a law of nature, progressives drew a very different set of lessons from the findings of evolutionary science. Progressives argued that, rather than diminishing the gap between human and animal life, evolutionary science allowed for greater insight into what is special about human life. The natural process of evolution had conferred unique intellectual capacities upon human beings that meant they might contemplate moral ends beyond narrow self-interest. Furthermore, evolutionary science demonstrated the role of the environment in shaping one's character and moral development. Individuals were not innately unequal, but only unequally educated and unequally resourced. Science did not prove the need for ever more aggressive economic competition. Rather, science provided a rational framework for social and institutional reform.

No one argued these points with more conviction than the so-called "father of American sociology," Lester Frank Ward, who forcefully rejected the idea that the laws of human society are identical to the laws of the natural world. At a time when capitalists such as Carnegie pointed to cheaply produced "luxuries" as a sign of progress, Ward pointed out that "the moral or emotional condition of man has scarcely advanced at all." Middle-class Americans living in urban centres lived alongside the "overworked millions" whose lives were defined by "poverty, drudgery, and nameless misery." Such conditions were not, as leading proponents of *laissez faire* capitalism argued, merely a sad but necessary evil. "In point of fact," Ward argued, "all things are now and always have been governed by force, and all the attempts to disguise it under the colour of abstract right have only served to make it easier for the unscrupulous to accomplish their personal aggrandizement" (32). In order to progressively improve society, Ward argued, Americans must level the playing field and enable all individuals—regardless of their background or family of origin—to participate, to improve together.

Gilman's *Women and Economics* contributes to the progressive effort to stymie economic individualism, and it does so in at least two ways. First, the text sets out to show how the American culture of selfish individualism can be tracked to mainstream domestic arrangements. Gilman disrupts the notion that marriage and private family contribute to the common good by asserting that the institution in fact maintains Americans in a primitive condition of selfish individualism. In the nineteenth century, many Americans subscribed to the view that the family provided the context for inculcating civic virtue in children and provided men with the emotional support that they needed to do battle in the external spheres of business and politics. To the contrary, Gilman argues, family life "developes personal selfishness" (p. 107). By encouraging wives and husbands to prioritize the needs of their own small family circle above all else, the institution makes servants of women and cowards of men, and it ultimately disincentivizes both from taking moral action that might benefit wider society.

Next, Gilman elaborates a new social conception of labour, one that highlights the dignity of diverse forms of work. In Chapter 7, she addresses the shared concerns of the women's movement and the labour movement, arguing that both movements demonstrate that men and women across American society share the "common consciousness of humanity" and are motivated by a shared "sense of social need and social duty" (p. 116). For Gilman, the major movements of the age emblematize America's dissatisfaction with the highly gendered and exclusive paradigm of capitalist acquisition. The middle-class–led women's movement and the working-class–led labour movement are, she argues, united in their recognition that individuals desire to engage in meaningful and useful activities that will draw them into community with their fellow citizens.

Progressivism was, among other things, an attempt to broaden democratic participation and build bonds of association across sharply demarcated class lines. In *Women and Economics*, Gilman preserves the nineteenth-century ideal of individual moral agency even as she attempts to dismantle the logic of economic self-seeking. The text seeks to demonstrate that women have a crucial role to play in advancing progress. Women must cultivate mental independence in order to transcend the family and engage in a relationship with the larger human society.

Socialist Feminism

For many ordinary Americans at the turn of the twentieth century, inequality and corruption were nothing less than an affront to American ideals of equality, and during the Progressive Era a small number of Americans, including Gilman, looked to socialism as an alternative to economic individualism. *Women and Economics* is, at its core, an attempt to bring economic analysis to bear on the woman question. Gilman famously declined to identify as a feminist, preferring "humanist" or "socialist," which she regarded as broader and more inclusive categories. To appreciate Gilman's significance to the history of feminist thought, it is constructive to situate her ideas on the spectrum of left economic thinking at the time.

In nineteenth-century America, as is still the case today, "socialism" meant different things to different people. In very basic terms, socialism refers to a system of social organization based on collective ownership of the production and distribution of goods for the common benefit of the group. Socialism is thus an alternative to capitalism, a system in which private individuals may own the means of production. In the nineteenth century, a small number of socialists identified as anarchists. Anarchist socialists subscribed to the basic idea of cooperation and mutual aid but believed that such cooperation among individuals ought to be voluntary and not coerced by a governing authority. A second group were the Marxist socialists who were followers of the German philosopher and economist Karl Marx (1818–83). Marxist socialists paid close attention to the relationship between two main groups: the propertied middle class (factory owners and employers of workers whom Marx referred to as the "bourgeoisie") and the working class (a group comprising those who sell their labour for a wage and whom Marx called the "proletariat"). Marxist socialists saw the proletariat as the most important agent of change and focused their attention on raising working-class consciousness.

Gilman subscribed to Nationalism, a third category of socialism that promoted the idea that the national government ought to play a major role in distributing wealth equally among all citizens. Her essays for Nationalist publications are included in Appendix A. In the 1890s, the most famous American Nationalist was Edward Bellamy (1850–98), whose commercially successful novel *Looking Backward* (1888) inspired the formation of Nationalist Clubs. Nationalists differed from anarchists, who distrusted all forms of hierarchy. They differed, too, from Marxist socialists, who were primarily concerned with maximizing the power of the working class. Nationalists argued that all Americans stood to gain from certain socialist provisions. Gilman was attracted to Nationalism, at least in part, because Nationalism provided a framework for uniting the working class and the middle class in common opposition to the ultra-rich, as scholar Mark W. Van Wienen has argued. Van Wienen writes that

"Gilman's work" can be interpreted as "an effort to show the bourgeois that their real, long-term interests lay not with the capitalist monopolists but with the common workers" (44). Gilman, as much as any American progressive of the time, recognized the divisions between different factions on the left. In the late nineteenth century, many socialists subscribed to the paradigm of separate spheres, arguing that a socialist revolution would enable working-class women to devote themselves more fully to their domestic duties as wives and mothers. Labour union activists, as historian Mari Jo Buhle has demonstrated, perceived capitalism and women's rights activism as dual threats to working-class female virtue (8). Meanwhile, middle-class women's movement activists argued that women's political equality would benefit all American women. Gilman's poem "The Socialist and the Suffragist" (p. 233) satirizes the rift, and it urges the two groups to unite behind their common goals.

In *Women and Economics*, one of Gilman's major aims is to convince women of all classes of their common experience of economic exploitation. Gilman set about writing her book with the guiding conviction that "[w]hat we do modifies us more than what is done to us" (p. 81), which is to say, our everyday activity—the work we perform—prominently determines our moral and physical development. The problem, in the nineteenth century, was that men and women spent their lives undertaking very different forms of activity. Thus, as Gilman argued, there was not one but, rather, two separate and distinct economies. One was the formal economy of productive labour, in which capitalists invested money to produce goods and services and hired wage labourers to produce those goods and services. The second was the informal economy of reproductive labour. This second economy comprised workers who performed essential tasks in their communities, such as birthing and raising children, caring for the elderly, and preparing food for their family. Gilman argues that both economies are crucial to human progress. But, while workers in the formal economy receive a wage, workers in the informal economy essentially provide labour for free, a phenomenon with grave implications for individuals and society alike.

Women and Economics calls for wide-reaching changes that were radical at the time and, as numerous twenty-first-century feminist economists continue to argue, are yet to be achieved today. Gilman argued that it is the duty of women as well as men to perform economically productive labour and, in so doing, contribute to the wellbeing of society. It is a "human impulse," she writes in Chapter 4, "to create ... to make, to do, to express one's new spirit in new forms" (p. 81). Dignified employment is an important source of self-esteem and, moreover, enables individuals to recognize their shared stake in the success of society's public ventures. Equally, though, as Gilman argues, it is essential that women and men should both undertake reproductive labour—women and men should fulfil their duties as mothers and fathers. Today this seems like common sense. But Gilman recognized that substantial changes to the prevailing social and economic structure would need to be made in order for women and men to live more balanced—as she saw it, happier and more equal—lives.

Gilman's analysis is carefully crafted to address the assumptions of sceptical readers who subscribed to the dominant view of marriage as a private partnership between two individuals performing separate functions but nonetheless working together toward a common goal, and it does so by demonstrating that the quality and quantity of women's labour bear no relation to their economic returns. In Chapter 1, she charts a theory of women's relation to labour that highlights forms of gendered dependency that women experience regardless of their socio-economic class status. Late-nineteenth-century readers may have been familiar with the ideas of Marx, who advanced the theory that human history is defined by the struggle between the owners of wealth (capitalists) and the working class (proletariat). Gilman radically complicates the Marxist class analysis by turning a spotlight on the forms of labour performed by women in the home. The "salient fact," Gilman writes, "is that, whatever the economic value of the domestic industry of women is, they do not get it" (p. 54). Women's work in the home, she argues, "is held to be their duty ... and their economic status bears no relation to their domestic labors, unless an inverse one" (pp. 54–55). For Gilman, women's work in the home was not, as many nineteenth-century Americans continued to believe, a labour of love performed by women possessing "natural" maternal instincts. Rather, marriage provided an infrastructure for the patriarchal appropriation of women's essential, although unpaid, reproductive labour.

But the problem, as Gilman saw it, went far deeper than mere labour exploitation, bad as that was. The effects of dependency on a woman's personality were truly monstrous. For centuries, Gilman maintained, men have achieved status by demonstrating their value to their communities—by generating wealth, for instance, or by proving themselves exceptionally learned or wise.

Women, on the other hand, have undertaken to secure their status as wives, which they have achieved by appealing to men's sexual tastes and, even worse, marketing themselves as ideal house servants. "Free creatures, getting their own food and maintaining their own lives, develop an active capacity for attaining their ends," Gilman writes in Chapter 4, while "[p]arasitic creatures, whose living is obtained by the exertions of others, develope powers of absorption and of tenacity,—the powers by which they profit most" (p. 79). Women's cultivated disregard for broader environmental currents, along with their "inordinate greed" for personal material gain, means that they are like no other living creature on earth, an argument that many middle-class women would no doubt have found startling.

But Gilman took her argument even further. She suggests that women's parasitic role in the sexual economy, though it sometimes rewards them with special privileges, essentially turns them into prostitutes. "We justify and approve the economic dependence of women upon the sex-relation in marriage. We condemn it unsparingly out of marriage. We follow it with our blame and scorn up to the very doors of marriage,—the mercenary bride,— but think no harm of the mercenary wife, filching her husband's pockets in the night," Gilman writes in Chapter 5 (p. 96). Some later feminist critics rejected the wife-as-prostitute paradigm, claiming it erases the diverse experiences of women across lines of race and class. Second Wave feminist Audre Lorde (1934–92), for instance, argued that the paradigm uncritically ignores the particular experiences of "poor women and women of Color" who "know there is a difference between the daily manifestations of marital slavery and prostitution because it is our daughters who line 42nd Street" (105). But Gilman's critique never suggests an equivalence in personal *experiences* among women, as Lorde seems to suggest. Rather, *Women and Economics* sets out to show that marriage is structurally embedded within a patriarchal order that rewards women as sexual sycophants and servants.

Gilman was optimistic that circumstances might change. As a committed socialist, she was conscious that work cultures in America could be punishingly difficult and knew that if women and men were to achieve greater equality, then more than minds and dispositions had to change. Like other progressives, she believed that the path to greater happiness lay with greater cooperation among individuals. To "feel in common and act in common," she writes, is "the deepest human joy" (p. 131). In Chapters 13 and 14, she lays out her proposals, which include apartment houses for working women and families that would put an end to traditional, gender-divided living arrangements. This new arrangement—essentially a community of assisted living units—would combine home comforts with around-the-clock childcare. For Gilman, remaking the home—finding ways to ensure that women and men can undertake productive activity while fulfilling their roles as loving parents—was the essential precondition of female economic independence.

Gilman's observation that female-coded sexual and reproductive labour is vulnerable to devaluation and appropriation would be developed by numerous twentieth-century left intellectuals and feminist theorists, including Simone de Beauvoir (1908–86), Christine Delphy (b. 1941), Leopoldina Fortunati (b. 1949), Nicole-Claude Mathieu (1937–2014), Mariarosa Dalla Costa (b. 1943), Selma James (b. 1930), and Marilyn Waring (b. 1952). Moreover, it remains an important reference point for twenty-first-century feminist economists who have expanded Gilman's analysis to consider why not only tasks associated with mothering but also particular forms of "feminized" waged labour such as nursing and hospitality remain vulnerable to exploitation.

Women and Economics

Fifteen years after the publication of *Women and Economics*, Gilman's vision of a society in which women combine care work with "active" waged labour was becoming more of a reality. In 1913, Gilman became involved in the so-called "teacher mother" controversy. In New York City, the Board of Education attempted to dismiss married female teachers when they became mothers. Gilman devoted columns in her magazine *The Forerunner* to promoting the League for the Civic Service of Women, an organization assembled to "advocate legislation for the protection of women in the performance of [maternal] functions, to protect against discharging women who marry and blacklisting those who bear children" ("Comment and Review" 26). Appendix C reproduces historical documents pertaining to the teacher-mother incident. The teachers' main opposition came from the City Schools' Superintendent John Martin, a Fabian socialist and one-time friend of Gilman's, who argued that working women, like all women, benefit more from paternalist protection than labour equality. Gilman's understanding of the real-life stakes of the teacher-mother incident was deeply informed by the ideas she had germinated in the book numerous critics consider her most enduring contribution to the history of feminist thought.

Gilman's *Women and Economics* is a remarkable treatise that documents the painful constraints imposed on nineteenth-century American women. Readers today will see that Gilman set out, first, to accurately describe and analyse the gendered dimensions of the economy and, second, to develop a practicable proposal for change.

Gilman's major achievement was casting light on the wide-ranging negative consequences of inter-generational cultures of female economic dependence. Economic disenfranchisement leaves women in a condition of mental confinement, she reveals, unable to contemplate matters of public concern. Additionally, women in a subordinate economic position do not improve family life, nor do they prepare their husbands and children to serve their society. Rather, women who are preoccupied with their own self-preservation, and who can secure material resources from superiors only by denying their own talents and desires, will, in the end, do harm to society, family, and self.

In her own life, Gilman resolved some of these issues even while confronting structural barriers that affected most women. While writing *Women and Economics*, Gilman was building a relationship with Houghton Gilman, the man who would become her second husband. Unlike her first husband, Houghton supported Gilman's writing career. They married in 1900 and, on their honeymoon, Houghton patiently encouraged his wife's creativity. In her biography, Gilman cheerfully notes that her second husband "bore ... nobly" the challenges of being married to a "philosopher" (*Living* 281). Gilman remained married to Houghton until his death in 1934. Gilman died in 1935. Her death was widely reported and generated public debate about the ethics of suicide.

Considering Gilman's life experiences alongside her work reveals an insight that has since become a central pillar of feminist economics, which is that economic knowledge is socially situated. Nineteenth-century patriarchy valued women as wives and mothers. Gilman observes in Chapter 4, "Wealth, power, social distinction, fame ... home and happiness, reputation, ease and pleasure, her bread and butter,—all, must come to her through a small gold ring" (p. 84). Many middle-class American women of Gilman's generation accepted marriage as a protective umbrella and highly valued the privileges and safeguards it provided. And yet Gilman's experiences taught her that this paradigm provided respectable cover for a number of inequities, including sexual domination and exploitation. Worst of all, perhaps, the protective umbrella paradigm convinced women to dispense with the characteristics required by every other living creature for survival—such as courage, ingenuity, and resilience.

Gilman's work offers a rational set of alternatives to the patriarchal family. She saw that structural problems require structural solutions, and her proposed new homes for working women sought to transform the economic foundation of family life. Whereas the traditional family maintained women in a state of economic precariousness, the housing proposal offered round-the-clock childcare that would sever the tie between marriage, reproduction, and economic dependence. This vision goes further than that of earlier nineteenth-century feminist writing about gendered labour, and it raises concerns about the sexual division of labour that would be more extensively developed by later feminists. In *The Second Sex* (1949), Simone de Beauvoir would provide a psychological portrait of middle-class marriage that would extend Gilman's economic critique. In this way, *Women and Economics* should be read as an important text that bridges nineteenth- and twentieth-century feminist thought.

Women in the twenty-first century continue to face many of the challenges that Gilman observed at the dawn of the twentieth. Reproductive care work continues to be unwaged or poorly waged. Women disproportionately remain caregivers for children and for the elderly, even as they are called upon to compete in the formal, productive economy. In her 1894 essay "Women as a Class" (Appendix A2), Gilman urges women who have succeeded professionally not to overlook the condition of women more generally. She writes, "Every woman [should] be proud to add her special strength to the growing power of women; to let her gain be theirs and to count in the average" (p. 267). In other words, Gilman believed that all people stand to benefit from a society and an economy built by collective enterprise of women and based on the values of fairness, reason, excellence, and even love.

A society based on love would treat productive and reproductive work as equally valuable, equally essential to human flourishing. And because productive and reproductive labour are equally essential, Gilman believed that society should be organized in order to enable people to choose those tasks that best suit their talents. Advocates of nineteenth-century family life imagined that women flourished best by performing unwaged work in the home and by depending exclusively on the wealth or wages of an individual man. But Gilman imagined a world in which people have the power to choose their own paths, and she imagined that this independence would be grounded in collective social arrangements. She did not merely want women to enter the formal economy of waged work, although she did want that. She also wanted a society that ensured that all work—productive and reproductive—enabled the worker to live a life of dignity and independence. *Women and Economics*, then, remains a book that will provoke us to think more deeply about how we might achieve a more humane and just society today.

Charlotte Perkins Gilman: A Brief Chronology

1846   Catharine Beecher (Gilman's paternal great-aunt) publishes *The Evils Suffered by American Women and Children: The Causes and Remedy*, which suggests the "cause of depression to [women] is found in the fact that there is no profession for women of education" and argues that women "ought never to be led to married life except under the promptings of pure affection."

1852   Harriet Beecher Stowe (Gilman's paternal great-aunt) publishes her anti-slavery novel *Uncle Tom's Cabin*.

1860   Charlotte Anna Perkins is born in Hartford, Connecticut, to Frederick Beecher Perkins and Mary Fitch Westcott Perkins. She is the second of two surviving children. Frederick worked as a teacher, a library director, and a newspaper editor.

1861–65   American Civil War

1863–69   Moves between family homes in Connecticut, Rhode Island, and Massachusetts. Frederick grows increasingly estranged from the family during these years before permanently abandoning his wife and children in 1869.

1868   Fourteenth Amendment to the US Constitution defines citizens as "all persons born or naturalized in the United States" but defines the electorate (citizens entitled to vote in elections) as "male."

1870   Fifteenth Amendment to the US Constitution prohibits the denial of a citizen's right to vote "on account of race, color, or previous condition of servitude." Women of all races continue to be denied the right to vote at the federal level.

1871   Beecher-Tilton Scandal: Beecher family embroiled in a widely publicized scandal when Henry Ward Beecher (Gilman's paternal great-uncle) is charged with committing adultery with Elizabeth Tilton.

1879	Beginning of friendship with Martha Luther, which was intimate and intense until Luther married in 1882. Beginning of lifelong friendship with Grace Channing.
1880	First publication, a poem titled "To D.G.," appears in *New England Journal of Education*.
1884	Marries the artist Charles Walter Stetson following a difficult two-year courtship.
1885	Gives birth to a daughter, Katharine Beecher Stetson, in March.
1886–87	Attends her first woman suffrage convention in October 1886; publishes articles for *Woman's Journal*, the official journal of the *American Woman Suffrage Association*.
1887	Suffers emotional and mental breakdown, following an extended period of depression. Travels to Philadelphia in spring 1887 to receive treatment from the neurological specialist S. Weir Mitchell. Mitchell prescribes the "rest cure" as a treatment for what was, at the time, called "neurasthenia."
1887–90	Marriage between Gilman and Charles Stetson breaks down. During this period, Gilman moves with her daughter to live with Grace Channing, first in Providence, Rhode Island, and after October 1888, in Pasadena, California. Gilman and Stetson formally separate in January 1890.
1890	Introduced to Nationalism. Lectures at the Nationalist Club of Pasadena and to audiences in Los Angeles. Publishes the poem "Similar Cases" in *Nationalist* magazine. Gains the attention of leading Nationalists, such as Edward Bellamy and William Dean Howells. Writes the short story "The Yellow Wall-paper." Gilman describes 1890 as a year of "great growth and gain."
1890–94	Continues residence in California. Publishes a book of poetry, *In This Our World*, in 1893, and takes over the journal *Impress* in 1894, two ventures which gained her a following among leading reform Darwinists such as Lester Frank Ward. Ward would initiate a friendship with Gilman in 1895.

1894	Sends daughter Katharine east to live with Walter Stetson and Grace Channing in May. Stetson and Channing announce their intention to marry.
1894–99	Undertakes a five-year period of travel around the United States and abroad. In her autobiography, Gilman describes her work during these years as "lecturing and preaching." Meets numerous leading intellectuals and reformers, including future British Prime Minister Ramsey Macdonald, American women's rights activists Susan B. Anthony and Elizabeth Cady Stanton, and founder of Chicago's Hull House Jane Addams. Speaks on "Equal Pay for Equal Work" at the 1899 Congress of the International Council of Women, held in London, England.
1898	Publishes *Women and Economics* with Small, Maynard, and Co.
1900	Marries George Houghton Gilman in June, following a three-year courtship. Houghton provides editorial support during the publication of *Women and Economics* and offers the physical and emotional companionship that Gilman had found lacking in her first marriage. Gilman and Houghton reside in New York City until 1922, and then in Norwich, Connecticut, until Houghton's death in 1934.
1903	Publishes *The Home: Its Work and Influences*, which expands on the ideas of *Women and Economics*.
1904–11	Travels and lectures abroad in countries including England, the Netherlands, Italy, Germany, Austria, and Hungary. Attends the 1911 International Congress of Women in Berlin, Germany.
1909–16	Writes, edits, and publishes *The Forerunner*, a monthly magazine comprising poems, essays, short stories, reviews, sermons, and serialized novels. Publishes a third book-length work, *The Man-Made World*, in 1911.
1919–20	Publishes several hundred articles with *New York Tribune* syndicated newspapers including the *Louisville Herald*, the *Baltimore Sun*, and the *Buffalo Evening News*.

1934   Moves to Pasadena, California, to live with daughter Katharine, Katharine's family, and Grace Channing Stetson.

1935   Dies in Pasadena on 17 August, ending her own life following a three-year struggle with cancer.

A Note on the Texts

This Broadview edition has been reproduced from the third American edition of Charlotte Perkins Gilman's *Women and Economics: A Study of the Relation Between Men and Women as a Factor in Social Evolution* (Small, Maynard and Company, January 1900). The text of this edition reproduces that of the third American edition, except for typographical errors, which have been silently corrected. The one-act play *Something to Vote For* has been reproduced from the original, which appeared in the June 1911 edition of *The Forerunner*, a magazine that Gilman wrote, edited, and self-published. This edition also includes a selection of poems, reproduced from Gilman's collections *In This Our World and Other Poems* (San Francisco, 1893) and *Suffrage Songs and Verses* (The Charlton Company, 1911). Over her lifetime, Gilman was known to her friends and readers by three different surnames: Perkins (1860–84), Stetson (1884–1900), and Gilman (1900–35). She published *Women and Economics* under the name Charlotte Perkins Stetson. She assumed the name Gilman on 11 June 1900, upon her marriage to George Houghton Gilman. I have chosen to follow the majority of scholars by referring to her as "Charlotte Perkins Gilman" or "Gilman."

WOMEN AND ECONOMICS
AND OTHER WRITINGS

WOMEN AND ECONOMICS
A Study of the Economic Relation Between Men and Women as a Factor in Social Evolution
By
Charlotte Perkins Stetson

PROEM[1]

In dark and early ages, through the primal forests faring,
Ere[2] the soul came shining into prehistoric night,
Twofold man was equal; they were comrades dear and daring,
Living wild and free together in unreasoning delight.

Ere the soul was born and consciousness came slowly,
Ere the soul was born, to man and woman, too,
Ere he found the Tree of Knowledge, that awful tree and holy,
Ere he knew he felt, and knew he knew.

Then said he to Pain, "I am wise now, and I know you!
No more will I suffer while power and wisdom last!"
Then said he to Pleasure, "I am strong, and I will show you
That the will of man can seize you,—aye, and hold you fast!"

Food he ate for pleasure, and wine he drank for gladness.
And woman? Ah, the woman! the crown of all delight!
His now,—he knew it! He was strong to madness
In that early dawning after prehistoric night.

His,—his forever! That glory sweet and tender!
Ah, but he would love her! And she should love but him!
He would work and struggle for her, he would shelter and defend her,—
She should never leave him, never, till their eyes in death were dim.

Close, close he bound her, that she should leave him never;
Weak still he kept her, lest she be strong to flee;
And the fainting flame of passion he kept alive forever
With all the arts and forces of earth and sky and sea.

---

1 Gilman's proem retells the story of Adam and Eve from the Book of Genesis.
2 Archaic expression: before.

*And, ah, the long journey! The slow and awful ages
They have labored up together, blind and crippled, all astray!
Through what a mighty volume, with a million shameful pages,
From the freedom of the forests to the prisons of to-day!*

*Food he ate for pleasure, and it slew him with diseases!
Wine he drank for gladness, and it led the way to crime!
And woman? He will hold her,—he will have her when he pleases,—
And he never once hath seen her since the prehistoric time!*

*Gone the friend and comrade of the day when life was younger,
She who rests and comforts, she who helps and saves.
Still he seeks her vainly, with a never-dying hunger;
Alone beneath his tyrants, alone above his slaves!*

*Toiler, bent and weary with the load of thine own making!
Thou who art sad and lonely, though lonely all in vain!
Who hast sought to conquer Pleasure and have her for the taking,
And found that Pleasure only was another name for Pain—*

*Nature hath reclaimed thee, forgiving dispossession!
God hath not forgotten, though man doth still forget!
The woman-soul is rising, in despite of thy transgression—
Loose her now, and trust her! She will love thee yet!*

*Love thee? She will love thee as only freedom knoweth!
Love thee? She will love thee while Love itself doth live!
Fear not the heart of woman! No bitterness it showeth!
The ages of her sorrow have but taught her to forgive!*

PREFACE

This book is written to offer a simple and natural explanation of one of the most common and most perplexing problems of human life,—a problem which presents itself to almost every individual for practical solution, and which demands the most serious attention of the moralist, the physician, and the sociologist—

To show how some of the worst evils under which we suffer, evils long supposed to be inherent and ineradicable in our natures, are but the result of certain arbitrary conditions of our own adoption, and how, by removing those conditions, we may remove the evils resultant—

To point out how far we have already gone in the path of improvement, and how irresistibly the social forces of to-day are compelling us further, even without our knowledge and against our violent opposition,—an advance which may be greatly quickened by our recognition and assistance—

To reach in especial the thinking women of to-day, and urge upon them a new sense, not only of their social responsibility as individuals, but of their measureless racial[1] importance as makers of men.

It is hoped also that the theory advanced will prove sufficiently suggestive to give rise to such further study and discussion as shall prove its error or establish its truth.

CHARLOTTE PERKINS STETSON.

---

1 The term *race* here denotes humankind or "the human race." Progressives like Gilman believed in building bonds of associations between diverse groups of people and sometimes supported segregation as a means of advancing reformist causes.

I.

Since we have learned to study the development of human life as we study the evolution of species throughout the animal kingdom, some peculiar phenomena which have puzzled the philosopher and moralist for so long, begin to show themselves in a new light.[1] We begin to see that, so far from being inscrutable problems, requiring another life to explain, these sorrows and perplexities of our lives are but the natural results of natural causes, and that, as soon as we ascertain the causes, we can do much to remove them.

In spite of the power of the individual will to struggle against conditions, to resist them for a while, and sometimes to overcome them, it remains true that the human creature is affected by his environment, as is every other living thing. The power of the individual will to resist natural law is well proven by the life and death of the ascetic.[2] In any one of those suicidal martyrs may be seen the will, misdirected by the ill-informed intelligence, forcing the body to defy every natural impulse,—even to the door of death, and through it.

But, while these exceptions show what the human will can do, the general course of life shows the inexorable effect of conditions upon humanity. Of these conditions we share with other living things the environment of the material universe. We are affected by climate and locality, by physical, chemical, electrical forces, as are all animals and plants. With the animals, we farther share the effect of our own activity, the reactionary force of exercise. What we do, as well as what is done to us, makes us what we are. But, beyond these forces, we come under the effect of a third set of conditions peculiar to our human status; namely, social conditions. In the organic interchanges which constitute social life, we are affected by each other to a degree beyond what is found even among the most gregarious of animals. This third factor, the social environment, is of enormous force as a modifier of human life. Throughout all these environing conditions, those which affect us through our economic necessities are most marked in their influence.

---

1 Charles Darwin's *On the Origin of Species by Means of Natural Selection, or the Preservation of Favoured Races in the Struggle for Life* was published in 1859. Reform Darwinists such as a Gilman engaged with the evolutionary ideas advanced by Darwin and his contemporaries even while they challenged the direct applicability of Darwinism to social questions.
2 A person who practices extreme self-discipline or is severely abstinent, particularly in regard to sex and other sensual pleasures.

Without touching yet upon the influence of the social factors, treating the human being merely as an individual animal, we see that he is modified most by his economic conditions, as is every other animal. Differ as they may in color and size, in strength and speed, in minor adaptation to minor conditions, all animals that live on grass have distinctive traits in common, and all animals that eat flesh have distinctive traits in common,—so distinctive and so common that it is by teeth, by nutritive apparatus in general, that they are classified, rather than by means of defence or locomotion. The food supply of the animal is the largest passive factor in his development; the processes by which he obtains his food supply, the largest active factor in his development. It is these activities, the incessant repetition of the exertions by which he is fed, which most modify his structure and develope his functions. The sheep, the cow, the deer, differ in their adaptation to the weather, their locomotive ability, their means of defence; but they agree in main characteristics, because of their common method of nutrition.

The human animal is no exception to this rule. Climate affects him, weather affects him, enemies affect him; but most of all he is affected, like every other living creature, by what he does for his living. Under all the influence of his later and wider life, all the reactive effect of social institutions, the individual is still inexorably modified by his means of livelihood: "the hand of the dyer is subdued to what he works in."[1] As one clear, world-known instance of the effect of economic conditions upon the human creature, note the marked race-modification of the Hebrew people[2] under the enforced restrictions of the last two thousand years. Here is a people rising to national prominence, first as a pastoral, and then as an agricultural nation; only partially commercial through race affinity with the Phœnicians, the pioneer traders of the world.[3] Under the social power of a united Christendom—united at least in this most unchristian deed—the Jew was forced to get his livelihood by commercial methods solely. Many effects can be traced in him to the fierce pressure of the

---

1 From William Shakespeare (1564–1616), Sonnet 111.7–6: "my nature is subdu'd / To what it works in, like the dyer's hand."
2 Jewish people.
3 A population who occupied the coast of the Levant (eastern Mediterranean). Gilman's line of discussion here indicates familiarity with nineteenth-century theological, historical, and anthropological scholarship, including works such as George Rawlinson's *History of the Phoenicians* (1889).

social conditions to which he was subjected: the intense family devotion of a people who had no country, no king, no room for joy and pride except the family; the reduced size and tremendous vitality and endurance of the pitilessly selected survivors of the Ghetto;[1] the repeated bursts of erratic genius from the human spirit so inhumanly restrained. But more patent still is the effect of the economic conditions,—the artificial development of a race of traders and dealers in money, from the lowest pawnbroker to the house of Rothschild;[2] a special kind of people, bred of the economic environment in which they were compelled to live.

One rough but familiar instance of the same effect, from the same cause, we can all see in the marked distinction between the pastoral, the agricultural, and the manufacturing classes in any nation, though their other conditions be the same. On the clear line of argument that functions and organs are developed by use, that what we use most is developed most, and that the daily processes of supplying economic needs are the processes that we most use, it follows that, when we find special economic conditions affecting any special class of people, we may look for special results, and find them.

In view of these facts, attention is now called to a certain marked and peculiar economic condition affecting the human race, and unparalleled in the organic world. We are the only animal species in which the female depends on the male for food, the only animal species in which the sex-relation is also an economic relation. With us an entire sex lives in a relation of economic dependence upon the other sex, and the economic relation is combined with the sex-relation. The economic status of the human female is relative to the sex-relation.

It is commonly assumed that this condition also obtains among other animals, but such is not the case. There are many birds among which, during the nesting season, the male helps the female feed the young, and partially feeds her; and, with certain of the higher carnivora, the male helps the female feed the young, and partially feeds her. In no case does she depend on him absolutely, even during this season, save in that of the hornbill, where the female, sitting on her nest in a hollow tree, is walled in with clay by the male, so that only her beak projects; and then he feeds her while the eggs are developing. But even the female

---

1 A quarter in a city occupied by a segregated group; areas to which Jews, specifically, were restricted.
2 A Jewish family that accumulated significant wealth through international banking.

hornbill does not expect to be fed at any other time. The female bee and ant are economically dependent, but not on the male. The workers are females, too, specialized to economic functions solely. And with the carnivora, if the young are to lose one parent, it might far better be the father: the mother is quite competent to take care of them herself. With many species, as in the case of the common cat, she not only feeds herself and her young, but has to defend the young against the male as well. In no case is the female throughout her life supported by the male.

In the human species the condition is permanent and general, though there are exceptions, and though the present century is witnessing the beginnings of a great change in this respect. We have not been accustomed to face this fact beyond our loose generalization that it was "natural," and that other animals did so, too.

To many this view will not seem clear at first; and the case of working peasant women or females of savage[1] tribes, and the general household industry of women, will be instanced against it. Some careful and honest discrimination is needed to make plain to ourselves the essential facts of the relation, even in these cases. The horse, in his free natural condition, is economically independent. He gets his living by his own exertions, irrespective of any other creature. The horse, in his present condition of slavery, is economically dependent. He gets his living at the hands of his master; and his exertions, though strenuous, bear no direct relation to his living. In fact, the horses who are the best fed and cared for and the horses who are the hardest worked are quite different animals. The horse works, it is true; but what he gets to eat depends on the power and will of his master. His living comes through another. He is economically dependent. So with the hard-worked savage or peasant women. Their labor is the property of another: they work under another will; and what they receive depends not on

---

1 A term used for describing hunter-gatherers and semi-nomadic populations. Nineteenth-century theorists, including Gilman, sometimes referred to such populations as *primitive*. In his 1884 work *The Origin of the Family: Private Property and the State* (English translation 1902), Friedrich Engels (1820–95) drew upon the earlier thought of the American anthropologist Lewis Henry Morgan (1818–81), identifying "savagery" as the first of the "three main epochs" in human economic evolutionary progress. The second epoch, according to Engels, is "barbarism" and the third is "civilization" (33). Researchers no longer use such terms to describe people in this context.

their labor, but on the power and will of another. They are economically dependent. This is true of the human female both individually and collectively.

In studying the economic position of the sexes collectively, the difference is most marked. As a social animal, the economic status of man rests on the combined and exchanged services of vast numbers of progressively specialized individuals. The economic progress of the race, its maintenance at any period, its continued advance, involve the collective activities of all the trades, crafts, arts, manufactures, inventions, discoveries, and all the civil and military institutions that go to maintain them. The economic status of any race at any time, with its involved effect on all the constituent individuals, depends on their world-wide labors and their free exchange. Economic progress, however, is almost exclusively masculine. Such economic processes as women have been allowed to exercise are of the earliest and most primitive[1] kind. Were men to perform no economic services save such as are still performed by women, our racial status in economics would be reduced to most painful limitations.

To take from any community its male workers would paralyze it economically to a far greater degree than to remove its female workers. The labor now performed by the women could be performed by the men, requiring only the setting back of many advanced workers into earlier forms of industry; but the labor now performed by the men could not be performed by the women without generations of effort and adaptation. Men can cook, clean, and sew as well as women; but the making and managing of the great engines of modern industry, the threading of earth and sea in our vast systems of transportation, the handling of our elaborate machinery of trade, commerce, government,— these things could not be done so well by women in their present degree of economic development.

This is not owing to lack of the essential human faculties necessary to such achievements, nor to any inherent disability of sex, but to the present condition of woman, forbidding the development of this degree of economic ability. The male human being is thousands of years in advance of the female in economic status. Speaking collectively, men produce and distribute wealth; and women receive it at their hands. As men hunt, fish, keep cattle, or raise corn, so do women eat game, fish, beef, or corn. As men go

---

1 From the French *primitif* (early or ancient): work that is simple, unsophisticated, or crude.

down to the sea in ships,[1] and bring coffee and spices and silks and gems from far away, so do women partake of the coffee and spices and silks and gems the men bring.

The economic status of the human race in any nation, at any time, is governed mainly by the activities of the male: the female obtains her share in the racial advance only through him.

Studied individually, the facts are even more plainly visible, more open and familiar. From the day laborer to the millionnaire, the wife's worn dress or flashing jewels, her low roof or her lordly one, her weary feet or her rich equipage,[2]—these speak of the economic ability of the husband. The comfort, the luxury, the necessities of life itself, which the woman receives, are obtained by the husband, and given her by him. And, when the woman, left alone with no man to "support" her, tries to meet her own economic necessities, the difficulties which confront her prove conclusively what the general economic status of the woman is. None can deny these patent facts,—that the economic status of women generally depends upon that of men generally, and that the economic status of women individually depends upon that of men individually, those men to whom they are related. But we are instantly confronted by the commonly received opinion that, although it must be admitted that men make and distribute the wealth of the world, yet women earn their share of it as wives. This assumes either that the husband is in the position of employer and the wife as employee, or that marriage is a "partnership," and the wife an equal factor with the husband in producing wealth.

Economic independence is a relative condition at best. In the broadest sense, all living things are economically dependent upon others,—the animals upon the vegetables, and man upon both. In a narrower sense, all social life is economically interdependent, man producing collectively what he could by no possibility produce separately. But, in the closest interpretation, individual economic independence among human beings means that the individual pays for what he gets, works for what he gets, gives to the other an equivalent for what the other gives him. I depend on the shoemaker for shoes, and the tailor for coats; but, if I give the shoemaker and the tailor enough of my own labor as a housebuilder to pay for the shoes and coats they give me, I retain my

---

1 Psalm 107.23: They that go down to the sea in ships, that do business in great waters; These see the works of the Lord, and His wonders in the deep.

2 Carriage with horses, attended by servants.

personal independence. I have not taken of their product, and given nothing of mine. As long as what I get is obtained by what I give, I am economically independent.

Women consume economic goods. What economic product do they give in exchange for what they consume? The claim that marriage is a partnership, in which the two persons married produce wealth which neither of them, separately, could produce, will not bear examination.[1] A man happy and comfortable can produce more than one unhappy and uncomfortable, but this is as true of a father or son as of a husband. To take from a man any of the conditions which make him happy and strong is to cripple his industry, generally speaking. But those relatives who make him happy are not therefore his business partners, and entitled to share his income.

Grateful return for happiness conferred is not the method of exchange in a partnership. The comfort a man takes with his wife is not in the nature of a business partnership, nor are her frugality and industry. A housekeeper, in her place, might be as frugal, as industrious, but would not therefore be a partner. Man and wife are partners truly in their mutual obligation to their children,—their common love, duty, and service. But a manufacturer who marries, or a doctor, or a lawyer, does not take a partner in his business, when he takes a partner in parenthood, unless his wife is also a manufacturer, a doctor, or a lawyer. In his business, she cannot even advise wisely without training and experience. To love her husband, the composer, does not enable her to compose; and the loss of a man's wife, though it may break his heart, does not cripple his business, unless his mind is affected by grief. She is in no sense a business partner, unless she contributes capital or experience or labor, as a man would in like relation. Most men would hesitate very seriously before entering a business partnership with any woman, wife or not.

If the wife is not, then, truly a business partner, in what way does she earn from her husband the food, clothing, and shelter she receives at his hands? By house service, it will be instantly replied. This is the general misty idea upon the subject,—that women earn all they get, and more, by house service. Here we come to a very practical and definite economic ground. Although

---

1 Following the American War of Independence (1775–83), contractual ideals enshrined in the Declaration of Independence were brought to bear on the institution of marriage, which was increasingly framed as an agreement between two contracting partners with mutual obligations, duties, and interests.

not producers of wealth, women serve in the final processes of preparation and distribution. Their labor in the household has a genuine economic value.

For a certain percentage of persons to serve other persons, in order that the ones so served may produce more, is a contribution not to be overlooked. The labor of women in the house, certainly, enables men to produce more wealth than they otherwise could; and in this way women are economic factors in society. But so are horses. The labor of horses enables men to produce more wealth than they otherwise could. The horse is an economic factor in society. But the horse is not economically independent, nor is the woman. If a man plus a valet can perform more useful service than he could minus a valet, then the valet is performing useful service. But, if the valet is the property of the man, is obliged to perform this service, and is not paid for it, he is not economically independent.

The labor which the wife performs in the household is given as part of her functional duty, not as employment. The wife of the poor man, who works hard in a small house, doing all the work for the family, or the wife of the rich man, who wisely and gracefully manages a large house and administers its functions, each is entitled to fair pay for services rendered.

To take this ground and hold it honestly, wives, as earners through domestic service, are entitled to the wages of cooks, housemaids, nursemaids, seamstresses, or housekeepers, and to no more. This would of course reduce the spending money of the wives of the rich, and put it out of the power of the poor man to "support" a wife at all, unless, indeed, the poor man faced the situation fully, paid his wife her wages as house servant, and then she and he combined their funds in the support of their children. He would be keeping a servant: she would be helping keep the family. But nowhere on earth would there be "a rich woman" by these means. Even the highest class of private housekeeper, useful as her services are, does not accumulate a fortune. She does not buy diamonds and sables[1] and keep a carriage. Things like these are not earned by house service.

But the salient fact in this discussion is that, whatever the economic value of the domestic industry of women is, they do not get it. The women who do the most work get the least money, and the women who have the most money do the least work. Their labor is neither given nor taken as a factor in economic exchange. It is held to be their duty as women to do this work; and their

---

1 Fur clothing and accessories.

economic status bears no relation to their domestic labors, unless an inverse one. Moreover, if they were thus fairly paid,—given what they earned, and—no more,—all women working in this way would be reduced to the economic status of the house servant. Few women—or men either—care to face this condition. The ground that women earn their living by domestic labor is instantly forsaken, and we are told that they obtain their livelihood as mothers. This is a peculiar position. We speak of it commonly enough, and often with deep feeling, but without due analysis.

In treating of an economic exchange, asking what return in goods or labor women make for the goods and labor given them,—either to the race collectively or to their husbands individually,—what payment women make for their clothes and shoes and furniture and food and shelter, we are told that the duties and services of the mother entitle her to support.

If this is so, if motherhood is an exchangeable commodity given by women in payment for clothes and food, then we must of course find some relation between the quantity or quality of the motherhood and the quantity and quality of the pay. This being true, then the women who are not mothers have no economic status at all; and the economic status of those who are must be shown to be relative to their motherhood. This is obviously absurd. The childless wife has as much money as the mother of many,—more; for the children of the latter consume what would otherwise be hers; and the inefficient mother is no less provided for than the efficient one. Visibly, and upon the face of it, women are not maintained in economic prosperity proportioned to their motherhood. Motherhood bears no relation to their economic status. Among primitive races, it is true,—in the patriarchal period,[1] for instance,—there was some truth in this position. Women being of no value whatever save as bearers of children, their favor and indulgence did bear direct relation to maternity; and they had reason to exult on more grounds than one when they could boast a son. To-day, however, the maintenance of the woman is not conditioned upon this. A man is not

---

1 While today's anthropologists recognize diversity in social organization during all periods, nineteenth-century theoretical works such as Lewis Morgan's *Ancient Society* (1877) and Friedrich Engels's *Origin of the Family* adopted a more universalizing approach, arguing that the earliest prehistoric human societies tracked descent through female lines but later prehistoric societies grew increasingly patriarchal—and patrilineal—over time.

allowed to discard his wife because she is barren. The claim of motherhood as a factor in economic exchange is false to-day. But suppose it were true. Are we willing to hold this ground, even in theory? Are we willing to consider motherhood as a business, a form of commercial exchange? Are the cares and duties of the mother, her travail[1] and her love, commodities to be exchanged for bread?

It is revolting so to consider them; and, if we dare face our own thoughts, and force them to their logical conclusion, we shall see that nothing could be more repugnant to human feeling, or more socially and individually injurious, than to make motherhood a trade. Driven off these alleged grounds of women's economic independence; shown that women, as a class, neither produce nor distribute wealth; that women, as individuals, labor mainly as house servants, are not paid as such, and would not be satisfied with such an economic status if they were so paid; that wives are not business partners or co-producers of wealth with their husbands, unless they actually practise the same profession; that they are not salaried as mothers, and that it would be unspeakably degrading if they were,—what remains to those who deny that women are supported by men? This (and a most amusing position it is),—that the function of maternity unfits a woman for economic production, and, therefore, it is right that she should be supported by her husband.

The ground is taken that the human female is not economically independent, that she is fed by the male of her species. In denial of this, it is first alleged that she is economically independent,—that she does support herself by her own industry in the house. It being shown that there is no relation between the economic status of woman and the labor she performs in the home, it is then alleged that not as house servant, but as mother, does woman earn her living. It being shown that the economic status of woman bears no relation to her motherhood, either in quantity or quality, it is then alleged that motherhood renders a woman unfit for economic production, and that, therefore, it is right that she be supported by her husband. Before going farther, let us seize upon this admission,—that she *is* supported by her husband.

Without going into either the ethics or the necessities of the case, we have reached so much common ground: the female of genus homo is supported by the male. Whereas, in other species

---

1 Childbirth.

of animals, male and female alike graze and browse, hunt and kill, climb, swim, dig, run, and fly for their livings, in our species the female does not seek her own living in the specific activities of our race, but is fed by the male.

Now as to the alleged necessity. Because of her maternal duties, the human female is said to be unable to get her own living. As the maternal duties of other females do not unfit them for getting their own living and also the livings of their young, it would seem that the human maternal duties require the segregation of the entire energies of the mother to the service of the child during her entire adult life, or so large a proportion of them that not enough remains to devote to the individual interests of the mother.

Such a condition, did it exist, would of course excuse and justify the pitiful dependence of the human female, and her support by the male. As the queen bee, modified entirely to maternity, is supported, not by the male, to be sure, but by her co-workers, the "old maids," the barren working bees, who labor so patiently and lovingly in their branch of the maternal duties of the hive, so would the human female, modified entirely to maternity, become unfit for any other exertion, and a helpless dependant.

Is this the condition of human motherhood? Does the human mother, by her motherhood, thereby lose control of brain and body, lose power and skill and desire for any other work? Do we see before us the human race, with all its females segregated entirely to the uses of motherhood, consecrated, set apart, specially developed, spending every power of their nature on the service of their children?

We do not. We see the human mother worked far harder than a mare, laboring her life long in the service, not of her children only, but of men; husbands, brothers, fathers, whatever male relatives she has; for mother and sister also; for the church a little, if she is allowed; for society, if she is able; for charity and education and reform,—working in many ways that are not the ways of motherhood.

It is not motherhood that keeps the housewife on her feet from dawn till dark; it is house service, not child service. Women work longer and harder than most men, and not solely in maternal duties. The savage mother carries the burdens, and does all menial service for the tribe. The peasant mother toils in the fields, and the workingman's wife in the home. Many mothers, even now, are wage-earners for the family, as well as bearers and rearers of it. And the women who are not so occupied, the women who belong to rich men,—here perhaps is the exhaustive devotion to maternity which is supposed to justify an admitted economic dependence. But we do not find it even among these. Women of ease and wealth provide for their children better care than the poor woman can; but they do not spend more time upon it themselves, nor more care and effort. They have other occupation.

In spite of her supposed segregation to maternal duties, the human female, the world over, works at extra-maternal duties for hours enough to provide her with an independent living, and then is denied independence on the ground that motherhood prevents her working!

If this ground were tenable, we should find a world full of women who never lifted a finger save in the service of their children, and of men who did *all* the work besides, and waited on the women whom motherhood prevented from waiting on themselves. The ground is not tenable. A human female, healthy, sound, has twenty-five years of life before she is a mother, and should have twenty-five years more after the period of such maternal service as is expected of her has been given. The duties of grandmotherhood are surely not alleged as preventing economic independence.

The working power of the mother has always been a prominent factor in human life. She is the worker *par excellence*, but her work is not such as to affect her economic status.[1] Her living, all that she gets,—food, clothing, ornaments, amusements, luxuries,—these bear no relation to her power to produce wealth, to her services in the house, or to her motherhood. These things bear relation only to the man she marries, the man she depends on,—to how much he has and how much he is willing to give her. The women whose splendid extravagance dazzles the world, whose economic goods are the greatest, are often neither houseworkers nor mothers, but simply the women who hold most power over the men who have the most money. The female of genus homo is economically dependent on the male. He is her food supply.

---

1 Gilman's analysis of the economic value of women's housework in this chapter is highly original. Contemporary male theorists, such as Lester Frank Ward (1841–1913), while attentive to women's economic status, did not recognize the importance of housework and childrearing in the economic system.

II.

Knowing how important a factor in the evolution of species is the economic relation, and finding in the human species an economic relation so peculiar, we may naturally look to find effects peculiar to our race. We may expect to find phenomena[1] in the sex-relation and in the economic relation of humanity of a unique character,—phenomena not traceable to human superiority, but singularly derogatory to that superiority; phenomena so marked, so morbid, as to give rise to much speculation as to their cause. Are these natural inferences fulfilled? Are these peculiarities in the sex-relation and in the economic relation manifested in human life? Indisputably these are,—so plain, so prominent, so imperiously demanding attention, that human thought has been occupied from its first consciousness in trying some way to account for them. To explain and relate these phenomena, separating what is due to normal race-development from what is due to this abnormal sexuo-economic[2] relation, is the purpose of the line of study here suggested.

As the racial distinction of humanity lies in its social relation, so we find the distinctive gains and losses of humanity to lie also in its social relation. We are more affected by our relation to each other than by our physical environment.

Disadvantages of climate, deficiencies in food supply, competition from other species,—all these conditions society, in its organic strength, is easily able to overcome or to adjust. But in our inter-human relations we are not so successful. The serious dangers and troubles of human life arise from difficulties of adjustment with our social environment, and not with our physical environment. These difficulties, so far, have acted as a continual check to social progress. The more absolutely a nation has triumphed over physical conditions, the more successful it has become in its conquest of physical enemies and obstacles, the more it has given rein to the action of social forces which have ultimately destroyed the nation, and left the long ascent to be begun again by others.

---

1 Facts, occurrences, or circumstances.
2 Gilman coined the term *sexuo-economic*. Her emphasis on the interrelationship between erotic and economic systems overlaps with but is distinct from Ward's analysis of the sociological effects of reproduction, which he described as a "sexuo-social" relation. See Ward 663–64.

There is the moral of all human tales:
'Tis but the same rehearsal of the past,—
First Freedom, and then Glory; when that fails,
Wealth, Vice, Corruption,—barbarism at last.
And History, with all her volumes vast,
Hath but *one* page.[1]

The path of history is strewn with fossils and faint relics of extinct races,—races which died of what the sociologist would call internal diseases rather than natural causes. This, too, has been clear to the observer in all ages. It has been easily seen that there was something in our own behavior which did us more harm than any external difficulty; but what we have not seen is the natural cause of our unnatural conduct, and how most easily to alter it.

Rudely[2] classifying the principal fields of human difficulty, we find one large proportion lies in the sex-relation, and another in the economic relation, between the individual constituents of society. To speak broadly, the troubles of life as we find them are mainly traceable to the heart or the purse. The other horror of our lives—disease—comes back often to these causes,—to something wrong either in economic relation or in sex-relation. To be ill-fed or ill-bred, or both, is largely what makes us the sickly race we are. In this wrong breeding, this maladjustment of the sex-relation in humanity, what are the principal features? We see in social evolution two main lines of action in this department of life. One is a gradual orderly development of monogamous marriage, as the form of sex-union best calculated to advance the interests of the individual and of society. It should be clearly understood that this is a natural development, inevitable in the course of social progress; not an artificial condition, enforced by laws of our making. Monogamy is found among birds and mammals: it is just as natural a condition as polygamy or promiscuity or any other form of sex-union; and its permanence and integrity are introduced and increased by the needs of the young and the advantage to the race, just as any other form of reproduction was introduced. Our moral concepts rest primarily on facts. The moral quality of monogamous marriage depends on its true advantage to the individual and to society. If it were not the best form of marriage for our racial good, it would not be right. All the way up, from the promiscuous horde of savages, with their

---

1 George Gordon Byron, *Childe Harold's Pilgrimage* (1812–18), 4.108.1–6.
2 Roughly, imperfectly.

miscellaneous matings, to the lifelong devotion of romantic love, social life has been evolving a type of sex-union best suited to develope and improve the individual and the race. This is an orderly process, and a pleasant one, involving only such comparative pain and difficulty as always attend the assumption of new processes and the extinction of the old; but accompanied by far more joy than pain.

But with the natural process of social advancement has gone an unnatural process,—an erratic and morbid action, making the sex-relation of humanity a frightful source of evil. So prominent have been these morbid actions and evil results that hasty thinkers of all ages have assumed that the whole thing was wrong, and that celibacy was the highest virtue. Without the power of complete analysis, without knowledge of the sociological data essential to such analysis, we have sweepingly condemned as a whole what we could easily see was so allied with pain and loss. But, like all natural phenomena, the phenomena of sex may be studied, both the normal and the abnormal, the physiological and the pathological; and we are quite capable of understanding why we are in such evil case,[1] and how we may attain more healthful conditions.

So far, the study of this subject has rested on the assumption that man must be just as we find him, that man behaves just as he chooses, and that, if he does not choose to behave as he does, he can stop. Therefore, when we discovered that human behavior in the sex-relation was productive of evil, we exhorted the human creature to stop so behaving, and have continued so to exhort for many centuries. By law and religion, by education and custom, we have sought to enforce upon the human individual the kind of behavior which our social sense so clearly showed was right.

But always there has remained the morbid action. Whatever the external form of sex-union to which we have given social sanction, however Bible and Koran and Vedas[2] have offered instruction, some hidden cause has operated continuously against the true course of social evolution, to pervert the natural trend toward a higher and more advantageous sex-relation; and to maintain lower forms, and erratic phases, of a most disadvantageous character.

Every other animal works out the kind of sex-union best adapted to the reproduction of his species, and peacefully practises it. We have worked out the kind that is best for us,—best for

---

1 Situation, circumstance.
2 Sacred texts.

the individuals concerned, for the young resultant, and for society as a whole; but we do not peacefully practise it. So palpable is this fact that we have commonly accepted it, and taken it for granted that this relation must be a continuous source of trouble to humanity. "Marriage is a lottery,"[1] is a common saying among us. "The course of true love never did run smooth."[2] And we quote with unction *Punch*'s advice to those about to marry,— "Don't!"[3] That peculiar sub-relation which has dragged along with us all the time that monogamous marriage has been growing to be the accepted form of sex-union—prostitution—we have accepted, and called a "social necessity." We also call it "the social evil." We have tacitly admitted that this relation in the human race must be more or less uncomfortable and wrong, that it is part of our nature to have it so.

Now let us examine the case fairly and calmly, and see whether it is as inscrutable and immutable as hitherto believed. What are the conditions? What are the natural and what the unnatural features of the case? To distinguish these involves a little study of the evolution of the processes of reproduction.

Very early in the development of species it was ascertained by nature's slow but sure experiments that the establishment of two sexes in separate organisms, and their differentiation, was to the advantage of the species. Therefore, out of the mere protoplasmic masses, the floating cells, the amorphous early forms of life, grew into use the distinction of the sexes,—the gradual development of masculine and feminine organs and functions in two distinct organisms. Developed and increased by use, the distinction of sex increased in the evolution of species. As the distinction increased, the attraction increased, until we have in all the higher races two markedly different sexes, strongly drawn together by the attraction of sex, and fulfilling their use in the reproduction of species. These are the natural features of sex-distinction and sex-union, and they are found in the human species as in others. The unnatural feature by which our race holds an unenviable distinction consists mainly in this,—a morbid excess in the exercise of this function.

It is this excess, whether in marriage or out, which makes the health and happiness of humanity in this relation so precarious.

---

1 This common proverb appears in numerous nineteenth-century publications, for example Charles Dickens's *Dombey and Son* (London: Bradbury and Evans, 1848), 353.
2 From Shakespeare, *A Midsummer Night's Dream* (c. 1595), 1.1.136.
3 British weekly satirical magazine *Punch; or, The London Charivari*.

It is this excess, always easily seen, which law and religion have mainly striven to check. Excessive sex-indulgence is the distinctive feature of humanity in this relation.

To define "excess" in this connection is not difficult. All natural functions that require our conscious co-operation for their fulfilment are urged upon our notice by an imperative desire. We do not have to desire to breathe or to digest or to circulate the blood, because that is done without our volition; but we do have to desire to eat and drink, because the stomach cannot obtain its supplies without in some way spurring the whole organism to secure them. So hunger is given us as an essential factor in our process of nutrition. In the same manner sex-attraction is an essential factor in the fulfilment of our processes of reproduction. In a normal condition the amount of hunger we feel is exactly proportioned to the amount of food we need. It tells us when to eat and when to stop. In some diseased conditions "an unnatural appetite" sets in; and we are impelled to eat far beyond the capacity of the stomach to digest, of the body to assimilate. This is an excessive hunger.

We, as a race, manifest an excessive sex-attraction, followed by its excessive indulgence, and the inevitable evil consequence. It urges us to a degree of indulgence which bears no relation to the original needs of the organism, and which is even so absurdly exaggerated as to react unfavorably on the incidental gratification involved; an excess which tends to pervert and exhaust desire as well as to injure reproduction.

The human animal manifests an excess in sex-attraction which not only injures the race through its morbid action on the natural processes of reproduction, but which injures the happiness of the individual through its morbid reaction on his own desires.

What is the cause of this excessive sex-attraction in the human species? The immediately acting cause of sex-attraction is sex-distinction. The more widely the sexes are differentiated, the more forcibly they are attracted to each other. The more highly developed becomes the distinction of sex in either organism, the more intense is its attraction for the other. In the human species we find sex-distinction carried to an excessive degree. Sex-distinction in humanity is so marked as to retard and confuse race-distinction, to check individual distinction, seriously to injure the race. Accustomed as we are simply to accept the facts of life as we find them, to consider people as permanent types instead of seeing them and the whole race in continual change according to the action of many forces, it seems strange at first to differentiate between familiar manifestations of sex-distinction, and to say: "This is normal, and should not be disturbed. This is abnormal, and should be removed." But that is precisely what must be done.

Normal sex-distinction manifests itself in all species in what are called primary and secondary sex-characteristics. The primary are those organs and functions essential to reproduction; the secondary, those modifications of structure and function which subserve the uses of reproduction ultimately, but are not directly essential,—such as the horns of the stag, of use in sex-combat; the plumage of the peacock, of use in sex-competition.[1] All the minor characteristics of beard or mane, comb, wattles, spurs, gorgeous color or superior size, which distinguish the male from the female,—these are distinctions of sex. These distinctions are of use to the species through reproduction only, the processes of race-preservation. They are not of use in self-preservation. The creature is not profited personally by his mane or crest or tail-feathers: they do not help him get his dinner or kill his enemies.

On the contrary, they react unfavorably upon his personal gains, if, through too great development, they interfere with his activity or render him a conspicuous mark for enemies. Such development would constitute excessive sex-distinction, and this is precisely the condition of the human race. Our distinctions of sex are carried to such a degree as to be disadvantageous to our progress as individuals and as a race. The sexes in our species are differentiated not only enough to perform their primal functions; not only enough to manifest all sufficient secondary sexual characteristics and fulfil their use in giving rise to sufficient sex-attraction; but so much as seriously to interfere with the processes of self-preservation on the one hand; and, more conspicuous still, so much as to react unfavorably upon the very processes of race-preservation which they are meant to serve. Our excessive sex-distinction, manifesting the characteristics of sex to an abnormal degree, has given rise to a degree of attraction which demands a degree of indulgence that directly injures motherhood and fatherhood. We are not better as parents, nor better as people, for our existing degree of sex-distinction, but visibly worse. To what conditions are we to look for the developing cause of these phenomena?

Let us first examine the balance of forces by which these two great processes, self-preservation and race-preservation, are conducted in the world. Self-preservation involves the expenditure of

---

1   Darwin argues that primary and secondary sex characteristics constitute prominent factors in evolution (*Descent of Man* 8.253–320).

energy in those acts, and their ensuing modifications of structure and function, which tend to the maintenance of the individual life. Race-preservation involves the expenditure of energy in those acts, and their ensuing modifications of structure and function, which tend to the maintenance of the racial life, even to the complete sacrifice of the individual. This primal distinction should be clearly held in mind. Self-preservation and race-preservation are in no way identical processes, and are often directly opposed. In the line of self-preservation, natural selection, acting on the individual, developes those characteristics which enable it to succeed in "the struggle for existence,"[1] increasing by use those organs and functions by which it directly profits. In the line of race-preservation, sexual selection, acting on the individual, developes those characteristics which enable it to succeed in what Drummond has called "the struggle for the existence of others,"[2] increasing by use those organs and functions by which its young are to profit, directly or indirectly. The individual has been not only modified to its environment, under natural selection, but modified to its mate, under sexual selection, each sex developing the qualities desired by the other by the simple process of choice, those best sexed being first chosen, and transmitting their sex-development as well as their racial development.

The order mammalia is the resultant of a primary sex-distinction developed by natural selection; but the gorgeous plumage of the peacock's tail is a secondary sex-distinction developed by sexual selection. If the peacock's tail were to increase in size and splendor till it shone like the sun and covered an acre,—if it tended so to increase, we will say,—such excessive sex-distinction would be so inimical to the personal prosperity of that peacock that he would die, and his tail-tendency would perish with him. If the pea-hen, conversely, whose sex-distinction attracts in the opposite direction, not by being large and splendid, but small and dull,—if she should grow so small and dull as to fail to keep herself and her young fed and defended, then she would die; and there would be another check to excessive sex-distinction. In herds of deer and cattle the male is larger and stronger, the female smaller and weaker; but, unless the latter is large and strong enough to keep up with the male in the search for food or

---

1 The phrase "struggle for existence" and the similar phrase "struggle for life" are used by Darwin frequently throughout *On the Origin of Species*.
2 Drummond (1851–97): "The Struggle for the Life of Others is the physiological name for the greatest word of ethics—Other-ism, Altruism, Love" (8.220).

the flight from foes, one is taken and the other left, and there is no more of that kind of animal. Differ as they may in sex, they must remain alike in species, equal in race-development, else destruction overtakes them. The force of natural selection, demanding and producing identical race-qualities, acts as a check on sexual selection, with its production of different sex-qualities. As sexes, they perform different functions, and therefore tend to develope differently. As species, they perform the same functions, and therefore tend to develope equally.

And as sex-functions are only used occasionally, and race-functions are used all the time,—as they mate but yearly or tri-monthly, but eat daily and hourly,—the processes of obtaining food or of opposing constant enemies act more steadily than the processes of reproduction, and produce greater effect.

We find the order mammalia accordingly producing and suckling its young in the same manner through a wide variety of species which obtain their living in a different manner. The calf and colt and cub and kitten are produced by the same process; but the cow and horse, the bear and cat, are produced by different processes. And, though cow and bull, mare and stallion, differ as to sex, they are alike in species; and the likeness in species is greater than the difference in sex. Cow, mare, and cat are all females of the order mammalia, and so far alike; but how much more different they are than similar!

Natural selection develops race. Sexual selection develops sex. Sex-development is one throughout its varied forms, tending only to reproduce what is. But race-development rises ever in higher and higher manifestation of energy. As sexes, we share our distinction with the animal kingdom almost to the beginning of life, and with the vegetable world as well. As races, we differ in ascending degree; and the human race stands highest in the scale of life so far.

When, then, it can be shown that sex-distinction in the human race is so excessive as not only to affect injuriously its own purposes, but to check and pervert the progress of the race, it becomes a matter for most serious consideration. Nothing could be more inevitable, however, under our sexuo-economic relation. By the economic dependence of the human female upon the male, the balance of forces is altered. Natural selection no longer checks the action of sexual selection, but co-operates with it. Where both sexes obtain their food through the same exertions, from the same sources, under the same conditions, both sexes are acted upon alike, and developed alike by their environment.

Where the two sexes obtain their food under different conditions, and where that difference consists in one of them being fed by the other, then the feeding sex becomes the environment of the fed. Man, in supporting woman, has become her economic environment. Under natural selection, every creature is modified to its environment, developing perforce the qualities needed to obtain its livelihood under that environment. Man, as the feeder of woman, becomes the strongest modifying force in her economic condition. Under sexual selection the human creature is of course modified to its mate, as with all creatures. When the mate becomes also the master, when economic necessity is added to sex-attraction, we have two great evolutionary forces acting together to the same end; namely, to develope sex-distinction in the human female. For, in her position of economic dependence in the sex-relation, sex-distinction is with her not only a means of attracting a mate, as with all creatures, but a means of getting her livelihood, as is the case with no other creature under heaven. Because of the economic dependence of the human female on her mate, she is modified to sex to an excessive degree. This excessive modification she transmits to her children; and so is steadily implanted in the human constitution the morbid tendency to excess in this relation, which has acted so universally upon us in all ages, in spite of our best efforts to restrain it. It is not the normal sex-tendency, common to all creatures, but an abnormal sex-tendency, produced and maintained by the abnormal economic relation which makes one sex get its living from the other by the exercise of sex-functions. This is the immediate effect upon individuals of the peculiar sexuo-economic relation which obtains among us.

III.

In establishing the claim of excessive sex-distinction in the human race, much needs to be said to make clear to the general reader what is meant by the term. To the popular mind, both the coarsely familiar and the over-refined, "sexual" is thought to mean "sensual"; and the charge of excessive sex-distinction seems to be a reproach. This should be at once dismissed, as merely showing ignorance of the terms used. A man does not object to being called "masculine," nor a woman to being called "feminine." Yet whatever is masculine or feminine is sexual. To be distinguished by femininity is to be distinguished by sex. To be over-feminine is to be over-sexed. To manifest in excess any of the distinctions of sex, primary or secondary, is to be over-sexed.[1] Our hypothetical peacock, with his too large and splendid tail, would be over-sexed, and no offence to his moral character! The primary sex-distinctions in our race as in others consist merely in the essential organs and functions of reproduction. The secondary distinctions, and this is where we are to look for our largest excess—consist in all those differences in organ and function, in look and action, in habit, manner, method, occupation, behavior, which distinguish men from women. In a troop of horses, seen at a distance, the sexes are indistinguishable. In a herd of deer the males are distinguishable because of their antlers. The male lion is distinguished by his mane, the male cat only by a somewhat heavier build. In certain species of insects the male and female differ so widely in appearance that even naturalists have supposed them to belong to separate species. Beyond these distinctions lies that of conduct. Certain psychic attributes are manifested by either sex. The intensity of the maternal passion is a sex-distinction as much as the lion's mane or the stag's horns. The belligerence and dominance of the male is a sex-distinction: the modesty and timidity of the female is a sex-distinction. The tendency to "sit" is a sex-distinction of the hen: the tendency to strut is a sex-distinction of the cock. The tendency to fight is a sex-distinction of males in general: the tendency to protect and provide for, is a sex-distinction of females in general.

With the human race, whose chief activities are social, the initial tendency to sex-distinction is carried out in many varied functions. We have differentiated our industries, our responsibilities, our very virtues,[2] along sex lines. It will therefore be clear that the claim of excessive sex-distinction in humanity, and especially in woman, does not carry with it any specific "moral" reproach, though it does in the larger sense prove a decided evil in its effect on human progress.

In primary distinctions our excess is not so marked as in the farther and subtler development; yet, even here, we have plain proof of it. Sex-energy in its primal manifestation is exhibited in the male of the human species to a degree far greater than is necessary for the processes of reproduction,—enough, indeed, to subvert and injure those processes. The direct injury to reproduction from the excessive indulgence of the male, and the indirect injury through its debilitating effect upon the female,

---

1 Darwin argues that primary and secondary sex characteristics constitute prominent factors in evolution (*Descent of Man* 8.253–320).
2 Moral qualities.

together with the enormous evil to society produced by extra-marital indulgence,—these are facts quite generally known.[1] We have recognized them for centuries, and sought to check the evil action by law, civil, social, moral. But we have treated it always as a field of voluntary action, not as a condition of morbid development. We have held it as right that man should be so, but wrong that man should do so. Nature does not work in that way. What it is right to be, it is right to do. What it is wrong to do, it is wrong to be. This inordinate demand in the human male is an excessive sex-distinction. In this, in a certain over-coarseness and hardness, a too great belligerence and pride, a too great subservience to the power of sex-attraction, we find the main marks of excessive sex-distinction in men. It has been always checked and offset in them by the healthful activities of racial life. Their energies have been called out and their faculties developed along all the lines of human progress. In the growth of industry, commerce, science, manufacture, government, art, religion, the male of our species has become human, far more than male. Strong as this passion is in him, inordinate as is his indulgence, he is a far more normal animal than the female of his species,—far less over-sexed. To him this field of special activity is but part of life,—an incident. The whole world remains besides. To her it is the world. This has been well stated in the familiar epigram of Madame de Staël,— "Love with man is an episode, with woman a history."[2] It is in woman that we find most fully expressed the excessive sex-distinction of the human species,—physical, psychical, social. See first the physical manifestation.

To make clear by an instance the difference between normal and abnormal sex-distinction, look at the relative condition of a wild cow and a "milch cow," such as we have made. The wild cow is a female. She has healthy calves, and milk enough for them; and that is all the femininity she needs. Otherwise than that she is bovine rather than feminine. She is a light, strong, swift, sinewy creature, able to run, jump, and fight, if necessary. We, for eco-

---

1   In the late nineteenth century, prostitution was referred to as the *social evil* in so-called polite society and sometimes held responsible for the spread of disease. Vice crusaders and medical doctors were particularly concerned about the spread of congenital and tertiary syphilis. Men sometimes contracted the disease during extra-marital sex and then passed the disease on to their wives.

2   Anne Louise Germaine Necker, Madame de Staël-Holstein (1766–1817): "L'amour est l'histoire de la vie des femmes; c'est un épisode dans celle des hommes" (170).

nomic uses, have artificially developed the cow's capacity for producing milk. She has become a walking milk-machine, bred and tended to that express end, her value measured in quarts. The secretion of milk is a maternal function,—a sex-function. The cow is over-sexed. Turn her loose in natural conditions, and, if she survive the change, she would revert in a very few generations to the plain cow, with her energies used in the general activities of her race, and not all running to milk.

Physically, woman belongs to a tall, vigorous, beautiful animal species, capable of great and varied exertion. In every race and time when she has opportunity for racial activity, she developes accordingly, and is no less a woman for being a healthy human creature. In every race and time where she is denied this opportunity,—and few, indeed, have been her years of freedom,—she has developed in the lines of action to which she was confined; and those were always lines of sex-activity. In consequence the body of woman, speaking in the largest generalization, manifests sex-distinction predominantly.

Woman's femininity—and "the eternal feminine"[1] means simply the eternal sexual—is more apparent in proportion to her humanity than the femininity of other animals in proportion to their caninity or felinity or equinity. "A feminine hand" or "a feminine foot" is distinguishable anywhere. We do not hear of "a feminine paw" or "a feminine hoof." A hand is an organ of prehension, a foot an organ of locomotion: they are not secondary sexual characteristics. The comparative smallness and feebleness of woman is a sex-distinction. We have carried it to such an excess that women are commonly known as "the weaker sex." There is no such glaring difference between male and female in other advanced species. In the long migrations of birds, in the ceaseless motion of the grazing herds that used to swing up and down over the continent each year, in the wild, steep journeys of the breeding salmon, nothing is heard of the weaker sex. And among the higher carnivora, where longer maintenance of the young brings their condition nearer ours, the hunter dreads the attack of the female more than that of the male. The disproportionate weakness is an excessive sex-distinction. Its injurious effect may be broadly shown in the Oriental nations, where the female in curtained harems is confined most exclusively to sex-functions and denied most fully the exercise of race-functions. In such peoples the weakness, the tendency to small bones and

---

1 The concept of the female as pure and immutable.

adipose tissue[1] of the over-sexed female, is transmitted to the male, with a retarding effect on the development of the race. Conversely, in early Germanic tribes the comparatively free and humanly developed women—tall, strong, and brave—transmitted to their sons a greater proportion of human power and much less of morbid sex-tendency.

The degree of feebleness and clumsiness common to women, the comparative inability to stand, walk, run, jump, climb, and perform other race-functions common to both sexes, is an excessive sex-distinction; and the ensuing transmission of this relative feebleness to their children, boys and girls alike, retards human development. Strong, free, active women, the sturdy, field-working peasant, the burden-bearing savage, are no less good mothers for their human strength. But our civilized "feminine delicacy," which appears somewhat less delicate when recognized as an expression of sexuality in excess,—makes us no better mothers, but worse. The relative weakness of women is a sex-distinction. It is apparent in her to a degree that injures motherhood, that injures wifehood, that injures the individual. The sex-usefulness and the human usefulness of women, their general duty to their kind, are greatly injured by this degree of distinction. In every way the over-sexed condition of the human female reacts unfavorably upon herself, her husband, her children, and the race.

In its psychic manifestation this intense sex-distinction is equally apparent. The primal instinct of sex-attraction has developed under social forces into a conscious passion of enormous power, a deep and lifelong devotion, overwhelming in its force. This is excessive in both sexes, but more so in women than in men,—not so commonly in its simple physical form, but in the unreasoning intensity of emotion that refuses all guidance, and drives those possessed by it to risk every other good for this one end. It is not at first sight easy, and it may seem an irreverent and thankless task, to discriminate here between what is good in the "master passion" and what is evil, and especially to claim for one sex more of this feeling than for the other; but such discrimination can be made.

It is good for the individual and for the race to have developed such a degree of passionate and permanent love as shall best promote the happiness of individuals and the reproduction of species. It is not good for the race or for the individual that this

---

1 Fatty tissue; fat deposits around organs in the body.

feeling should have become so intense as to override all other human faculties, to make a mock of the accumulated wisdom of the ages, the stored power of the will; to drive the individual—against his own plain conviction—into a union sure to result in evil, or to hold the individual helpless in such an evil union, when made.

Such is the condition of humanity, involving most evil results to its offspring and to its own happiness. And, while in men the immediate dominating force of the passion may be more conspicuous, it is in women that it holds more universal sway. For the man has other powers and faculties in full use, whereby to break loose from the force of this; and the woman, specially modified to sex and denied racial activity, pours her whole life into her love, and, if injured here, she is injured irretrievably. With him it is frequently light and transient, and, when most intense, often most transient. With her it is a deep, all-absorbing force, under the action of which she will renounce all that life offers, take any risk, face any hardships, bear any pain. It is maintained in her in the face of a lifetime of neglect and abuse. The common instance of the police court trials—the woman cruelly abused who will not testify against her husband—shows this. This devotion, carried to such a degree as to lead to the mismating of individuals with its personal and social injury, is an excessive sex-distinction.

But it is in our common social relations that the predominance of sex-distinction in women is made most manifest. The fact that, speaking broadly, women have, from the very beginning, been spoken of expressively enough as "the sex," demonstrates clearly that this is the main impression which they have made upon observers and recorders. Here one need attempt no farther proof than to turn the mind of the reader to an unbroken record of facts and feelings perfectly patent to every one, but not hitherto looked at as other than perfectly natural and right. So utterly has the status of woman been accepted as a sexual one that it has remained for the woman's movement of the nineteenth century to devote much contention to the claim that women are persons![1] That women are persons as well as females,—an unheard of proposition!

---

[1] In *Minor v. Happersett* (1875), the United States Supreme Court unanimously rejected Virginia Minor's claim that the Fourteenth Amendment prohibited the disenfranchisement of women as citizens of the United States. The Court acknowledged that women are persons and citizens but found that suffrage was not coextensive with citizenship.

In a "Handbook of Proverbs of All Nations,"[1] a collection comprising many thousands, these facts are to be observed: first, that the proverbs concerning women are an insignificant minority compared to those concerning men; second, that the proverbs concerning women almost invariably apply to them in general,—to the sex. Those concerning men qualify, limit, describe, specialize. It is "a lazy man," "a violent man," "a man in his cups." Qualities and actions are predicated of man individually, and not as a sex, unless he is flatly contrasted with woman, as in "A man of straw is worth a woman of gold," "Men are deeds, women are words," or "Man, woman, and the devil are the three degrees of comparison." But of woman it is always and only "a woman," meaning simply a female, and recognizing no personal distinction: "As much pity to see a woman weep as to see a goose go barefoot." "He that hath an eel by the tail and a woman by her word hath a slippery handle." "A woman, a spaniel, and a walnut-tree,—the more you beat 'em, the better they be." Occasionally a distinction is made between "a fair woman" and "a black woman"; and Solomon's "virtuous woman," who commanded such a high price, is familiar to us all.[2] But in common thought it is simply "a woman" always. The boast of the profligate that he knows "the sex," so recently expressed by a new poet,—"The things you will learn from the Yellow and Brown, they'll 'elp you an' 'eap with the White";[3] the complaint of the angry rejected that "all women are just alike!"—the consensus of public opinion of all time goes to show that the characteristics common to the sex have predominated over the characteristics distinctive of the individual,—a marked excess in sex-distinction.

From the time our children are born, we use every means known to accentuate sex-distinction in both boy and girl; and the reason that the boy is not so hopelessly marked by it as the girl is that he has the whole field of human expression open to him besides. In our steady insistence on proclaiming sex-distinction we have grown to consider most human attributes as masculine attributes, for the simple reason that they were allowed to men and forbidden to women.

A clear and definite understanding of the difference between race-attributes and sex-attributes should be established. Life consists of action. The action of a living thing is along two main lines,—self-preservation and race-preservation. The processes

---

1 Possibly Walter Keating Kelly's *Proverbs of All Nations* (1859).
2 Proverbs 31.10–31.
3 Rudyard Kipling, "The Ladies" (1896), 15–16.

that keep the individual alive, from the involuntary action of his internal organs to the voluntary action of his external organs,—every act, from breathing to hunting his food, which contributes to the maintenance of the individual life,—these are the processes of self-preservation. Whatever activities tend to keep the race alive, to reproduce the individual, from the involuntary action of the internal organs to the voluntary action of the external organs; every act from the development of germ-cells to the taking care of children, which contributes to the maintenance of the racial life,—these are the processes of race-preservation. In race-preservation, male and female have distinctive organs, distinctive functions, distinctive lines of action. In self-preservation, male and female have the same organs, the same functions, the same lines of action. In the human species our processes of race-preservation have reached a certain degree of elaboration; but our processes of self-preservation have gone farther, much farther.

All the varied activities of economic production and distribution, all our arts and industries, crafts and trades, all our growth in science, discovery, government, religion,—these are along the line of self-preservation: these are, or should be, common to both sexes. To teach, to rule, to make, to decorate, to distribute,—these are not sex-functions: they are race-functions. Yet so inordinate is the sex-distinction of the human race that the whole field of human progress has been considered a masculine prerogative. What could more absolutely prove the excessive sex-distinction of the human race? That this difference should surge over all its natural boundaries and blazon itself across every act of life, so that every step of the human creature is marked "male" or "female,"—surely, this is enough to show our over-sexed condition.

Little by little, very slowly, and with most unjust and cruel opposition, at cost of all life holds most dear, it is being gradually established by many martyrdoms that human work is woman's as well as man's. Harriet Martineau[1] must conceal her writing under her sewing when callers came, because "to sew" was a feminine verb, and "to write" a masculine one. Mary Somerville[2] must struggle to hide her work from even relatives, because mathematics was a "masculine" pursuit. Sex has been made to dominate the whole human world,—all the main avenues of life marked "male," and the female left to be a female, and nothing else.

---

1   British social theorist Harriet Martineau (1802–76).
2   Scottish scientist Mary Somerville (1780–1872).

But while with the male the things he fondly imagined to be "masculine" were merely human, and very good for him, with the female the few things marked "feminine" were feminine, indeed; and her ceaseless reiterance of one short song, however sweet, has given it a conspicuous monotony. In garments whose main purpose is unmistakably to announce her sex; with a tendency to ornament which marks exuberance of sex-energy, with a body so modified to sex as to be grievously deprived of its natural activities; with a manner and behavior wholly attuned to sex-advantage, and frequently most disadvantageous to any human gain; with a field of action most rigidly confined to sex-relations; with her overcharged sensibility, her prominent modesty, her "eternal femininity,"—the female of genus homo is undeniably oversexed.

This excessive distinction shows itself again in a marked precocity of development. Our little children, our very babies, show signs of it when the young of other creatures are serenely asexual in general appearance and habit. We eagerly note this precocity. We are proud of it. We carefully encourage it by precept and example, taking pains to develope the sex-instinct in little children, and think no harm. One of the first things we force upon the child's dawning consciousness is the fact that he is a boy or that she is a girl, and that, therefore, each must regard everything from a different point of view. They must be dressed differently, not on account of their personal needs, which are exactly similar at this period, but so that neither they, nor any one beholding them, may for a moment forget the distinction of sex.

Our peculiar inversion of the usual habit of species, in which the male carries ornament and the female is dark and plain, is not so much a proof of excess indeed, as a proof of the peculiar reversal of our position in the matter of sex-selection. With the other species the males compete in ornament, and the females select. With us the females compete in ornament, and the males select. If this theory of sex-ornament is disregarded, and we prefer rather to see in masculine decoration merely a form of exuberant sex-energy, expending itself in non-productive excess, then, indeed, the fact that with us the females manifest such a display of gorgeous adornment is another sign of excessive sex-distinction. In either case the forcing upon girl-children of an elaborate ornamentation which interferes with their physical activity and unconscious freedom, and fosters a premature sex-consciousness, is as clear and menacing a proof of our condition as could be mentioned. That the girl-child should be so dressed as to require a difference in care and behavior, resting wholly on the fact that she is a girl,—a fact not otherwise present to her thought at that age,—is a precocious insistence upon sex-distinction, most unwholesome in its results. Boys and girls are expected, also, to behave differently to each other, and to people in general,—a behavior to be briefly described in two words. To the boy we say, "Do"; to the girl, "Don't." The little boy must "take care" of the little girl, even if she is larger than he is. "Why?" he asks. Because he is a boy. Because of sex. Surely, if she is the stronger, she ought to take care of him, especially as the protective instinct is purely feminine in a normal race. It is not long before the boy learns his lesson. He is a boy, going to be a man; and that means all. "I thank the Lord that I was not born a woman,"[1] runs the Hebrew prayer. She is a girl, "only a girl," "nothing but a girl," and going to be a woman,—only a woman. Boys are encouraged from the beginning to show the feelings supposed to be proper to their sex. When our infant son bangs about, roars, and smashes things, we say proudly that he is "a regular boy!" When our infant daughter coquettes[2] with visitors, or wails in maternal agony because her brother has broken her doll, whose sawdust remains she nurses with piteous care, we say proudly that "she is a perfect little mother already!" What business has a little girl with the instincts of maternity? No more than the little boy should have with the instincts of paternity. They are sex-instincts, and should not appear till the period of adolescence. The most normal girl is the "tom-boy,"—whose numbers increase among us in these wiser days,—a healthy young creature, who is human through and through, not feminine till it is time to be. The most normal boy has calmness and gentleness as well as vigor and courage. He is a human creature as well as a male creature, and not aggressively masculine till it is time to be. Childhood is not the period for these marked manifestations of sex. That we exhibit them, that we admire and encourage them, shows our over-sexed condition.

IV.

Having seen the disproportionate degree of sex-distinction in humanity and its greater manifestation in the female than in

---

1 Text found in the Talmud, recited by traditional Jewish men at the beginning of morning prayers.
2 Flirts.

the male, and having seen also the unique position of the human female as an economic dependant on the male of her species, it is not difficult to establish a relation between these two facts. The general law acting to produce this condition of exaggerated sex-development was briefly referred to in the second chapter. It is as follows: the natural tendency of any function to increase in power by use causes sex-activity to increase under the action of sexual selection. This tendency is checked in most species by the force of natural selection, which diverts the energies into other channels and developes race-activities. Where the female finds her economic environment in the male, and her economic advantage is directly conditioned upon the sex-relation, the force of natural selection is added to the force of sexual selection, and both together operate to develope sex-activity. In any animal species, free from any other condition, such a relation would have inevitably developed sex to an inordinate degree, as may be readily seen in the comparatively similar cases of those insects where the female, losing economic activity and modified entirely to sex, becomes a mere egg-sac, an organism with no powers of self-preservation, only those of race-preservation. With these insects the only race-problem is to maintain and reproduce the species, and such a condition is not necessarily evil; but with a race like ours, whose development as human creatures is but comparatively begun, it is evil because of its check to individual and racial progress. There are other purposes before us besides mere maintenance and reproduction.

It should be clear to any one accustomed to the working of biological laws that all the tendencies of a living organism are progressive in their development, and are held in check by the interaction of their several forces. Each living form, with its dominant characteristics, represents a balance of power, a sort of compromise. The size of earth's primeval monsters was limited by the tensile strength of their material. Sea monsters can be bigger, because the medium in which they move offers more support. Birds must be smaller for the opposite reason. The cow requires many stomachs of a liberal size, because her food is of low nutritive value; and she must eat large quantities to keep her machine going. The size of arboreal animals, such as monkeys or squirrels, is limited by the nature of their habitat: creatures that live in trees cannot be so big as creatures that live on the ground. Every quality of every creature is relative to its condition, and tends to increase or decrease accordingly; and each quality tends to increase in proportion to its use, and to decrease in proportion to its disuse. Primitive man and his female were animals, like other animals. They were strong, fierce, lively beasts; and she was as nimble and ferocious as he, save for the added belligerence of the males in their sex-competition. In this competition, he, like the other male creatures, fought savagely with his hairy rivals; and she, like the other female creatures, complacently viewed their struggles, and mated with the victor. At other times she ran about in the forest, and helped herself to what there was to eat as freely as he did.

There seems to have come a time when it occurred to the dawning intelligence of this amiable savage that it was cheaper and easier to fight a little female, and have it done with, than to fight a big male every time. So he instituted the custom of enslaving the female; and she, losing freedom, could no longer get her own food nor that of her young. The mother ape, with her maternal function well fulfilled, flees leaping through the forest,— plucks her fruit and nuts, keeps up with the movement of the tribe, her young one on her back or held in one strong arm. But the mother woman, enslaved, could not do this. Then man, the father, found that slavery had its obligations: he must care for what he forbade to care for itself, else it died on his hands. So he slowly and reluctantly shouldered the duties of his new position. He began to feed her, and not only that, but to express in his own person the thwarted uses of maternity: he had to feed the children, too. It seems a simple arrangement. When we have thought of it at all, we have thought of it with admiration. The naturalist defends it on the ground of advantage to the species through the freeing of the mother from all other cares and confining her unreservedly to the duties of maternity. The poet and novelist, the painter and sculptor, the priest and teacher, have all extolled this lovely relation. It remains for the sociologist, from a biological point of view, to note its effects on the constitution of the human race, both in the individual and in society.[1]

When man began to feed and defend woman, she ceased proportionately to feed and defend herself. When he stood between her and her physical environment, she ceased proportionately to feel the influence of that environment and respond to it. When he became her immediate and all-important environment, she began proportionately to respond to this new influence and to be mod-

---

1 In her effort to ground sociological enquiry in biology, Gilman sides with reform Darwinists such as Ward.

ified accordingly. In a free state, speed was of as great advantage to the female as to the male, both in enabling her to catch prey and in preventing her from being caught by enemies; but, in her new condition, speed was a disadvantage. She was not allowed to do the catching, and it profited her to be caught by her new master. Free creatures, getting their own food and maintaining their own lives, develope an active capacity for attaining their ends. Parasitic creatures, whose living is obtained by the exertions of others, develope powers of absorption and of tenacity,— the powers by which they profit most. The human female was cut off from the direct action of natural selection, that mighty force which heretofore had acted on male and female alike with inexorable and beneficial effect, developing strength, developing skill, developing endurance, developing courage,—in a word, developing species. She now met the influence of natural selection acting indirectly through the male, and developing, of course, the faculties required to secure and obtain a hold on him. Needless to state that these faculties were those of sex-attraction, the one power that has made him cheerfully maintain, in what luxury he could, the being in whom he delighted. For many, many centuries she had no other hold, no other assurance of being fed. The young girl had a prospective value, and was maintained for what should follow; but the old woman, in more primitive times, had but a poor hold on life. She who could best please her lord was the favorite slave or favorite wife, and she obtained the best economic conditions.

With the growth of civilization, we have gradually crystallized into law the visible necessity for feeding the helpless female; and even old women are maintained by their male relatives with a comfortable assurance. But to this day—save, indeed, for the increasing army of women wage-earners, who are changing the face of the world by their steady advance toward economic independence—the personal profit of women bears but too close a relation to their power to win and hold the other sex. From the odalisque[1] with the most bracelets to the débutante[2] with the most bouquets, the relation still holds good,—woman's economic profit comes through the power of sex-attraction.

When we confront this fact boldly and plainly in the open market of vice, we are sick with horror. When we see the same economic relation made permanent, established by law, sanctioned and sanctified by religion, covered with flowers and

---

1 Female slave in a harem.
2 A young woman appearing in society for the first time.

incense and all accumulated sentiment, we think it innocent, lovely, and right. The transient trade[1] we think evil. The bargain for life we think good. But the biological effect remains the same. In both cases the female gets her food from the male by virtue of her sex-relationship to him. In both cases, perhaps even more in marriage because of its perfect acceptance of the situation, the female of genus homo, still living under natural law, is inexorably modified to sex in an increasing degree.

Followed in specific detail, the action of the changed environment upon women has been in given instances as follows: In the matter of mere passive surroundings she has been immediately restricted in her range. This one factor has an immense effect on man and animal alike. An absolutely uniform environment, one shape, one size, one color, one sound, would render life, if any life could be, one helpless, changeless thing. As the environment increases and varies, the development of the creature must increase and vary with it; for he acquires knowledge and power, as the material for knowledge and the need for power appear. In migratory species the female is free to acquire the same knowledge as the male by the same means, the same development by the same experiences. The human female has been restricted in range from the earliest beginning. Even among savages, she has a much more restricted knowledge of the land she lives in. She moves with the camp, of course, and follows her primitive industries in its vicinity; but the war-path and the hunt are the man's. He has a far larger habitat. The life of the female savage is freedom itself, however, compared with the increasing constriction of custom closing in upon the woman, as civilization advanced, like the iron torture chamber of romance. Its culmination is expressed in the proverb: "A woman should leave her home but three times,—when she is christened, when she is married, and when she is buried." Or this: "The woman, the cat, and the chimney should never leave the house." The absolutely stationary female and the wide-ranging male are distinctly human institutions, after we leave behind us such low forms of life as the gypsy moth, whose female seldom moves more than a few feet from the pupa moth. She has aborted wings, and cannot fly. She waits humbly for the winged male, lays her myriad eggs, and dies,—a fine instance of modification to sex.

To reduce so largely the mere area of environment is a great check to race-development; but it is not to be compared in its

---

1 Prostitution.

effects with the reduction in voluntary activity to which the human female has been subjected. Her restricted impression, her confinement to the four walls of the home, have done great execution, of course, in limiting her ideas, her information, her thought-processes, and power of judgment; and in giving a disproportionate prominence and intensity to the few things she knows about; but this is innocent in action compared with her restricted expression, the denial of freedom to act. A living organism is modified far less through the action of external circumstances upon it and its reaction thereto, than through the effect of its own exertions. Skin may be thickened gradually by exposure to the weather; but it is thickened far more quickly by being rubbed against something, as the handle of an oar or of a broom. To be surrounded by beautiful things has much influence upon the human creature: to make beautiful things has more. To live among beautiful surroundings and make ugly things is more directly lowering than to live among ugly surroundings and make beautiful things. What we do modifies us more than what is done to us. The freedom of expression has been more restricted in women than the freedom of impression, if that be possible. Something of the world she lived in she has seen from her barred windows. Some air has come through the purdah's[1] folds, some knowledge has filtered to her eager ears from the talk of men. Desdemona learned somewhat of Othello. Had she known more, she might have lived longer.[2] But in the ever-growing human impulse to create, the power and will to make, to do, to express one's new spirit in new forms,—here she has been utterly debarred. She might work as she had worked from the beginning,—at the primitive labors of the household; but in the inevitable expansion of even those industries to professional levels we have striven to hold her back. To work with her own hands, for nothing, in direct body-service to her own family,—this has been permitted,—yes, compelled. But to be and do anything further from this she has been forbidden. Her labor has not only been limited in kind, but in degree. Whatever she has been allowed to do must be done in private and alone, the first-hand industries of savage times.

Our growth in industry has been not only in kind, but in class. The baker is not in the same industrial grade with the house-

---

1 A curtain used to screen women from public view.
2 In Shakespeare's *Othello*, Desdemona was enthralled by the tales of her husband Othello's travels. Othello murders his wife Desdemona when he believes wrongly that she has committed adultery.

cook, though both make bread. To specialize any form of labor is a step up: to organize it is another step. Specialization and organization are the basis of human progress, the organic methods of social life. They have been forbidden to women almost absolutely. The greatest and most beneficent change of this century is the progress of women in these two lines of advance. The effect of this check in industrial development, accompanied as it was by the constant inheritance of increased racial power, has been to intensify the sensations and emotions of women, and to develope great activity in the lines allowed. The nervous energy that up to present memory has impelled women to labor incessantly at something, be it the veriest folly of fancy work, is one mark of this effect.

In religious development the same dead-line has held back the growth of women through all the races and ages. In dim early times she was sharer in the mysteries and rites; but, as religion developed, her place receded, until Paul commanded her to be silent in the churches.[1] And she has been silent until to-day. Even now, with all the ground gained, we have but the beginnings—the slowly forced and disapproved beginnings—of religious equality for the sexes. In some nations, religion is held to be a masculine attribute exclusively, it being even questioned whether women have souls. An early Christian council settled that important question by vote, fortunately deciding that they had.[2] In a church whose main strength has always been derived from the adherence of women, it would have been an uncomfortable reflection not to have allowed them souls. Ancient family worship ran in the male line. It was the son who kept the sacred grandfathers in due respect, and poured libations to their shades. When the woman married, she changed her ancestors, and had to worship her husband's progenitors instead of her own. This is why the Hindu and the Chinaman[3] and many others of like stamp must have a son to keep them in countenance,—a deep-seated sex-prejudice, coming to slow extinction as women rise in economic importance.

It is painfully interesting to trace the gradual cumulative effect of these conditions upon women: first, the action of large natural laws, acting on her as they would act on any other animal; then

---

1 Let your women keep silence in the churches: for it is not permitted unto them to speak; but they are commanded to be under obedience, as also saith the law (1 Corinthians 14.34).

2 An unproven report of the deliberations of an early council of Roman Catholic bishops.

3 This term is considered offensive today.

the evolution of social customs and laws (with her position as the active cause), following the direction of mere physical forces, and adding heavily to them; then, with increasing civilization, the unbroken accumulation of precedent, burnt into each generation by the growing force of education, made lovely by art, holy by religion, desirable by habit; and, steadily acting from beneath, the unswerving pressure of economic necessity upon which the whole structure rested. These are strong modifying conditions, indeed.

The process would have been even more effective and far less painful but for one important circumstance. Heredity has no Salic law.[1] Each girl child inherits from her father a certain increasing percentage of human development, human power, human tendency; and each boy as well inherits from his mother the increasing percentage of sex-development, sex-power, sex-tendency. The action of heredity has been to equalize what every tendency of environment and education made to differ. This has saved us from such a female as the gypsy moth. It has held up the woman, and held down the man. It has set iron bounds to our absurd effort to make a race with one sex a million years behind the other. But it has added terribly to the pain and difficulty of human life,—a difficulty and a pain that should have taught us long since that we were living on wrong lines. Each woman born, re-humanized by the current of race activity carried on by her father and re-womanized by her traditional position, has had to live over again in her own person the same process of restriction, repression, denial; the smothering "no" which crushed down all her human desires to create, to discover, to learn, to express, to advance.[2] Each woman has had, on the other hand, the same single avenue of expression and attainment; the same one way in which alone she might do what she could, get what she might. All other doors were shut, and this one always open; and the whole pressure of advancing humanity was upon her. No wonder that young Daniel in the apocryphal tale proclaimed: "The king is strong! Wine is strong! But women are stronger!"[3]

To the young man confronting life the world lies wide. Such powers as he has he may use, must use. If he chooses wrong at

---

1 Law of the French monarchy that excluded females from succession to the Crown.
2 For the Son of God, Jesus Christ ... was not yea and nay, but in him was yea ... For all the promises of God in him are yea, and in him Amen, unto the glory of God by us (2 Corinthians 1.19–20).
3 1 Esdras 3.10–13.

first, he may choose again, and yet again. Not effective or successful in one channel, he may do better in another. The growing, varied needs of all mankind call on him for the varied service in which he finds his growth. What he wants to be, he may strive to be. What he wants to get, he may strive to get. Wealth, power, social distinction, fame,—what he wants he can try for.

To the young woman confronting life there is the same world beyond, there are the same human energies and human desires and ambition within. But all that she may wish to have, all that she may wish to do, must come through a single channel and a single choice. Wealth, power, social distinction, fame,—not only these, but home and happiness, reputation, ease and pleasure, her bread and butter,—all, must come to her through a small gold ring. This is a heavy pressure. It has accumulated behind her through heredity, and continued about her through environment. It has been subtly trained into her through education, till she herself has come to think it a right condition, and pours its influence upon her daughter with increasing impetus. Is it any wonder that women are over-sexed? But for the constant inheritance from the more human male, we should have been queen bees, indeed, long before this. But the daughter of the soldier and the sailor, of the artist, the inventor, the great merchant, has inherited in body and brain her share of his development in each generation, and so stayed somewhat human for all her femininity.

All morbid conditions tend to extinction. One check has always existed to our inordinate sex-development,—nature's ready relief, death. Carried to its furthest excess, the individual has died, the family has become extinct, the nation itself has perished, like Sodom and Gomorrah.[1] Where one function is carried to unnatural excess, others are weakened, and the organism perishes. We are familiar with this in individual cases,—at least, the physician is. We can see it somewhat in the history of nations. From younger races, nearer savagery, nearer the healthful equality of pre-human creatures, has come each new start in history. Persia was older than Greece, and its highly differentiated sexuality had produced the inevitable result of enfeebling the racial qualities. The Greek commander stripped the rich robes and jewels from his Persian captives, and showed their unmanly feebleness to his men. "You have such bodies as these to fight for such plunder as this," he said. In

---

1 Two cities that were destroyed by God as punishment for the sins committed by the people (Genesis 19).

the country, among peasant classes, there is much less sex-distinction than in cities, where wealth enables the women to live in absolute idleness; and even the men manifest the same characteristics. It is from the country and the lower classes that the fresh blood pours into the cities, to be weakened in its turn by the influence of this unnatural distinction until there is none left to replenish the nation.

The inevitable trend of human life is toward higher civilization; but, while that civilization is confined to one sex, it inevitably exaggerates sex-distinction, until the increasing evil of this condition is stronger than all the good of the civilization attained, and the nation falls. Civilization, be it understood, does not consist in the acquisition of luxuries. Social development is an organic development. A civilized State is one in which the citizens live in organic industrial relation. The more full, free, subtle, and easy that relation; the more perfect the differentiation of labor and exchange of product, with their correlative institutions,—the more perfect is that civilization. To eat, drink, sleep, and keep warm,—these are common to all animals, whether the animal couches in a bed of leaves or one of eiderdown, sleeps in the sun to avoid the wind or builds a furnace-heated house, lies in wait for game or orders a dinner at a hotel. These are but individual animal processes. Whether one lays an egg or a million eggs, whether one bears a cub, a kitten, or a baby, whether one broods its chickens, guards its litter, or tends a nursery full of children, these are but individual animal processes. But to serve each other more and more widely; to live only by such service; to develope special functions, so that we depend for our living on society's return for services that can be of no direct use to ourselves,—this is civilization, our human glory and race-distinction.

All this human progress has been accomplished by men. Women have been left behind, outside, below, having no social relation whatever, merely the sex-relation, whereby they lived. Let us bear in mind that all the tender ties of family are ties of blood, of sex-relationship. A friend, a comrade, a partner,—this is a human relative. Father, mother, son, daughter, sister, brother, husband, wife,—these are sex-relatives. Blood is thicker than water, we say. True. But ties of blood are not those that ring the world with the succeeding waves of progressive religion, art, science, commerce, education, all that makes us human. Man is the human creature. Woman has been checked, starved, aborted in human growth; and the swelling forces of race-development have been driven back in each generation to work in her through sex-functions alone.

This is the way in which the sexuo-economic relation has operated in our species, checking race-development in half of us, and stimulating sex-development in both.

V.

The facts stated in the foregoing chapters are familiar and undeniable, the argument seems clear; yet the mind reacts violently from the conclusions it is forced to admit, and tries to find relief in the commonplace conditions of every-day life. From this looming phantom of the over-sexed female of genus homo we fly back in satisfaction to familiar acquaintances and relatives,—to Mrs. John Smith and Miss Imogene Jones, to mothers and sisters and daughters and sweethearts and wives. We feel that such a dreadful state of things cannot be true, or we should surely have noticed it. We may even perform that acrobatic feat so easy to most minds,—admit that the statement may be theoretically true, but practically false!

Two simple laws of brain action are responsible for the difficulty of convincing the human race of any large general truths concerning itself. One is common to all brains, to all nerve sensations indeed, and is cheerfully admitted to have nothing to do with the sexuo-economic relation. It is this simple fact, in popular phrase,—that what we are used to we do not notice. This rests on the law of adaptation, the steady, ceaseless pressure that tends to fit the organism to the environment. A nerve touched for the first time with a certain impression feels this first impression far more than the hundredth or thousandth, though the thousandth be far more violent than the first. If an impression be constant and regular, we become utterly insensitive to it, and only respond under some special condition, as the ticking of a clock, the noise of running water or waves on the beach, even the clatter of railroad trains, grows imperceptible to those who hear it constantly. It is perfectly possible for an individual to become accustomed to the most disadvantageous conditions, and fail to notice them.

It is equally possible for a race, a nation, a class, to become accustomed to most disadvantageous conditions, and fail to notice them. Take, as an individual instance, the wearing of corsets by women. Put a corset, even a loose one, on a vigorous man or woman who never wore one, and there is intense discomfort, and a vivid consciousness thereof. The healthy muscles of the trunk resent the pressure, the action of the whole body is checked in the middle, the stomach is choked, the process of digestion interfered with; and the victim says, "How can you bear such a thing?"

But the person habitually wearing a corset does not feel these evils. They exist, assuredly, the facts are there, the body is not deceived; but the nerves have become accustomed to these disagreeable sensations, and no longer respond to them. The person "does not feel it." In fact, the wearer becomes so used to the sensations that, when they are removed,—with the corset,—there is a distinct sense of loss and discomfort. The heavy folds of the cravat, stock, and neckcloth of earlier men's fashions, the heavy horse-hair peruke,[1] the stiff high collar of to-day, the kind of shoes we wear,—these are perfectly familiar instances of the force of habit in the individual.

This is equally true of racial habits. That a king should rule because he was born, passed unquestioned for thousands of years. That the eldest son should inherit the titles and estates was a similar phenomenon as little questioned. That a debtor should be imprisoned, and so entirely prevented from paying his debts, was common law. So glaring an evil as chattel slavery was an unchallenged social institution from earliest history to our own day among the most civilized nations of the earth. Christ himself let it pass unnoticed. The hideous injustice of Christianity to the Jew attracted no attention through many centuries. That the serf went with the soil, and was owned by the lord thereof, was one of the foundations of society in the Middle Ages.

Social conditions, like individual conditions, become familiar by use, and cease to be observed. This is the reason why it is so much easier to criticise the customs of other persons or other nations than our own. It is also the reason why we so naturally deny and resent the charges of the critic. It is not necessarily because of any injustice on the one side or dishonesty on the other, but because of a simple and useful law of nature. The Englishman coming to America is much struck by America's political corruption; and, in the earnest desire to serve his brother, he tells us all about it. That which he has at home he does not observe, because he is used to it. The American in England finds also something to object to, and omits to balance his criticism by memories of home.

When a condition exists among us which began in those unrecorded ages back of tradition even, which obtains in varying degree among every people on earth, and which begins to act

---

1 A skullcap covered with hair; a wig.

upon the individual at birth, it would be a miracle past all belief if people should notice it. The sexuo-economic relation is such a condition. It began in primeval savagery. It exists in all nations. Each boy and girl is born into it, trained into it, and has to live in it. The world's progress in matters like these is attained by a slow and painful process, but one which works to good ends.

In the course of social evolution there are developed individuals so constituted as not to fit existing conditions, but to be organically adapted to more advanced conditions. These advanced individuals respond in sharp and painful consciousness to existing conditions, and cry out against them according to their lights. The history of religion, of political and social reform, is full of familiar instances of this. The heretic, the reformer, the agitator, these feel what their compeers do not, see what they do not, and, naturally, say what they do not. The mass of the people are invariably displeased by the outcry of these uneasy spirits. In simple primitive periods they were promptly put to death. Progress was slow and difficult in those days. But this severe process of elimination developed the kind of progressive person known as a martyr; and this remarkable sociological law was manifested: that the strength of a current of social force is increased by the sacrifice of individuals who are willing to die in the effort to promote it. "The blood of the martyrs is the seed of the church."[1] This is so commonly known to-day, though not formulated, that power hesitates to persecute, lest it intensify the undesirable heresy. A policy of "free speech" is found to let pass most of the uneasy pushes and spurts of these stirring forces, and lead to more orderly action. Our great anti-slavery agitation, the heroic efforts of the "women's rights" supporters, are fresh and recent proofs of these plain facts: that the mass of the people do not notice existing conditions, and that they are not pleased with those who do. This is one strong reason why the sexuo-economic relation passes unobserved among us, and why any statement of it will be so offensive to many.

The other law of brain action which tends to prevent our perception of general truth is this: it is easier to personalize than to generalize. This is due primarily to the laws of mental development, but it is greatly added to by the very relation under discussion. As a common law of mental action, the power to observe

---

1 Early Christian author Tertullian (155–240 CE): "The Christian blood you spill is like the seed you sow, it springs from the earth again, and fructifies the more" (*Apology for the Christians* 143).

and retain an individual impression marks a lower degree of development than the power to classify and collate impressions and make generalizations therefrom. There are savages who can say "hot fire," "hot stone," "hot water," but cannot say "heat," cannot think it. Similarly, they can say "good man," "good knife," "good meat"; but they cannot say "goodness," they cannot think it. They have observed specific instances, but are unable to collate them, to generalize therefrom. So, in our common life, individual instances of injustice or cruelty are observed long before the popular mind is able to see that it is a condition which causes these things, and that the condition must be altered before the effects can be removed. A bad priest, a bad king, a bad master, were long observed and pointedly objected to before it began to be held that the condition of monarchy or the condition of slavery must needs bear fruit, and that, if we did not like the fruit, we might better change the tree. Any slaveholder would admit that there were instances of cruelty, laziness, pride, among masters, and of deceit, laziness, dishonesty, among slaves. What the slaveholder did not see was that, given the relation of chattel slavery, it inevitably tended to produce these evils, and did produce them, in spite of all the efforts of the individual to the contrary. To see the individual instance is easy. To see the general cause is harder, requires a further brain development. We, as a race, have long since reached the degree of general intelligence which ought to enable us to judge more largely and wisely of social questions; but here the deteriorating effect of the sexuo-economic relation is shown.

The sex relation is intensely personal. All the functions and relations ensuing are intensely personal. The spirit of "me and my wife, my son John and his wife, us four, and no more," is the natural spirit of this phase of life. By confining half the world to this one set of functions, we have confined it absolutely to the personal. And man that is born of woman is reared by her in this same atmosphere of concentrated personality, and afterward spends a large part of his life in it. This condition tends to magnify the personal and minimize the general in our minds, with results that are familiar to us all. The difficulty of enforcing sanitary laws, where personal convenience must be sacrificed to general safety, the size of the personal grievance as against the general, the need of "having it brought home to us," which hinders every step of public advancement, and our eager response when it is "brought home to us,"—these are truisms. So far as a comparison can be made, women are in this sense more personal than men, more personally sensitive, less willing to "stand in line" and "take turns," less able to see why a general restriction is just when it touches them or their children. This is natural enough, inevitable enough, and only mentioned here as partially explaining why people do not see the general facts as to our over-sexed condition. Yet they are patent everywhere, not only patent, but painful. Being used to them, we do not notice them, or, forced to notice them, we attribute the pain we feel to the evil behavior of some individual, and never think of it as being the result of a condition common to us all.

If we have among us such a condition as has been stated,—a state of morbid and excessive sex-development,—it must, of course, show itself in daily life in a thousand ways. The non-observer, not having seen any such manifestation, concludes that there is none, and so denies the alleged condition,—says it sounds all right, but he does not see any proof of it! Having clearly in mind that, if such proof exists, such commensurate evil in common life as would naturally result from an abnormal sex-distinction, these evils must be so common and habitual as to pass unobserved; and, farther, that, when forced upon our notice, we only see them as matters of personal behavior,—let us, in spite of these hindrances, see if the visible results among us are not such as must follow such a cause, and let us seek them merely in the phenomena of every-day life as we know it, not in the deeper sexual or social results.

A concrete instance, familiar as the day, and unbelievable in its ill effects, is the attitude of the mother toward her children in regard to the sex-relation. With very few exceptions, the mother gives her daughter no warning or prevision of what life holds for her, and so lets innocence and ignorance go on perpetuating sickness and sin and pain through ceaseless generations. A normal motherhood wisely and effectively guards its young from evil. An abnormal motherhood, over-anxious and under-wise, hovers the child to its harm, and turns it out defenceless to the worst of evils. This is known to millions and millions personally. Only very lately have we thought to consider it generally. And not yet do we see that it is not the fault of the individual mother, but of her economic status. Because of our abnormal sex-development, the whole field has become something of an offence,—a thing to be hidden and ignored, passed over without remark or explanation. Hence this amazing paradox of mothers ashamed of motherhood, unable to explain it, and—measure this well—lying to their children about the primal truths of life,—mothers lying to their own children about motherhood!

The pressure under which this is done is an economic one. The girl must marry: else how live? The prospective husband prefers the girl to know nothing. He is the market, the demand. She is the supply. And with the best intentions the mother serves her child's economic advantage by preparing her for the market. This is an excellent instance. It is common. It is most evil. It is plainly traceable to our sexuo-economic relation.

Another instance of so grossly unjust, so palpable, so general an evil that it has occasionally aroused some protest even from our dull consciousness is this: the enforced attitude of the woman toward marriage. To the young girl, as has been previously stated, marriage is the one road to fortune, to life. She is born highly specialized as a female: she is carefully educated and trained to realize in all ways her sex-limitations and her sex-advantages. What she has to gain even as a child is largely gained by feminine tricks and charms. Her reading, both in history and fiction, treats of the same position for women; and romance and poetry give it absolute predominance. Pictorial art, music, the drama, society, everything, tells her that she is *she*, and that all depends on whom she marries. Where young boys plan for what they will achieve and attain, young girls plan for whom they will achieve and attain. Little Ellie and her swan's nest among the reeds is a familiar illustration. It is the lover on the red roan steed she planned for.[1] It is Lancelot riding through the sheaves that called the Lady from her loom at Shalott: "he" is the coming world.[2]

With such a prospect as this before her; with an organization specially developed to this end; with an education adding every weight of precept and example, of wisdom and virtue, to the natural instincts; with a social environment the whole machinery of which is planned to give the girl a chance to see and to be seen, to provide her with "opportunities"; and with all the pressure of personal advantage and self-interest added to the sex-instinct,—what one would logically expect is a society full of desperate and eager husband-hunters, regarded with popular approval.

Not at all! Marriage is the woman's proper sphere, her divinely ordered place, her natural end. It is what she is born for, what she is trained for, what she is exhibited for. It is, moreover, her means of honorable livelihood and advancement. *But*—she must not even look as if she wanted it! She must not turn her hand over to

---

[1] Allusion to Elizabeth Barrett Browning's "The Romance of the Swan's Nest" (1844).
[2] Allusion to Alfred, Lord Tennyson's "The Lady of Shalott" (1833).

get it. She must sit passive as the seasons go by, and her "chances" lessen with each year. Think of the strain on a highly sensitive nervous organism to have so much hang on one thing, to see the possibility of attaining it grow less and less yearly, and to be forbidden to take any step toward securing it! This she must bear with dignity and grace to the end.

To what end? To the end that, if she does not succeed in being chosen, she becomes a thing of mild popular contempt, a human being with no further place in life save as an attachée, a dependant upon more fortunate relatives, an old maid. The open derision and scorn with which unmarried women used to be treated is lessening each year in proportion to their advance in economic independence. But it is not very long since the popular proverb, "Old maids lead apes in hell,"[1] was in common use; since unwelcome lovers urged their suit with the awful argument that they might be the last askers; since the hapless lady in the wood prayed for a husband, and, when the owl answered, "Who? who?" cried, "Anybody, good Lord!"[2] There is still a pleasant ditty afloat as to the "Three Old Maids of Lynn," who did not marry when they could, and could not when they would.

The cruel and absurd injustice of blaming the girl for not getting what she is allowed no effort to obtain seems unaccountable; but it becomes clear when viewed in connection with the sexuo-economic relation. Although marriage is a means of livelihood, it is not honest employment where one can offer one's labor without shame, but a relation where the support is given outright, and enforced by law in return for the functional service of the woman, the "duties of wife and mother." Therefore no honorable woman can ask for it. It is not only that the natural feminine instinct is to retire, as that of the male is to advance, but that, because marriage means support, a woman must not ask a man to support her. It is economic beggary as well as a false attitude from a sex point of view.

Observe the ingenious cruelty of the arrangement. It is just as humanly natural for a woman as for a man to want wealth. But, when her wealth is made to come through the same channels as her love, she is forbidden to ask for it by her own sex-nature and by business honor. Hence the millions of mismade marriages with "anybody, good Lord!" Hence the million broken hearts which must let all life pass, unable to make any attempt to stop it. Hence the many "maiden aunts," elderly sisters and daughters,

---

1 Proverbial fate of women who died unmarried.
2 From the poem "An Old Maid's Prayer" (anonymous, n.d.).

unattached women everywhere, who are a burden on their male relatives and society at large. This is changing for the better, to be sure, but changing only through the advance of economic independence for women. A "bachelor maid" is a very different thing from "an old maid."

This, then, is the reason for the Andromeda[1] position of the possibly-to-be-married young woman, and for the ridicule and reproach meted out to her. Since women are viewed wholly as creatures of sex even by one another, and since everything is done to add to their young powers of sex-attraction; since they are marriageable solely on this ground, unless, indeed, "a fortune" has been added to their charms,—failure to marry is held a clear proof of failure to attract, a lack of sex-value. And, since they have no other value, save in a low order of domestic service, they are quite naturally despised. What else is the creature good for, failing in the functions for which it was created? The scorn of male and female alike falls on this sexless thing: she is a human failure.

It is not strange, therefore, though just as pitiful,—this long chapter of patient, voiceless, dreary misery in the lives of women; and it is not strange, either, to see the marked and steady change in opinion that follows the development of other faculties in woman besides those of sex. Now that she is a person as well as a female, filling economic relation to society, she is welcomed and accepted as a human creature, and need not marry the wrong man for her bread and butter. So sharp is the reaction from this unlovely yoke that there is a limited field of life to-day wherein women choose not to marry, preferring what they call "their independence,"—a new-born, hard-won, dear-bought independence. That any living woman should prefer it to home and husband, to love and motherhood, throws a fierce light on what women must have suffered for lack of freedom before.

This tendency need not be feared, however. It is merely a reaction, and a most natural one. It will pass as naturally, as more and more women become independent, when marriage is not the price of liberty. The fear exhibited that women generally, once fully independent, will not marry, is proof of how well it has been known that only dependence forced them to marriage as it was. There will be needed neither bribe nor punishment to force women to true marriage with independence.

Along this line it is most interesting to mark the constant struggle between natural instinct and natural law, and social habit

---

1 In Greek myth, Andromeda was chained to a rock and left to be devoured by a sea monster but was saved from death by Perseus.

and social law, through all our upward course. Beginning with the natural functions and instincts of sex, holding her great position as selector of the best among competing males, woman's beautiful work is to improve the race by right marriage. The feeling by which this is accomplished, growing finer as we become more civilized, develops into that wide, deep, true, and lasting love which is the highest good to individual human beings. Following its current, we have always reverenced and admired "true love"; and our romances, from the earliest times, abound in praise of the princess who marries the page or prisoner, venerating the selective power in woman, choosing "the right man" for his own sake. Directly against this runs the counter-current, resulting in the marriage of convenience, a thing which the true inner heart of the world has always hated. Young Lochinvar[1] is not an eternal hero for nothing. The personified type of a great social truth is sure of a long life. The poor young hero, handsome, brave, good, but beset with difficulties, stands ever against the wealth and power of the bad man. The woman is pulled hither and thither between them, and the poor hero wins in the end. That he is heaped with honor and riches, after all, merely signifies our recognition that he is the higher good. This is better than a sun-myth.[2] It is a race-myth, and true as truth.

So we have it among us in life to-day, endlessly elaborated and weakened by profuse detail, as is the nature of that life, but there yet. The girl who marries the rich old man or the titled profligate is condemned by the popular voice; and the girl who marries the poor young man, and helps him live his best, is still approved by the same great arbiter. And yet why should we blame the woman for pursuing her vocation? Since marriage is her only way to get money, why should she not try to get money in that way? Why cast the weight of all self-interest on the "practical" plane so solidly against the sex-interest of the individual and of the race? The mercenary marriage is a perfectly natural consequence of the economic dependence of women.

On the other hand, note the effect of this dependence upon men. As the excessive sex-distinction and economic dependence of women increase, so do the risk and difficulty of marriage increase, so is marriage deferred and avoided, to the direct injury of both sexes and society at large. In simpler relations, in the

---

1 "So faithful in love, and so dauntless in war / There never was knight like the young Lochinvar" (Sir Walter Scott, "Marmion" [1808] 5–6).
2 Sun worship, practiced throughout history.

country, wherever women have a personal value in economic relation as well as a feminine value in sex-relation, an early marriage is an advantage. The young farmer gets a profitable servant when he marries. The young business man gets nothing of the kind,—a pretty girl, a charming girl, ready for "wifehood and motherhood"—so far as her health holds out,—but having no economic value whatever. She is merely a consumer, and he must wait till he can "afford to marry." These are instances frequent everywhere, and familiar to us all, of the palpable effects in common life of our sexuo-economic relation.

If there is one unmixed evil in human life, it is that known to us in all ages, and popularly called "the social evil," consisting of promiscuous and temporary sex-relations. The inherent wrong in these relations is sociological before it is legal or moral. The recognition by the moral sense of a given thing as wrong requires that it be wrong, to begin with. A thing is not wrong merely because it is called so. The wrongness of this form of sex-relation in an advanced social state rests solidly on natural laws. In the evolution of better and better means of reproducing the species, a longer period of infancy was developed. This longer period of infancy required longer care, and it was accordingly developed that the best care during this time was given by both parents. This induced a more permanent mating. And the more permanent mating, bound together by the common interests and duties, developed higher psychic attributes in the parents by use, in the children by heredity. That is why society is right in demanding of its constituent individuals the virtue of chastity, the sanctity of marriage. Society is perfectly right, because social evolution is as natural a process as individual evolution; and the permanent parent is proven an advantageous social factor. But social evolution, deep, unconscious, slow, is one thing; and self-conscious, loud-voiced society is another.

The deepest forces of nature have tended to evolve pure, lasting, monogamous marriage in the human race. But our peculiar arrangement of feeding one sex by the other has tended to produce a very different thing, and has produced it. In no other animal species is the female economically dependent on the male. In no other animal species is the sex-relation for sale. A coincidence. Where, on the one hand, every condition of life tends to develop sex in women, to crush out the power and the desire for economic production and exchange, and to develop also the age-long habit of seeking all earthly good at a man's hands and of making but one return; where, on the other hand, man inherits the excess in sex-energy, and is never blamed for exercising it, and where he develops also the age-long habit of taking what he wants from women, for whose helpless acquiescence he makes an economic return,—what should naturally follow? Precisely what has followed. We live in a world of law, and humanity is no exception to it. We have produced a certain percentage of females with inordinate sex-tendencies and inordinate greed for material gain. We have produced a certain percentage of males with inordinate sex-tendencies and a cheerful willingness to pay for their gratification. And, as the percentage of such men is greater than the percentage of such women, we have worked out most evil methods of supplying the demand. But always in the healthy social heart we have known that it was wrong, a racial wrong, productive of all evil. Being a man's world, it was quite inevitable that he should blame woman for their mutual misdoing. There is reason in it, too. Bad as he is, he is only seeking gratification natural in kind, though abnormal in degree. She is not only in some cases doing this, but in most cases showing the falseness of the deed by doing it for hire,—physical falsehood,—a sin against nature.

It is a true instinct that revolts against obtaining bread by use of the sex-functions. Why, then, are we so content to do this in marriage? Legally and religiously, we say that it is right; but in its reactionary effect on the parties concerned and on society at large it is wrong. The physical and psychical effects are evil, though modified by our belief that it is right. The physical and psychical effects of prostitution were still evil when the young girls of Babylon earned their dowries thereby in the temple of Bela, and thought it right.[1] What we think and feel alters the moral quality of an act in our consciousness as we do it, but does not alter its subsequent effect. We justify and approve the economic dependence of women upon the sex-relation in marriage. We condemn it unsparingly out of marriage. We follow it with our blame and scorn up to the very doors of marriage,—the mercenary bride,—but think no harm of the mercenary wife, filching her husband's pockets in the night. Love sanctifies it, we say: love must go with it.

Love never yet went with self-interest. The deepest antagonism lies between them: they are diametrically opposed forces. In the beautiful progress of evolution we find constant opposition between the instincts and processes of self-preservation and the

---

1 Sacred rituals described in ancient literature.

instinct and processes of race-preservation. From those early forms where birth brought death, as in the flowering aloe, the ephemeral may-fly, up to the highest glory of self-effacing love; these two forces work in opposition. We have tied them together. We have made the woman, the mother,—the very source of sacrifice through love,—get gain through love,—a hideous paradox. No wonder that our daily lives are full of the flagrant evils produced by this unnatural state. No wonder that men turn with loathing from the kind of women they have made.

VI.

The peculiar combination of functions which we are studying has not only an immediate effect on individuals through sex-action, and through the sex-affected individuals upon society, but also an effect upon society through economic action, and through the economically affected society upon the individual.

The economic aspect of the question brings it prominently forward to-day as influencing not only our private health and happiness and the processes of reproduction, but our public health and happiness and the processes of social economics as well. Society is confronted in this age with most pressing problems in economics, and we need the fullest understanding of the factors involved. These problems are almost wholly social rather than physical, and concern not the capacity of a given society to produce and distribute enough wealth for its maintenance, but some maladjustment of internal processes which checks that production and distribution, and developes such irregular and morbid processes of innutrition, malnutrition, and over-nutrition as continually to injure the health and activity of the social organism. Our difficulty about wealth is not in getting it out of the earth, but in getting it away from one another. We have phenomena before us in the development of social economic relations analogous to those accompanying our development in sex-relation.

In the original constituents of society, the human animal in its primitive state, economic processes were purely individual. The amount of food obtained by a given man bore direct relation to his own personal exertions. Other men were to him merely undesirable competitors for the same goods; and, the fewer these competitors were, the more goods remained for him. Therefore, he killed as many of his rivals as possible. Given a certain supply of needed food, as the edible beasts or fruits in a forest, and a certain number of individuals to get this food, each by his own exertions, it follows that, the more numerous the individuals, the less food to be obtained by each; and, conversely, the fewer the individuals, the more food to be obtained by each. Wherefore, the primitive savage slew his fellow-man at sight, on good economic grounds. This is the extreme of individual competition, perfectly logical, and, in its time, economically right. That time is forever past. The basic condition of human life is union; the organic social relation, the interchange of functional service, wherein the individual is most advantaged, not by his own exertions for his own goods, but by the exchange of his exertions with the exertions of others for goods produced by them together. We are not treating here of any communistic theory as to the equitable division of the wealth produced, but of a clear truth in social economics,—that wealth is a social product. Whatever one may believe as to what should be done with the wealth of the world, no one can deny that the production of this wealth requires the combined action of many individuals. From the simplest combination of strength that enables many men to overcome the mammoth or to lift the stone—an achievement impossible to one alone—to the subtle and complex interchange of highly specialized skilled labor which makes possible our modern house; the progress of society rests upon the increasing collectivity of human labor.

The evolution of organic life goes on in geometrical progression: cells combine, and form organs; organs combine, and form organisms; organisms combine, and form organizations. Society is an organization. Society is the fourth power of the cell. It is composed of individual animals of genus homo, living in organic relation. The course of social evolution is the gradual establishment of organic relation between individuals, and this organic relation rests on purely economic grounds. In the simplest combination of primordial cells the force that drew and held them together was that of economic necessity. It profited them to live in combination. Those that did so survived, and those that did not perished. So with the appearance of the most elaborate organisms: it profited them to become a complex bundle of members and organs in indivisible relation. A creature so constructed survived, where the same amount of living matter unorganized would have perished. And so it is, literally and exactly, in a complex society, with all its elaborate specialization of individuals in arts and crafts, trades and professions. A society so constructed survives, where the same number of living beings, unorganized, would perish. The specialization of labor and exchange of product in a social body is identical in its nature with the specialization and exchange of function in an individual body. This process, on orderly lines of evolution, involves the gradual subordination of individual effort for individual good to the collective effort for the collective good,—not from any so-called "altruism," but from the economic necessities of the case. It is as natural, as "selfish," for society so to live, the individual citizens working together for the social good, as for one's own body to live by the hands and feet, teeth and eyes, heart and lungs, working together for the individual good. Social evolution tends to an increasing specialization in structure and function, and to an increasing interdependence of the component parts, with a correlative decrease through disuse of the once valuable process of individual struggle for success; and this is based absolutely on the advantage to the individual as well as to the social body.

But, as we study this process of development, noting with admiration the progressive changes in human relation, the new functions, the extended structure, the increase of sensation in the socialized individuals with its enormous possibilities of joy and healthful sensitiveness to pain, we are struck by the visible presence of some counter-force, acting against the normal development and producing most disadvantageous effects. As in our orderly progress in social sex-development we are checked by the tenacious hold of rudimentary impulses artificially maintained by false conditions, so in our orderly progress in social economic development we see the same peculiar survival of rudimentary impulses, which should have been long since easily outgrown. It is no longer of advantage to the individual to struggle for his own gain at the expense of others: his gain now requires the co-ordinate efforts of these others; yet he continues so to struggle.

In this lack of adjustment between the individual and the social interest lies our economic trouble. An illustration of this may be seen in the manufacture of prepared foods. This is a process impossible to the individual singly, and of great advantage to the individual in collective relation,—a perfectly natural economic process, advantageous in proportion to the amount and quality of the food manufactured. This we constantly find accompanied by a morbid process of dilution and adulteration, by which society is injured, in order that the individual concerned in the manufacture may be benefited. This is as though one of the organs of the body—the liver, for instance—should deliberately weaken or poison its quota of secretion, in order that by giving less it might retain more, and become large and fat individually.

An organ can do so, does do so; but such action is morbid action, and constitutes disease. The body is injured, weakened, destroyed, and so ultimately the organ perishes also. It is a false conception of gain, and the falsehood lies in not recognizing the true relation between individual and social interests. This failure to recognize or, at least, to act up to a recognition of social interests, owing to the disproportionate pressure of individual interests, is the underlying cause of our economic distress. As society is composed of individuals, we must look to them for the action causing these morbid social processes; and, as individuals act under the pressure of conditions, we must look to the conditions affecting the individuals for the causes of their action.

In general, under social law, men develope right action; but some hidden spring seems to force them continually into wrong action. We have our hand upon this hidden spring in the sexuo-economic relation. If we had remained on an individual economic basis, the evil influence would have had far less ill effect; but, as we grow into the social economic relation, it increases with our civilization. The sex-relation is primarily and finally individual. It is a physical relation between individual bodies; and, while it may also extend to a psychical relation between individual souls, it does not become a social relation, though it does change its personal development to suit social needs.

In all its processes, to all its results, the sex-relation is personal, working through individuals upon individuals, and developing individual traits and characteristics, to the great advantage of society. The qualities developed by social relation are built into the race through the sex-relation, but the sex-relation itself is wholly personal. Our economic relation, on the contrary, though originally individual, becomes through social evolution increasingly collective. By combining the human sex-relation with the human economic relation, we have combined a permanently individual process with a progressively collective one. This involves a strain on both, which increases in direct proportion to our socialization, and, so far, has resulted in the ultimate destruction of the social organism acted upon by such irreconcilable forces.

As has been shown, this combination has affected the sex-relation of individuals by bringing into it a tendency to collectivism with economic advantage, best exhibited in our distinctive racial phenomenon of prostitution. On the other hand, it has affected the economic relation of society by bringing into it a tendency to individualism with sex-advantage, best exhibited in the frequent practice of sacrificing public good to personal gain, that the individual may thereby "support his family." We are so used to considering it the first duty of a man to support his family that it takes a very glaring instance of bribery and corruption in their interests to shake our conviction; but, as a sociological law, every phase of the prostitution of public service to private gain, from the degradation of the artist to the exploitation of the helpless unskilled laborer, marks a diseased social action. Our social status rests upon our common consent, common action, common submission to the common will. No individual interests can stand for a moment against the interests of the common weal, either when war demands the last sacrifice of individual property and life or when peace requires the absolute submission of individual property and life to common law,—the fixed expression of the people's will. The maintenance of "law and order" involves the very spirit of socialism,—the sinking of personal interest in common interest. All this rests upon the evolution of the social spirit, the keen sense of social duty, the conscientious fulfilment of social service; and it is here that the excessive individualism maintained by our sexuo-economic relation enters as a strong and increasingly disadvantageous social factor. We have dimly recognized the irreconcilability of the sex-relation with economic relations on both sides,—in our sharp condemnation of making the sex-functions openly commercial, and in the drift toward celibacy in collective institutions. Bodies of men or women, actuated by the highest religious impulses, desiring to live nobly and to serve society, have always recognized something antagonistic in the sex-relation. They have thought it inherent in the relation itself, not seeing that it was the economic side which made it reactionary. Yet this action was practically admitted by the continued existence of communal societies where the sex-relation did exist, in an unacknowledged form, and without the element of economic exchange. It is admitted also by the noble and self-sacrificing devotion of married missionaries of the Protestant Church, who are supported by contributions. If the missionary were obliged to earn his wife's living and his own, he could do little mission work.

The highest human attributes are perfectly compatible with the sex-relation, but not with the sexuo-economic relation. We see this opposition again in the tendency to collectivity in bodies of single men,—their comradeship, equality, and mutual helpfulness as compared with the attitude of the same men toward one another, when married. This is why the quality of "organizability" is stronger in men than in women; their common economic interests force them into relation, while the isolated and even antagonistic economic interests of women keep them from it. The condition of individual economic dependence in which women live resembles that of the savage in the forest. They obtain their economic goods by securing a male through their individual exertions, all competing freely to this end. No combination is possible. The numerous girls at a summer resort, in their attitude toward the scant supply of young men, bear an unconscious resemblance to the emulous savages in a too closely hunted forest. And here may be given an economic reason for the oft-noted bitterness with which the virtuous women regard the vicious. The virtuous woman stands in close ranks with her sisters, refusing to part with herself—her only economic goods—until she is assured of legal marriage, with its lifelong guarantee of support. Under equal proportions of birth in the two sexes, every woman would be tolerably sure of obtaining her demands. But here enters the vicious woman, and offers the same goods—though of inferior quality, to be sure—for a far less price. Every one of such illegitimate competitors lowers the chances of the unmarried women and the income of the married. No wonder those who hold themselves highly should be moved to bitterness at being undersold in this way. It is the hatred of the trade-unionist for "scab labor."[1]

On the woman's side we are steadily maintaining the force of primitive individual competition in the world as against the tendency of social progress to develope co-operation in its place, and this tendency of course is inherited by their sons.[2] On the man's side the same effect is produced through another feature of the relation. The tendency to individualism with sex-advantage is developed in man by an opposite process to that operating on the woman. She gets her living by getting a husband. He gets his wife by getting a living. It is to her individual economic advantage to secure a mate. It is to his individual sex-advantage to secure economic gain. The sex-functions to her have become economic functions. Economic functions to him have become sex-functions. This has confounded our natural economic competition, inevitably growing into economic co-operation, with the element of sex-competition,—an entirely different force.

---

1 A worker who refuses to join a labor union or who accepts employment to replace a union worker during a strike.
2 According to French naturalist Jean-Baptiste Lamarck (1744–1829), traits acquired in one's lifetime could be transmitted to one's descendants.

Competition among males, with selection by the female of the superior male, is the process of sexual selection, and works to racial improvement. So far as the human male competes freely with his peers in higher and higher activities, and the female chooses the winner, so far we are directly benefited. But there is a radical distinction between sex-competition and marriage by purchase. In the first the male succeeds by virtue of what he can do; in the second, by virtue of what he can get. The increased power to do, transmitted to the young, is of racial advantage. But mere possessions, with no question as to the method of their acquisition, are not necessarily of advantage to the individual as a father. To make the sexual gain of the male rest on his purchasing power puts the immense force of sex-competition into the field of social economics, not only as an incentive to labor and achievement, which is good, but as an incentive to individual gain, however obtained, which is bad; thus accounting for our multiplied and intensified desire to get,—the inordinate greed of our industrial world. The tournament of the Middle Ages was a brutal sport perhaps, with its human injury, pain, and death, under the cry of: "Fight on, brave knights! Fair eyes are looking on you!" but it represents a healthier process than our modern method of securing the wherewithal to maintain the sex-relation. As so beautifully phrased by Jean Ingelow:—

> "I worked afar that I might rear
> A happy home on English soil;
> I labored for the gold and gear,
> I loved my toil.

> "Forever in my spirit spake
> The natural whisper, 'Well 'twill be
> When loving wife and children break
> Their bread with thee!'"[1]

Or, put more broadly by Kipling:—

> "But since our women must walk gay,
> And money buys their gear,
> The sealing vessels filch this way
> At hazard, year by year."[2]

---

1 "The Letter L" (1863), 155.7–13.
2 "The Rhyme of the Three Sealers" (1896), 26–27.

The contest in every good man's heart to-day between the "ought to" and the "must," between his best work and the "potboiler," is his personal share of this incessant struggle between social interest and self-interest. For himself and by himself he would be glad to do his best work, to be true to his ideals, to be brave in meeting loss for that truth's sake. But as the compromising capitalist says in "Put Yourself in His Place," when his sturdy young friend—a bachelor—wonders at his giving in to unjust demands, "Marriage makes a mouse of a man."[1] To the young business man who falls into evil courses in the sex-relation the open greed of his fair dependant is a menace to his honesty, to his business prospects. On the same man married the needs of his wife often operate in the same way. The sense of the dependence of the helpless creature whose food must come through him does not stimulate courage, but compels submission.

The foregoing distinction should be clearly held in mind. Legitimate sex-competition brings out all that is best in man. To please her, to win her, he strives to do his best. But the economic dependence of the female upon the male, with its ensuing purchasability, does not so affect a man: it puts upon him the necessity for getting things, not for doing them. In the lowest grades of labor, where there is no getting without doing and where the laborer always does more than he gets, this works less palpable evil than in the higher grades, the professions and arts, where the most valuable work is always ahead of the market, and where to work for the market involves a lowering of standards. The young artist or poet or scientific student works for his work's sake, for art, for science, and so for the best good of society. But the artist or student married must get gain, must work for those who will pay; and those who will pay are not those who lift and bear forward the standard of progress. Community of interest is quite possible with those who are working most disinterestedly for the social good; but bring in the sex-relation, and all such solidarity disintegrates,—resolves itself into the tiny groups of individuals united on a basis of sex-union, and briskly acting in their own immediate interests at anybody's or everybody's expense.

The social perception of the evil resultant from the intrusion of sex-influence upon racial action has found voice in the heartless proverb, "There is no evil without a woman at the bottom of

---

1 "I've got a wife and children; and they make a man a mouse" (Mr. Cheetham in Charles Reade, *Put Yourself in His Place* [1870]).

it."[1] When a man's work goes wrong, his hopes fail, his ambitions sink, cynical friends inquire, "Who is she?" It is not for nothing that a man's best friends sigh when he marries, especially if he is a man of genius. This judgment of the world has obtained side by side with its equal faith in the ennobling influence of woman. The world is quite right. It does not have to be consistent. Both judgments are correct. Woman affecting society through the sex-relation or through her individual economic relation is an ennobling influence. Woman affecting society through our perverse combination of the two becomes a strange influence, indeed.

One of the amusing minor results of these conditions is that, while we have observed the effect of marriage upon social economic relation and the effect of social economic relation upon marriage,—seeing that the devoted servant of the family was a poor servant of society and that the devoted servant of society was a poor servant of the family, seeing the successful collectivity of celibate institutions,—we have jumped to the conclusion that collective prosperity was conditioned upon celibacy, and that we did not want it. That is why the popular mind is so ready to associate socialistic theories with injury to marriage. Having seen that marriage makes us less collective, we infer conversely that collectivity will make us less married,—that it will "break up the home," "strike at the roots of the family."

When we make plain to ourselves that a pure, lasting, monogamous sex-union can exist without bribe or purchase, without the manacles of economic dependence, and that men and women so united in sex-relation will still be free to combine with others in economic relation, we shall not regard devotion to humanity as an unnatural sacrifice, nor collective prosperity as a thing to fear.

Besides this maintenance of primeval individualism in the growing collectivity of social economic process and the introduction of the element of sex-combat into the narrowing field of industrial competition, there is another side to the evil influence of the sexuo-economic relation upon social development. This is in the attitude of woman as a non-productive consumer.

In the industrial evolution of the human race, that marvellous and subtle drawing out and interlocking of special functions which constitute the organic life of society, we find that production and consumption go hand in hand; and production comes first. One cannot consume what has not been produced. Eco-

---

1 Cf. "There's no mischief in the world but there's a woman or a priest at the bottom of it" (Kelly 210).

nomic production is the natural expression of human energy,—not sex-energy at all, but race-energy,—the unconscious functioning of the social organism. Socially organized human beings tend to produce, as a gland to secrete: it is the essential nature of the relation. The creative impulse, the desire to make, to express the inner thought in outer form, "just for the work's sake, no use at all i' the work!" this is the distinguishing character of humanity. "I want to mark!" cries the child, demanding the pencil. He does not want to eat. He wants to mark. He is not seeking to get something into himself, but to put something out of himself. He generally wants to do whatever he sees done,—to make pie-crust or to make shavings, as it happens. The pie he may eat, the shavings not; but he likes to make both. This is the natural process of production, and is followed by the natural process of consumption, where practicable. But consumption is not the main end, the governing force. Under this organic social law, working naturally, we have the evolution of those arts and crafts in the exercise of which consists our human living, and on the product of which we live. So does society evolve within itself—secrete as it were—the social structure with all its complex machinery; and we function therein as naturally as so many glands, other things being equal.

But other things are not equal. Half the human race is denied free productive expression, is forced to confine its productive human energies to the same channels as its reproductive sex-energies. Its creative skill is confined to the level of immediate personal bodily service, to the making of clothes and preparing of food for individuals. No social service is possible. While its power of production is checked, its power of consumption is inordinately increased by the showering upon it of the "unearned increment"[1] of masculine gifts. For the woman there is, first, no free production allowed; and, second, no relation maintained between what she does produce and what she consumes. She is forbidden to make, but encouraged to take. Her industry is not the natural output of creative energy, not the work she does because she has the inner power and strength to do it; nor is her industry even the measure of her gain. She has, of course, the natural desire to consume; and to that is set no bar save the capacity or the will of her husband.

---

1 The amount added to the selling value of land or property due to social or developmental factors rather than expenditure on behalf of the proprietor.

Thus we have painfully and laboriously evolved and carefully maintain among us an enormous class of non-productive consumers,—a class which is half the world, and mother of the other half. We have built into the constitution of the human race the habit and desire of taking, as divorced from its natural precursor and concomitant of making. We have made for ourselves this endless array of "horse-leech's daughters, crying, Give! give!"[1] To consume food, to consume clothes, to consume houses and furniture and decorations and ornaments and amusements, to take and take and take forever,—from one man if they are virtuous, from many if they are vicious, but always to take and never to think of giving anything in return except their womanhood,—this is the enforced condition of the mothers of the race. What wonder that their sons go into business "for what there is in it"! What wonder that the world is full of the desire to get as much as possible and to give as little as possible! What wonder, either, that the glory and sweetness of love are but a name among us, with here and there a strange and beautiful exception, of which our admiration proves the rarity!

Between the brutal ferocity of excessive male energy struggling in the market-place as in a battlefield and the unnatural greed generated by the perverted condition of female energy, it is not remarkable that the industrial evolution of humanity has shown peculiar symptoms. One of the minor effects of this last condition—this limiting of female industry to close personal necessities, and this tendency of her over-developed sex-nature to overestimate the so-called "duties of her position"—has been to produce an elaborate devotion to individuals and their personal needs,—not to the understanding and developing of their higher natures, but to the intensification of their bodily tastes and pleasure. The wife and mother, pouring the rising tide of racial power into the same old channels that were allowed her primitive ancestors, constantly ministers to the physical needs of her family with a ceaseless and concentrated intensity. They like it, of course. But it maintains in the individuals of the race an exaggerated sense of the importance of food and clothes and ornaments to themselves, without at all including a knowledge of their right use and value to us all. It developes personal selfishness.

Again, the consuming female, debarred from any free production, unable to estimate the labor involved in the making of what she so lightly destroys, and her consumption limited mainly to

---

1 Proverbs 30.15.

those things which minister to physical pleasure, creates a market for sensuous decoration and personal ornament, for all that is luxurious and enervating, and for a false and capricious variety in such supplies, which operates as a most deadly check to true industry and true art. As the priestess of the temple of consumption, as the limitless demander of things to use up, her economic influence is reactionary and injurious. Much, very much, of the current of useless production in which our economic energies run waste—man's strength poured out like water on the sand—depends on the creation and careful maintenance of this false market, this sink into which human labor vanishes with no return. Woman, in her false economic position, reacts injuriously upon industry, upon art, upon science, discovery, and progress. The sexuo-economic relation in its effect on the constitution of the individual keeps alive in us the instincts of savage individualism which we should otherwise have well outgrown. It sexualizes our industrial relation and commercializes our sex-relation. And, in the external effect upon the market, the over-sexed woman, in her unintelligent and ceaseless demands, hinders and perverts the economic development of the world.

VII.

A condition so long established, so wide-spread, so permanent as the sexuo-economic relation in the human species could not have been introduced and maintained in the course of social evolution without natural causes and uses. No wildest perversion of individual will could permanently maintain a condition wholly injurious to society. Church and State and social forms move and change with our growth, and we cannot hinder them long after the time has come for further progress. Once it was of advantage to society that the sexuo-economic relation should be established. Now that it is no longer of advantage to society, the "woman's movement" has set in; and the relation is changing under our eyes from year to year, from day to day, in spite of our traditional opposition. The change considered in these pages is not one merely to be prophesied and recommended: it is already taking place under the forces of social evolution; and only needs to be made clear to our conscious thought, that we may withdraw the futile but irritating resistance of our misguided will.

The original necessity for this distinctive human phenomenon lies very deep among the primal forces of social life. The relations required to develop individual organisms failed in the further development of the social organism of organization. Co-ordination requires first a common interest, and then the establishment of a common consciousness. It was for the common interest of the individual cells to obtain food easily, and this drew them into closer relation. That relation being established, their co-existence became a unit, an entity, a thing with a conscious life of its own. In the fullest development of the most elaborate organisms, this holds good. There must be a common interest to be served by all this co-ordinate activity; and there must be a common consciousness established, whereby to serve most easily the common interest. When the component cells in our tissues shrink and fail for lack of nutrition, when the several organs weary of inaction and fretfully demand their natural exercise, the man does not say, "My tissues need replenishment" or "My organs need exercise": he says, "I am hungry." And that "I," the personal consciousness directing the smooth interaction of all its parts, goes to work to get food. Social evolution rests on this common interest. Individual men are profited by social relation; and, therefore, they enter into social relation. Such relation requires a common consciousness, through which the co-ordinate action may take place; and the whole course of social development is marked by the constant extension of this social consciousness and its necessary vehicles. Language is our largest common medium, and leads on into literature, which is but preserved speech. The brain of man is the social organ, the organ of communication. Through it flows the current of thought, whereby we are enabled to work together. By so much as our brains hold in common, we can understand each other; and, therefore, some degree of common education is essential to free social development.

At the very beginning of this process, when the human animal was still but an animal,—but an individual,—came the imperative demand for the establishment of a common consciousness between these hitherto irreconcilable individuals. The first step in nature toward this end is found in the relation between mother and child. Where the young, after birth, are still dependent on the mother, the functions of the one separate living body needing the service of another separate living body, we have the overlapping of personality, the mutual need, which brings with it the essential instinct that holds together these interacting personalities. That instinct we call love. The child must have the mother's breast. The mother's breast must have the child. Therefore, between mother and child was born love, long before fatherhood was anything more than a momentary incident. But the common consciousness, the mutual attraction between mother and child, stopped there absolutely. It was limited in range to this closest relation; in duration, to the period of infancy.

The common interest of human beings must be served by racial faculties, not merely by the sex-functions of the female, or the duties of mother to child. As the male, acting through his natural instincts, steadily encroached upon the freedom of the female until she was reduced to the state of economic dependence, he thereby assumed the position of provider for this creature no longer able to provide for herself. He was not only compelled to serve her needs, but to fulfil in his own person the thwarted uses of maternity. He became, and has remained, a sort of man-mother, alone in creation in his remarkable position. By this common interest, existing now not only between mother and child, but between father, mother, and child, grew up a wider common consciousness. And, as the father served the child not through sex-function, but through race-function, this service was open to far wider development and longer duration than the mother's alone could ever have reached. Maternal energy is the force through which have come into the world both love and industry. It is through the tireless activity of this desire, the mother's wish to serve the young, that she began the first of the arts and crafts whereby we live. While the male savage was still a mere hunter and fighter, expressing masculine energy, the katabolic force, along its essential line, expanding, scattering, the female savage worked out in equally natural ways the conserving force of female energy.[1] She gathered together and saved nutrition for the child, as the germ-cell gathers and saves nutrition in the unconscious silences of nature. She wrapped it in garments and built a shelter for its head as naturally as the same maternal function had loved, clothed, and sheltered the unborn. Maternal energy, working externally through our elaborate organism, is the source of productive industry, the main current of social life.

But not until this giant force could ally itself with others and work co-operatively, overcoming the destructive action of male energy in its blind competition, could our human life enter upon its full course of racial evolution. This is what was accomplished through the suppression of the free action of maternal energy in

---

1   In the *Evolution of Sex* (1889), Patrick Geddes and John Arthur Thomson associate male reproduction with the destructive changes (katabolism) and female reproduction with the constructive changes (anabolism) of living matter.

the female and its irresistible expression through the male. The two forces were combined, and he was the active factor in their manifestation. It was one of nature's calm, unsmiling miracles, no more wonderful than where she makes the guileless, greedy bee, who thinks he is merely getting his dinner, serve as an agent of reproduction to countless flowers. The bee might resent it if he knew what office he performed, and that his dinner was only there that he might fulfil that office. The subjection of woman has involved to an enormous degree the maternalizing of man. Under its bonds he has been forced into new functions, impossible to male energy alone. He has had to learn to love and care for some one besides himself. He has had to learn to work, to serve, to be human. Through the sex-passion, mightily overgrown, the human race has been led and driven up the long, steep path of progress, over all obstacles, through all dangers, carrying its accompanying conditions of disease and sin (and surmounting them), up and up in spite of all, until at last a degree of evolution is reached in which the extension of human service and human love makes possible a better way.

By the action of his own desires, through all its by-products of evil, man was made part mother; and so both man and woman were enabled to become human. It was an essential step in our racial progress, a means to an end. It should not be considered as an extreme maternal sacrifice, but as a novel and thorough system of paternal sacrifice,—the male of genus homo coerced by sex-necessity into the expression of maternal energy. The naturally destructive tendencies of the male have been gradually subverted to the conservative tendencies of the female, and this so palpably that the process is plainly to be observed throughout history. Into the male have been bred, by natural selection and unbroken training, the instincts and habits of the female, to his immense improvement. The female was dependent upon the male in individual economic relation. She was in a state of helpless slavery. She was treated with unspeakable injustice and cruelty. But nature's processes go on quite undisturbed among incidents like these. To blend the opposing sex-tendencies of two animals into the fruitful powers of a triumphant race was a painful process, but that does not matter. It was essential, and it has been fulfilled. There should be an end to the bitterness of feeling which has arisen between the sexes in this century. Right as is the change of attitude in the woman of to-day, she need feel no resentment as to the past, no shame, no sense of wrong. With a full knowledge of the initial superiority of her sex and the sociological necessity for its temporary subversion, she should feel only a deep and tender pride in the long patient ages during which she has waited and suffered, that man might slowly rise to full racial equality with her. She could afford to wait. She could afford to suffer.

It is high time that women began to understand their true position, primarily and eternally, and to see how little the long years of oppression have altered it. It was not well for the race to have the conservative processes of life so wholly confined to the female, the male being merely a temporary agent in reproduction and of no further use. His size, strength, and ferocity—admirable qualities in maintaining the life of an individual animal—were not the most desirable to develope the human race. We needed most the quality of co-ordination,—the facility in union, the power to make and to save rather than to spend and to destroy. These were female qualities. Acting from his own nature, man could not manifest traits that he did not possess. Throned as woman's master, chained as her servant, he has, through this strange combination of functions, acquired these traits under the heavy law of necessity. Originally, the two worked on divers[1] lines, he spending and scattering, she saving and building. She was the deep, steady, main stream of life, and he the active variant, helping to widen and change that life, but rather as an adjunct than as an essential. Races there were and are which reproduce themselves without the masculine organism,—by hermaphroditism and parthenogenesis.[2]

As the evolution of species progressed, we find a long series of practical experiments in males,—very tiny, transient, and inferior devices at first, but gradually developed into fuller and fuller equality with the female. In some of the lower forms, as in rotifers, insects, and crustaceans, are found the most inferior males, often none at all; and, where they do exist, they have no use save as an agent in reproduction. The most familiar instance of this is among the bees, where the drone, after fulfilling his functions, dies or is destroyed by the sturdy co-mothers of the hive. The common spider, too, has a tiny male, who tremblingly achieves his one brief purpose, and is then eaten up by his mate. She is the spider, a permanent flycatcher. He is merely a fertiliz-

---

1 Diverse.
2 Hermaphroditism: having both male and female sex organs; parthenogenesis: the natural process of reproduction in which the growth of an embryo occurs without fertilization.

ing agent. The little green aphis, so numerous on our rosebushes, can reproduce parthenogenetically so long as conditions are good,—while it is warm and there is enough to eat; but, when conditions grow hard, males are developed, and the dual method of reproduction is introduced.

In the two great activities of life, self-preservation and race-preservation, the female in these lower species is better equipped than the male for the first, and carries almost the whole burden of the second. His short period of functional use is as nothing compared to her long period of gestation, and the services she performs, in many cases, in providing for her young after their birth. Race-preservation has been almost entirely a female function, sometimes absolutely so. But it has been proven better for the race to have two highly developed parents rather than to have one. Therefore, sexual equality has been slowly evolved, not only by increasing the importance of the male element in reproduction, but by developing race-qualities in the male, so long merely a reproductive agent. The last step of this process has been the elevation of the male of genus homo to full racial equality with the female, and this has involved her temporary subjection. Both her physical and psychical tendencies have been transplanted into the organism of the male. He has been made the working mother of the world. The sexuo-economic relation was necessary to raise and broaden, to deepen and sweeten, to make more feminine, and so more human, the male of the human race. If the female had remained in full personal freedom and activity, she would have remained superior to him, and both would have remained stationary. Since the female had not the tendency to vary which distinguished the male, it was essential that the expansive forces of masculine energy be combined with the preservative and constructive forces of feminine energy. The expansive and variable male energy, struggling under its new necessity for constructive labor, has caused that labor to vary and progress more than it would have done in feminine hands alone. Out of her wealth of power and patience, liking to work, to give, she toils on forever in the same primitive industries. He, impatient of obstacles, not liking to work, desirous to get rather than to give, splits his task into a thousand specialties, and invents countless ways to lighten his labors. Male energy made to expend itself in performing female functions is what has brought our industries to their present development. Without the economic dependence of the female, the male would still be merely the hunter and fighter, the killer, the destroyer; and she would continue to be the industrious mother, without change or progress.

"What the children of Israel delighted in making
The children of Egypt delighted in breaking,"

runs the old rhyme; but there is small gain in such a process. In her subordinate position, under every disadvantage, through the very walls of her prison, the constructive force of woman has made man its instrument, and worked for the upbuilding of the world. As his energy was purely individualistic, and only to be controlled by the power of sex-attraction, it needed precisely this form of union, with its peculiar exaggeration of sex-faculty, to hold him to his task. Woman's abnormal development of sex, restrained and imprisoned by every law, has acted like a coiled spring upon the only free agent in society,—man. Under its intense stimulus he has moved mountains. All the world has seen it; and we have always murmured admiringly, "Oh, 'tis love, 'tis love, 'tis love that makes the world go round." It has done so, indeed, or, at least, has driven man round the world in one long range of struggle and conquest, of work and war. And every man who loves, and says, "I am yours: do with me what you will," knows the power, and honors it.

Human development thus far has proceeded in the male line, under the force of male energy, spurred by sex-stimulus, and by the vast storage battery of female energy suppressed. Women can well afford their period of subjection for the sake of a conquered world, a civilized man. In spite of the agony of the process, the black, long ages of shame and pain and horror, women should remember that they are still here; and, thanks to the blessed power of heredity, they are not so far aborted that a few generations of freedom will not set them abreast of the age. When the centuries of slavery and dishonor, of torture and death, of biting injustice and slow, suffocating repression, seem long to women, let them remember the geologic ages, the millions and millions of years when puny, pygmy, parasitic males struggled for existence, and were used or not, as it happened, like a half-tried patent medicine. What train of wives and concubines was ever so ignominiously placed as the extra husbands carried among the scales of the careful female cirriped,[1] lest she lose one or two! What neglect of faded wives can compare with the scorned, unnoticed

---

1 A marine animal.

death of the drone bee, starved, stung, shut out, walled up in wax, kept only for his momentary sex-function, and not absolutely necessary for that! What Bluebeard tragedy[1] or cruelty of bride-murdering Eastern king can emulate the ruthless slaughter of the hapless little male spider, used by his ferocious mate "to coldly furnish forth a marriage breakfast"![2] Never once in the history of humanity has any outrage upon women compared with these sweeping sacrifices of helpless males in earlier species. The female has been dominant for the main duration of life on earth. She has been easily equal always up to our own race; and in our race she has been subjugated to the male during the earlier period of development for such enormous racial gain, such beautiful and noble uses, that the sacrifice should never be mentioned nor thought of by a womanhood that knows its power. For the upbuilding of human life on earth she could afford to have her own held back; and—closer, tenderer, lovelier service—for the raising of her fierce sex-mate to a free and gentle brotherhood, for the uplifting of the human soul in her dear son, she could have borne not only this, but more,—borne it smilingly, ungrudgingly, gladly, for his sake and the world's.

And now that the long strain is over, now that the time has come when neither he nor the world is any longer benefited by her subordination, now that she is coming steadily out into direct personal expression, into the joy of racial action in full freedom, of power upon the throne instead of behind it, it is unworthy of this supreme new birth to waste one regret upon the pain that had to be.

Thus it may be seen that, even allowing for the injury to the individual and to society through the check to race-development and the increase of sex-development in woman, with its transmitted effects; allowing, further, that our highly specialized motherhood cannot be shown to be an advantage to humanity,—still it remains true that our sexuo-economic relation, with its effect of carrying on human life through the male side only, in activities driven by intensified sex-energy, has reacted to the benefit of the individual and of the race in many ways, as already suggested: in the extension of female function through the male; in the blending of faculties which have resulted in the possibility of our civilization; in the superior fighting power developed in the male, and

---

1 "Bluebeard" is a French folktale that tells the story of a wealthy nobleman who murders each of his successive wives.
2 "The funeral baked meats did coldly furnish forth the marriage tables" (Hamlet in Shakespeare's *Hamlet*, 1.2).

its effects in race-conquest, military and commercial; in the increased productivity developed by his assumption of maternal function; and by the sex-relation becoming mainly proportioned to his power to pay for it. Even motherhood has been indirectly the gainer in that, although the mother herself has been checked in direct maternal service, serving the race far more through her stimulation of male activities than through any activities of her own; yet the child has ultimately profited more by the materno-paternal services than he would have done by the maternal services alone.

All this may be granted as having been true in the past. And many, reassured by this frank admission, will ask, if it is so clear that the subjection of woman was useful, that this evil-working, monstrous sexuo-economic relation was after all of racial advantage, how we know that it is time to change. Principally, because we are changing. Social development is not caused by the promulgators of theories and by the writers of books. When Rousseau[1] wrote of equality, free France was being born,—the spirit of the times thrilled through the human mind; and those who had ears to hear heard, those who had pens to write wrote.[2] The condition of chattel slavery, working to its natural end, roused Garrison and Phillips and Harriet Beecher Stowe.[3] They did not make the movement. The period of women's economic dependence is drawing to a close, because its racial usefulness is wearing out. We have already reached a stage of human relation where we feel the strength of social duty pull against the sex-ties that have been for so long the only ties that we have recognized. The common consciousness of humanity, the sense of social need and social duty, is making itself felt in both men and women. The time has come when we are open to deeper and wider impulses than the sex-instinct; the social instincts are strong enough to come into full use at last. This is shown by the twin struggle that convulses the world to-day,—in sex and economics,—the "woman's movement" and the "labor movement." Neither name is wholly correct. Both make a class issue of what is in truth a social issue, a question involving every human interest. But the women natu-

---

1 Enlightenment philosopher Jean-Jacques Rousseau (1712–78).
2 Ezekiel 12.2: Son of man, you dwell in the midst of a rebellious house, which has eyes to see but does not see, and ears to hear but does not hear; for they are a rebellious house.
3 American abolitionists William Lloyd Garrison (1805–79), Wendell Phillips (1811–84), and Harriet Beecher Stowe (1811–96).

rally feel most the growing healthful pain of their position. They personally revolt, and think it is they who are most to be benefited. Similarly, since the "laboring classes" feel most the growing healthful pain of their position, they as naturally revolt under the same conviction. Sociologically, these conditions, which some find so painful and alarming, mean but one thing,—the increase of social consciousness. The progress of social organization has produced a corresponding degree of individualization, which has reached at last even to women,—even to the lowest grade of unskilled labor. This higher degree of individualization means a sharp personal consciousness of the evils of a situation hitherto little felt. With this higher growth of individual consciousness, and forming a part of it, comes the commensurate growth of social consciousness. We have grown to care for one another.

The woman's movement rests not alone on her larger personality, with its tingling sense of revolt against injustice, but on the wide, deep sympathy of women for one another. It is a concerted movement, based on the recognition of a common evil and seeking a common good. So with the labor movement. It is not alone that the individual laborer is a better educated, more highly developed man than the stolid peasant of earlier days, but also that with this keener personal consciousness has come the wider social consciousness, without which no class can better its conditions. The traits incident to our sexuo-economic relation have developed till they forbid the continuance of that relation. In the economic world, excessive masculinity, in its fierce competition and primitive individualism; and excessive femininity, in its inordinate consumption and hindering conservatism; have reached a stage where they work more evil than good.

The increasing specialization of the modern woman, acquired by inheritance from the ceaselessly specializing male, makes her growing racial faculties strain against the primitive restrictions of a purely sexual relation. The desire to produce—the distinctive human quality—is no longer satisfied with a status that allows only reproduction. In our present stage of social evolution it is increasingly difficult and painful for women to endure their condition of economic dependence, and therefore they are leaving it. This does not mean that at a given day all women will stand forth free together, but that in slowly gathering numbers, now so great that all the world can see, women in the most advanced races are so standing free. Great advances along social lines come slowly, like the many-waved progress of the tide: they are not sudden jumps over yawning chasms.

But, besides this first plain perception that our strange relation is coming to an end, we may see how in its own working it developes forces which must end it or us. The method of action of our peculiar cat's-paw combination of the sexes—the mother-father doing the work of the helpless creature he carries on his back; the parasite mate devouring even when she should most feed—has been this, as repeatedly shown: because of sex-desire the male subjugates the female. Lest he lose her, he feeds her, and, perforce, her young. She, obtaining food through the sex-relation, becomes over-sexed, and acts with constantly increasing stimulus on his sex-activities; and, as these activities are made economic by their relation, she so stimulates industry and all progress. But,—and here is the natural end of an unnatural position, a position that serves its purpose for a time, but holds in itself the seeds of its own destruction,—through the unchecked sex-energy, accumulated under the abnormal pressure of the economic side of the relation, such excess is developed as tends to destroy both individual and race; and such psychic qualities are developed as tend also to our injury and extinction.

A relation that inevitably produces abnormal development cannot be permanently maintained. The intensification of sex-energy as a social force results in such limitless exaggeration of sex-instinct as finds expression sexually in the unnatural vices of advanced civilization, and, socially, in the strained economic relation between producer and consumer which breaks society in two. The sexuo-economic relation serves to bring social development to a certain level. After that level is reached, a higher relation must be adopted, or the lifting process comes to an end; and either the race succumbs to the morbid action of its own forces or some fresher race comes in, and begins the course of social evolution anew.

Under the stimulus of the sexuo-economic relation, one civilization after another has climbed up and fallen down in weary succession. It remains for us to develop a newer, better form of sex-relation and of economic relation therewith, and so to grasp the fruits of all previous civilizations, and grow on to the beautiful results of higher ones. The true and lasting social progress, beyond that which we have yet made, is based on a spirit of inter-human love, not merely the inter-sexual; and it requires an economic machinery organized and functioned for human needs, not sexual ones. The sexuo-economic relation drives man up to where he can become fully human. It deepens and develops the human soul until it is able to conceive and fulfil the larger social uses in which our further life must find expression. But, unless the human soul sees these new forces, feels them, gives way to them in loyal service, it fails to reach the level from which all further progress must proceed, and falls back. Again and again society has so risen, so failed to grasp new duties, so fallen back.

To-day it will not so fall again, because the social consciousness is at last so vital a force in both men and women that we feel clearly that our human life cannot be fully lived on sex-lines only. We are so far individualized, so far socialized, that men can work without the tearing spur of exaggerated sex-stimulus, work for some one besides mate and young; and women can love and serve without the slavery of economic dependence,—love better and serve more. Sex-stimulus begins and ends in individuals. The social spirit is a larger thing, a better thing, and brings with it a larger, nobler life than we could ever know on a sex-basis solely.

Moreover, it should be distinctly understood, as it is already widely and vaguely felt, that the higher development of social life following the economic independence of women makes possible a higher sex-life than has ever yet been known. As fast as the human individual rises in social progress to a certain degree of development, so fast this primitive form of sex-union chafes and drags: it is felt to be unsatisfying and injurious. This is a marked feature in modern life. The long, sure, upward trend of the human race toward monogamous marriage is no longer helped, but hindered by the economic side of the relation. The best marriage is between the best individuals; and the best individuals of both sexes to-day are increasingly injured by the economic basis of our marriage, which produces and maintains those qualities in men and women and their resultant industrial conditions which make marriage more difficult and precarious every day.[1]

The woman's movement, then, should be hailed by every right-thinking, far-seeing man and woman as the best birth of our century. The banner advanced proclaims "equality before the law,"[2] woman's share in political freedom; but the main line of progress is and has been toward economic equality and freedom. While life exists on earth, the economic conditions must under-

---

[1] In late-nineteenth-century America, college-educated women married at significantly lower rates than the general population, differing by 35 to 50 percent.

[2] Equality before the law, the idea that each individual person should be subject to the same legal standards of fairness and justice, was a (radical) goal of some nineteenth-century American feminists.

lie and dominate each existing form and its activities; and social life is no exception. A society whose economic unit is a sex-union can no more develope beyond a certain point industrially than a society like the patriarchal, whose political unit was a sex-union, could develope beyond a certain point politically.

The last freeing of the individual makes possible the last combination of individuals. While sons must bend to the will of a patriarchal father, no democracy is possible. Democracy means, requires, is, individual liberty. While the sexuo-economic relation makes the family the centre of industrial activity, no higher collectivity than we have to-day is possible. But, as women become free, economic, social factors, so becomes possible the full social combination of individuals in collective industry. With such freedom, such independence, such wider union, becomes possible also a union between man and woman such as the world has long dreamed of in vain.

VIII.

In the face of so vital and radical a change in human life as this change of economic base in the position of women, it is well to call attention more at length to the illustrations of every-day facts in our common lives, which he who runs may read, if he knows how to read.[1] We do not, as a rule, know how to read the most important messages to humanity,—the signs of the times. Historic crises, which have been slowly maturing, burst upon us in sudden birth before the majority of the people imagine that anything is going on. The first gun fired at Fort Sumter[2] was an extreme surprise to most of the citizens of the Union. The Boston Tea Party[3] was, no doubt, an unaccountable piece of insolence to many worthy Britons. When "the deluge" did pour over the *noblesse* of France,[4] few had been really foreseeing enough to avoid it.

---

1 Habakkuk 2.2: Write the vision and make it plain upon tables ... that he may run that readeth it.

2 The opening engagement of the American Civil War (12–14 April 1861).

3 On 16 December 1773, American colonists, protesting "taxation without representation," dumped tea imported by the British East India Company into the harbour at Boston, Massachusetts.

4 "After me, the deluge" (French: Après moi, le déluge). An expression attributed to Louis XV of France (r. 1715–74), often used in retrospect as a foreshadowing of the French Revolution (1789–99).

Fortunately, the laws of social evolution do not wait for our recognition or acceptance: they go straight on. And this greater and more important change than the world has ever seen, this slow emergence of the long-subverted human female to full racial equality, has been going on about us full long enough to be observed. It is seen more prominently in this country than in any other, for many reasons.

The Anglo-Saxon blood, that English mixture of which Tennyson sings,—"Saxon and Norman and Dane though we be,"[1]— is the most powerful expression of the latest current of fresh racial life from the north,—from those sturdy races where the women were more like men, and the men no less manly because of it. The strong, fresh spirit of religious revolt in the new church that protested against and broke loose from the old, woke and stirred the soul of woman as well as the soul of man, and in the equality of martyrdom the sexes learned to stand side by side.[2] Then, in the daring and exposure, the strenuous labor and bitter hardship of the pioneer life of the early settlers, woman's very presence was at a premium; and her labor had a high economic value. Sex-dependence was almost unfelt. She who moulded the bullets, and loaded the guns while the men fired them, was co-defender of the home and young. She who carded and dyed and wove and spun was co-provider for the family. Men and women prayed together, worked together, and fought together in comparative equality. More than all, the development of democracy has brought to us the fullest individualization that the world has ever seen. Although politically expressed by men alone, the character it has produced is inherited by their daughters. The Federal Democracy[3] in its organic union, reacting upon individuals, has so strengthened, freed, emboldened, the human soul in America

---

1 "A Welcome to Alexandra" (1879).
2 English Protestants in the sixteenth and seventeenth centuries sought to purify the Church of England of Roman Catholic practices. During this period, hundreds of Protestants, including numerous women, were burned at the stake, choosing martyrdom over compliance with monarchical rule.
3 A system of government in which power is constitutionally divided between a central governing authority and constituent political units (such as states or provinces). While often categorized as a democracy, the United States is more accurately defined as a constitutional federal republic. Progressives including Gilman sought to strengthen and deepen American democracy, often through institution building and reform.

that we have thrown off slavery, and with the same impulse have set in motion the long struggle toward securing woman's fuller equality before the law.

This struggle has been carried on unflaggingly for fifty years, and fast nears its victorious end. It is not only in the four States where full suffrage is exercised by both sexes,[1] nor in the twenty-four where partial suffrage is given to women, that we are to count progress; but in the changes legal and social, mental and physical, which mark the advance of the mother of the world toward her full place. Have we not all observed the change even in size of the modern woman, with its accompanying strength and agility? The Gibson Girl and the Duchess of Towers,[2]—these are the new women; and they represent a noble type, indeed. The heroines of romance and drama to-day are of a different sort from the Evelinas and Arabellas[3] of the last century. Not only do they look differently, they behave differently. The false sentimentality, the false delicacy, the false modesty, the utter falseness of elaborate compliment and servile gallantry which went with the other falsehoods,—all these are disappearing. Women are growing honester, braver, stronger, more healthful and skilful and able and free, more human in all ways.

The change in education is in large part a cause of this, and progressively a consequence. Day by day the bars go down. More and more the field lies open for the mind of woman to glean all it can, and it has responded most eagerly. Not only our pupils, but our teachers, are mainly women. And the clearness and strength of the brain of the woman prove continually the injustice of the clamorous contempt long poured upon what was scornfully called "the female mind." There is no female mind. The brain is not an organ of sex. As well speak of a female liver.

Woman's progress in the arts and sciences, the trades and professions, is steady; but it is most unwise to claim from these relative advances the superiority of women to men, or even their equality, in these fields. What is more to the purpose and easily to

---

1   By 1900, four US states had granted women the right to vote: Wyoming (1890), Colorado (1893), Utah (1896), and Idaho (1896).
2   Gibson Girl: originally portrayed by the pen-and-ink illustrations of artist Charles Dana Gibson (1867–1944), the ideal personification of American womanhood in the late nineteenth and early twentieth centuries; The Duchess of Towers: Mary, Duchess of Towers, in George Du Maurier's novel *Peter Ibbetson* (1891).
3   Evelina: in Fanny Burney's *Evelina* (1778); Arabella: in Charlotte Lennox's *The Female Quixote* (1752).

be shown is the superiority of the women of to-day to those of earlier times, the immense new development of racial qualities in the sex. No modern proverbs, if we expressed ourselves in proverbs now, would speak with such sweeping, unbroken contumely[1] of the women of to-day as did those unerring exhibitors of popular feeling in former times.

The popular thought of our day is voiced in fiction, fluent verse, and an incessant play of humor. By what is freely written by most authors and freely read by most people is shown our change in circumstances and change in feeling. In old romances the woman was nothing save beautiful, high-born, virtuous, and perhaps "accomplished." She did nothing but love and hate, obey or disobey, and be handed here and there among villain, hero, and outraged parent, screaming, fainting, or bursting into floods of tears as seemed called for by the occasion

In the fiction of to-day women are continually taking larger place in the action of the story. They are given personal characteristics beyond those of physical beauty. And they are no longer content simply to *be*: they *do*. They are showing qualities of bravery, endurance, strength, foresight, and power for the swift execution of well-conceived plans. They have ideas and purposes of their own; and even when, as in so many cases described by the more reactionary novelists, the efforts of the heroine are shown to be entirely futile, and she comes back with a rush to the self-effacement of marriage with economic dependence, still the efforts were there. Disapprove as he may, use his art to oppose and contemn as he may, the true novelist is forced to chronicle the distinctive features of his time; and no feature is more distinctive of this time than the increasing individualization of women. With lighter touch, but with equally unerring truth, the wit and humor of the day show the same development. The majority of our current jokes on women turn on their "newness," their advance.

No sociological change equal in importance to this clearly marked improvement of an entire sex has ever taken place in one century. Under it all, the *crux* of the whole matter, goes on the one great change, that of the economic relation. This follows perfectly natural lines. Just as the development of machinery constantly lowers the importance of mere brute strength of body and raises that of mental power and skill, so the pressure of industrial conditions demands an ever-higher specialization, and tends to

---

1 Insult.

break up that relic of the patriarchal age,—the family as an economic unit.

Women have been led under pressure of necessity into a most reluctant entrance upon fields of economic activity. The sluggish and greedy disposition bred of long ages of dependence has by no means welcomed the change. Most women still work only as they "have to," until they can marry and "be supported." Men, too, liking the power that goes with money, and the poor quality of gratitude and affection bought with it, resent and oppose the change; but all this disturbs very little the course of social progress.

A truer spirit is the increasing desire of young girls to be independent, to have a career of their own, at least for a while, and the growing objection of countless wives to the pitiful asking for money, to the beggary of their position. More and more do fathers give their daughters, and husbands their wives, a definite allowance,—a separate bank account,—something which they can play[1] is all their own. The spirit of personal independence in the women of to-day is sure proof that a change has come.

For a while the introduction of machinery which took away from the home so many industries deprived woman of any importance as an economic factor; but presently she arose, and followed her lost wheel and loom to their new place, the mill. To-day there is hardly an industry in the land in which some women are not found. Everywhere throughout America are women workers outside the unpaid labor of the home, the last census[2] giving three million of them. This is so patent a fact, and makes itself felt in so many ways by so many persons, that it is frequently and widely discussed. Without here going into its immediate advantages or disadvantages from an industrial point of view, it is merely instanced as an undeniable proof of the radical change in the economic position of women that is advancing upon us. She is assuming new relations from year to year before our eyes; but we, seeing all social facts from a personal point of view, have failed to appreciate the nature of the change.

Consider, too, the altered family relation which attends this movement. Entirely aside from the strained relation in marriage, the other branches of family life feel the strange new forces, and respond to them. "When I was a girl," sighs the gray-haired mother, "we sisters all sat and sewed while mother read to us.

---

1 Pretend.
2 The Eleventh Census of the United States (June 1890).

Now every one of my daughters has a different club!" She sighs, be it observed. We invariably object to changed conditions in those departments of life where we have established ethical values. For all the daughters to sew while the mother read aloud to them was esteemed right; and, therefore, the radiating diffusion of daughters among clubs is esteemed wrong,—a danger to home life. In the period of the common sewing and reading the women so assembled were closely allied in industrial and intellectual development as well as in family relationship. They all could do the same work, and liked to do it. They all could read the same book, and liked to read it. (And reading, half a century ago, was still considered half a virtue and the other half a fine art.) Hence the ease with which this group of women entered upon their common work and common pleasure.

The growing individualization of democratic life brings inevitable change to our daughters as well as to our sons. Girls do not all like to sew, many do not know how. Now to sit sewing together, instead of being a harmonizing process, would generate different degrees of restlessness, of distaste, and of nervous irritation. And, as to the reading aloud, it is not so easy now to choose a book that a well-educated family of modern girls and their mother would all enjoy together. As the race become more specialized, more differentiated, the simple lines of relation in family life draw with less force, and the more complex lines of relation in social life draw with more force; and this is a perfectly natural and desirable process for women as well as for men.

It may be suggested, in passing, that one of the causes of "Americanitis"[1] is this increasing nervous strain in family relation, acting especially upon woman. As she becomes more individualized, she suffers more from the primitive and indifferentiated conditions of the family life of earlier times. What "a wife" and "a mother" was supposed to find perfectly suitable, this newly specialized wife and mother, who is also a personality, finds clumsy and ill-fitting,—a mitten where she wants a glove. The home cares and industries, still undeveloped, give no play for her increasing specialization. Where the embryonic combination of cook-nurse-laundress-chambermaid-housekeeper-waitress-governess was content to be "jack of all trades" and mistress of none,[2] the woman who is able to be one of these things perfectly,

---

1 A condition defined by American psychologist William James (1842–1910) to describe fatigue, irritability, and stress; neurasthenia.
2 A play on the term "Jack of all trades, master of none."

and by so much less able to be all the others, suffers doubly from not being able to do what she wants to do, and from being forced to do what she does not want to do. To the delicately differentiated modern brain the jar and shock of changing from trade to trade a dozen times a day is a distinct injury, a waste of nervous force. With the larger socialization of the woman of to-day, the fitness for and accompanying desire for wider combinations, more general interest, more organized methods of work for larger ends, she feels more and more heavily the intensely personal limits of the more primitive home duties, interests, methods. And this pain and strain must increase with the advance of women until the new functional power makes to itself organic expression, and the belated home industries are elevated and organized, like the other necessary labors of modern life.

In the meantime, however, the very best and foremost women suffer most; and a heavy check is placed on social progress by this difficulty in enlarging old conditions to suit new powers. It should still be remembered it is not the essential relations of wife and mother which are thus injurious, but the industrial conditions born of the economic dependence of the wife and mother, and hitherto supposed to be part of her functions. The change we are making does not in any way militate against the true relations of the family, marriage, and parentage, but only against those sub-relations belonging to an earlier period and now in process of extinction. The family as an entity, an economic and social unit, does not hold as it did. The ties between brother and sister, cousins and relatives generally, are gradually lessening their hold, and giving way under pressure of new forces which tend toward better things.

The change is more perceptible among women than among men, because of the longer survival of more primitive phases of family life in them. One of its most noticeable features is the demand in women not only for their own money, but for their own work for the sake of personal expression. Those who object to women's working on the ground that they should not compete with men or be forced to struggle for existence look only at work as a means of earning money. They should remember that human labor is an exercise of faculty, without which we should cease to be human; that to do and to make not only gives deep pleasure, but is indispensable to healthy growth. Few girls to-day fail to manifest some signs of this desire for individual expression. It is not only in the classes who are forced to it: even among the rich we find this same stirring of normal race-energy. To carve in wood, to hammer brass, to do "art dressmaking," to raise mushrooms in the cellar,—our girls are all wanting to do something individually. It is a most healthy state, and marks the development of race-distinction in women with a corresponding lowering of sex-distinction to its normal place.

In body and brain, wherever she touches life, woman is changing gloriously from the mere creature of sex, all her race-functions held in abeyance, to the fully developed human being, none the less true woman for being more truly human. What alarms and displeases us in seeing these things is our funny misconception that race-functions are masculine. Much effort is wasted in showing that women will become "unsexed" and "masculine" by assuming these human duties. We are told that a slight sex-distinction is characteristic of infancy and old age, and that the assumption of opposite traits by either sex shows either a decadent or an undeveloped condition. The young of any race are less marked by sex-distinction; and in old age the distinguishing traits are sometimes exchanged, as in the crowing of old hens and in the growing of the beard on old women. And we are therefore assured that the endeavor of women to perform these masculine economic functions marks a decadent civilization, and is greatly to be deprecated. There would be some reason in this objection if the common racial activities of humanity, into which women are now so eagerly entering, were masculine functions. But they are not. There is no more sublimated expression of our morbid ideas of sex-distinction than in this complacent claiming of all human life-processes as sex-functions of the male. "Masculine" and "feminine" are only to be predicated of reproductive functions,—processes of race-preservation. The processes of self-preservation are racial, peculiar to the species, but common to either sex.

If it could be shown that the women of to-day were growing beards, were changing as to pelvic bones, were developing bass voices, or that in their new activities they were manifesting the destructive energy, the brutal combative instinct, or the intense sex-vanity of the male, then there would be cause for alarm. But the one thing that has been shown in what study we have been able to make of women in industry is that they are women still, and this seems to be a surprise to many worthy souls. A female horse is no less female than a female starfish, but she has more functions. She can do more things, is a more highly specialized organism, has more intelligence, and, with it all, is even more feminine in her more elaborate and farther-reaching processes of reproduction. So the "new woman" will be no less female than the "old" woman, though she has more functions, can do more things, is a more highly specialized organism, has more intelligence. She will be, with it all, more feminine, in that she will develope far more efficient processes of caring for the young of the human race than our present wasteful and grievous method, by which we lose fifty per cent. of them, like a codfish. The average married pair, says the scientific dictator,[1] in all sobriety, should have four children merely to preserve our present population, two to replace themselves and two to die,—a pleasant method this, and redounding greatly to the credit of our motherhood.

The rapid extension of function in the modern woman has nothing to do with any exchange of masculine and feminine traits: it is simply an advance in human development of traits common to both sexes, and is wholly good in its results. No one who looks at the life about us can fail to see the alteration going on. It is a pity that we so fail to estimate its value. On the other hand, the growth and kindling intensity of the social consciousness among us all is as conspicuous a feature of modern life as the change in woman's position, and closely allied therewith.

Never before have people cared so much about other people. From its first expression in greater kindliness and helpfulness toward individual human beings to its last expression in the vague, blind, groping movements toward international justice and law, the heart of the world is alive and stirring to-day. The whole social body is affected with sudden shudders of feeling over some world calamity or world rejoicing. When the message of "Uncle Tom's Cabin"[2] ran from heart to heart around the world, kindling a streak of fire, the fire of human love and sympathy which is latent in us all and longing always for some avenue of common expression, it proved that in every civilized land of our time the people are of one mind on some subjects. Nothing could have so spread and so awakened a response in the Periclean, the Augustan, or even the Elizabethan age;[3] for humanity was not then so far socialized and so far individualized as to be capable of such a general feeling.

---

1   British academic and essayist Grant Allen (1848–99), who argued for a higher birth rate among Americans.
2   Harriet Beecher Stowe, *Uncle Tom's Cabin* (1852).
3   "Golden ages" named for Greek statesman and general of Athens, Pericles (495–429 BCE); Roman statesman and first emperor of the Roman Empire, Augustus (63 BCE–14 CE); Queen Elizabeth I of England (r. 1558–1603).

Invention and the discoveries of science are steadily unifying the world to-day. The statement is frequently advanced that the minds of the men of Greece or of the great thinkers of the Middle Ages were stronger and larger than the minds of the men of to-day. Perhaps they were. So were the bodies of the megatherium and the ichthyosaurus stronger and larger than the bodies of the animals of to-day. Yet they were lower in the scale of organic evolution. The ability of the individual is not so much the criterion of social progress as that organic relation of individuals which makes the progress of each available to all. Emerson has done more for America than Plato[1] could do for Greece. Indeed, Plato has done more for America than he could do for Greece, because the printing-press and the public school have made thought more freely and easily transmissible.

Human progress lies in the perfecting of the social organization, and it is here that the changes of our day are most marked. Whereas, in more primitive societies, injuries were only felt by the individual as they affected his own body or direct personal interests, and later his own nation or church, to-day there is a growing sensitiveness to social injuries, even to other nations. The civilized world has suffered in Armenia's agony,[2] even though the machinery of social expression is yet unable fully to carry out the social feeling or the social will. Function comes before organ always; and the human heart and mind, which are the social heart and mind, must feel and think long before the social body can act in full expression.

Social sympathy and thought are growing more intense and active every day. In our cumbrous[3] efforts at international arbitration, in the half-hearted alliances and agreements between great peoples, in the linking of humanity together across ocean and mountain and desert plain by steam and electricity, in the establishment of such world-functions as the international postal

---

1 American essayist, philosopher, and poet Ralph Waldo Emerson (1803–82); Athenian philosopher Plato (c. 429–347 BCE).
2 Gilman is referring to the Armenian massacres (1894–96). Beginning in the fifteenth century, the Armenians were ruled by the Ottoman Empire. By the late nineteenth century, many Armenians began demanding greater rights, and the Armenian Revolutionary Federation, a nationalist political party, was founded in 1890. In the years following, Ottoman forces carried out a series of atrocities that resulted in the deaths of many thousands of Armenian people.
3 Presenting obstruction; cumbersome.

service,[1]—in these, externally, our social unity has begun to act. In the more familiar field of personal life, who has not seen how unceasingly many of us are occupied in the interests of the community, even to the injury of our own? The rising manifestations of social interest among women were covered with ridicule at first, through such characters as Mrs. Jellyby or Mrs. Pardiggle,[2] although a few women who were so great and so identified with religion and philanthropy as to command respect, women like the saintly Elizabeth Fry, Florence Nightingale, and Clara Barton, escaped.[3] But both belong to the same age, are part of the same phenomena. To-day there is hardly a woman of intelligence in all America, to say nothing of other countries, who is not definitely and actively concerned in some social interest, who does not recognize some duty besides those incident to her own blood relationship.

The woman's club movement[4] is one of the most important sociological phenomena of the century,—indeed, of all centuries,—marking as it does the first timid steps toward social organization of these so long unsocialized members of our race. Social life is absolutely conditioned upon organization. The military organizations which promote peace, the industrial organizations which maintain life, and all the educational, religious, and charitable organizations which serve our higher needs constitute the essential factors of that social activity in which, as individuals, we live and grow; and it is plain, therefore, that while women had no part in these organizations they had no part in social life. Their main relation to society was an individual one, an animal one, a sexual one. They produced the people of whom society was made, but they were not society. Of course, they were indispensable in this capacity; but one might as well call food a part of society because people could not exist without eating as to call women a social factor because people could not exist without

---

1 In 1874, the Treaty of Bern established the General Postal Union (later the Universal Postal Union) and was signed by twenty-one nation states including the United States.
2 Mrs. Jellyby and Mrs. Pardiggle: in Charles Dickens, *Bleak House* (1852–53).
3 Fry: British prison reformer and Quaker philanthropist (1780–1845); Nightingale: British social reformer and founder of modern nursing (1820–1910); Barton: American nurse and founder of the American Red Cross (1821–1912).
4 In nineteenth-century America, women's clubs were important vehicles for female-led policy reform.

being born. Women have made the people who made the world, and will always continue so to do. But they have heretofore had a most insignificant part in the world their sons have made.

The only form of organization possible to women was for long the celibate religious community. This has always been dear to them; and, as to-day many avoid undesired marriage for the sake of "independence," so in earlier times many fled from undesired marriage to the communal independence of the convent. The fondness of women for the church has been based, not only on religious feeling, but on the force of the human longing for co-ordinate interest and activities; and only here could this be gratified. In the church at least they could be together. They could feel in common and act in common,—the deepest human joy. As the church has widened its activities, it has found everywhere in women its most valuable and eager workers. To labor together, together to raise funds for a common end, for a new building or a new minister, for local charities or for foreign missions,—but to labor together, and for other needs than those of the family relation,—this has always met glad response from the struggling human soul in woman. When it became possible to work together for other than religious ends,—when large social service was made possible to women, as in our sanitary commission during the last war,—women everywhere rose to meet the need. The rise and spread of that greatest of women's organizations, the Woman's Christian Temperance Union,[1] has shown anew how ready is the heart of woman to answer the demands of other than personal relations.

And now the whole country is budding into women's clubs. The clubs are uniting and federating by towns, States, nations: there are even world organizations.[2] The sense of human unity is growing daily among women. Not to see it is impossible. Not to watch with pleasure and admiration this new growth in social life, this sudden and enormous re-enforcement of our best forces from the very springs of life, only shows how blind we are to true human advantage, how besotted in our fondness for sex-distinction in excess.

One of the most valuable features of this vast line of progress is the new heroism it is pouring into life. The crumbling and flattening of ambitions and ideals under pressure of our modern

---

1 An evangelical Christian women's organization founded in 1874 to combat the abuse of alcohol through prohibition of alcoholic beverages.
2 Jane Cunningham Croly (1829–1901) founded the General Federation of Women's Clubs (GFWC) in 1890.

business life is a patent fact. We are growing to surrender taste and conscience and honor itself to the demands of business success, prostituting the noblest talents to the most ignoble uses with that last excuse of cowardice,—"A man must live." Into this phase of life comes a new spirit,—the spirit of such women as Elizabeth Cady Stanton and Susan B. Anthony; of Dr. Elizabeth Blackwell and her splendid sisterhood;[1] of all the women who have battled and suffered for half a century, forcing their way, with sacrifices never to be told, into the field of freedom so long denied them,—not for themselves alone, but for one another. We have loudly cried out at the injury to the home and family which are supposed to follow such a course. We have unsparingly ridiculed the unattractive and unfeminine among these vanguard workers. But few have thought what manner of spirit it must take to leave the dear old easy paths so long trodden by so many feet, and go to hew out new ones alone. The nature of the effort involved and the nature of the opposition incurred conduced to lessen the soft charms and graces of the ultra-feminine state; but the women who follow and climb swiftly up the steps which these great leaders so laboriously built may do the new work in the new places, and still keep much of what these strenuous heroes had to lose.

It is not being a doctor that makes a woman unwomanly, but the treatment which the first women medical students and physicians received was such as to make even men unmanly. That time is largely past. The gates are nearly all open, at least in some places; and the racial activities of women are free to develop as rapidly as the nature of the case will allow. The main struggle now is with the distorted nature of the creature herself. Grand as are the women who embody at whatever cost the highest spirit of the age, there still remains to us the heavy legacy of the years behind,—the innumerable weak and little women, with the aspirations of an affectionate guinea pig. The soul of woman must speak through the long accumulations of her intensified sex-nature, through the uncertain impulses of a starved and thwarted class. She must recognize that she is handicapped. She must understand her difficulty, and meet it bravely and firmly.

But this is a matter for personal volition, for subjective consciousness. The thing to see and to rejoice in is that, with and without their conscious volition, with or without the approval and

---

1 Stanton (1815–1902) and Anthony (1820–1906): nineteenth-century woman's movement activists; Blackwell (1821–1910): the first woman to receive a medical degree in the United States.

assistance of men, in spite of that crowning imbecility of history,—the banded opposition of some women to the advance of the others,—the female of our race is making sure and rapid progress in human development.

IX.

The main justification for the subjection of women, which is commonly advanced, is the alleged advantage to motherhood resultant from her extreme specialization to the uses of maternity under this condition.

There are two weak points in this position. One is that the advantage to motherhood cannot be proved: the other, that it is not the uses of maternity to which she is specialized, but the uses of sex-indulgence. So far from the economic dependence of women working in the interests of motherhood, it is the steadily acting cause of a pathological maternity and a decreasing birth-rate.[1]

In simple early times there was a period when women were economically profited by child-bearing; when, indeed, that was their sole use, and, failing it, they were entitled to no respect or profit whatever. Such a condition tended to increase the quantity of children, if not the quality. With industrial development and the increasing weight of economic cares upon the shoulders of the man, children come to be looked upon as a burden, and are dreaded instead of desired by the hard-worked father. They subtract from the family income; and the mother, absolutely dependent upon that income and also overworked in her position of unpaid house-servant, is not impelled to court maternity by any economic pressure. In the working classes—to which the great majority of people belong—the woman is by no means "segregated to the uses of maternity." Among the most intelligent and conscientious workingmen to-day there is a strong feeling against large families, and a consistent effort is made to prevent them.

Lest this be considered as not bearing directly upon the economic position of women, but rather on the general status of the working classes, let us examine the same condition among the wealthy. It is here that the economic dependence of women is

---

1 Numerous nineteenth-century commentators expressed concern about decreasing birth rates, particularly among native-born populations. From 1873 onward, purity crusader Anthony Comstock (1844–1915) led a nation-wide push to criminalize contraceptive devices and information.

carried to its extreme. The daughters and wives of the rich fail to perform even the domestic service expected of the women of poorer families. They are from birth to death absolutely non-productive in goods or labor of economic value, and consumers of such goods and labor to an extent limited only by the purchasing power of their male relatives. In this condition the economic advantage of the woman, married or unmarried, not merely in food and clothes, but in such social advantage as she desires, lies in her power to attract and hold the devotion of men; and this power is not the power of maternity. On the contrary, maternity, by lowering the personal charms and occupying the time of the mother, fails to bring her the pleasure and profit obtainable by the woman who is not a mother. It is through the sex-relation minus its natural consequence[1] that she profits most; and, therefore, the force of economic advantage acts against maternity instead of toward it.

In the last extreme this is clear to all in the full flower of the sexuo-economic relation,—prostitution, than which nothing runs more absolutely counter to the improvement of the race through maternity. Specialization to uses of maternity, as in the queen bee, is one thing. Specialization to uses of sex without maternity is quite another. Yet this popular opinion, that we as a race are greatly benefited by having all our women saved from direct economic activity, and so allowed to concentrate all their energies on the beautiful work of motherhood, remains strong among us.

In *The Forum* for November, 1888, Lester F. Ward published a paper called "Our Better Halves," in which was clearly shown the biological supremacy of the female sex. This naturally aroused much discussion; and in an answering article, "Woman's Place in Nature" (*The Forum*, May 1889), Mr. Grant Allen very thoroughly states the general view on this subject. He says of woman: "I believe it to be true that she is very much less the race than man; that she is, indeed, not even half the race at present, but rather a part of it told specially off[2] for the continuance of the species, just as truly as drones or male spiders are parts of their species told off for the performance of male-functions, or as 'rotund' honey ants are individual insects told off to act as living honey jars to the community. She is the sex sacrificed to reproductive necessities."

Since biological facts point to the very gradual introduction and development of the male organism solely as a reproductive

---

1 I.e., pregnancy.
2 Set apart; assigned to a special duty.

necessity, and since women are sacrificed not to reproductive necessities, but to a most unnecessary and injurious degree of sex-indulgence under economic necessity, such a statement as Mr. Grant Allen's has elements of humor. The opinion is held, however, not only by the special students of biology and sociology, but by the general public, and demands most careful attention. Those holding such a view may admit the over-development of sex consequent upon the economic relation between men and women, and the train of evils, individual and social, following that over-development. They may even admit, further, something of the alleged injury to economic evolution. But they will claim in answer that these morbid conditions are essential to human progress, and that the good to humanity through the segregation of the female to the uses of maternity overbalances the evil, great as this is; also, conversely, that the gain to the individual and to society to be obtained by the economic freedom of the female would be more than offset by the loss to the race caused by the removal of our highly specialized motherhood.

To meet this, it is necessary to show that our highly specialized motherhood is not so advantageous as believed; that it is below rather than above the efficacy of motherhood in other species; that its deficiency is due to the sexuo-economic relation; that the restoration of economic freedom to the female will improve motherhood; and, finally, to indicate in some sort the lines of social and individual development along which this improvement may be "practically" manifested.

In approaching this subject, we need something of special mental preparation. We need to realize that our ideas upon this theme are peculiarly colored by prejudice, that in no other field of thought are we so blinded by our emotions. We have felt more on this subject than on any other, and thought less. We have also felt much on the relation of the sexes; but it has been made a subject of study, of comparison, of speculation. There are differences of feeling on the sex question, but as to motherhood none. Here and there, to be sure, some isolated philosopher, a Plato, a Rousseau, dares advance some thought on this ground; but, on the whole, no theme of commensurate importance has been so little studied. More sacred than religion, more binding than the law, more habitual than methods of eating, we are each and all born into the accepted idea of motherhood and trained in it; and in maturity we hand it down unquestioningly. A man may question the purposes and methods of his God with less danger of outcry against him than if he dare to question the purposes and methods of his mother. This matriolatry[1] is a sentiment so deep-seated, wide-spread, and long-established as to be dominant in every class of minds. It is so associated with our religious instincts, on the one hand, and our sex-instincts, on the other, both of which we have long been forbidden to discuss,—the one being too holy and the other too unholy,—that it is well-nigh impossible to think clearly and dispassionately on the subject. It is easy to understand why we are so triple-plated with prejudice in the case.

The instinct that draws the child to its mother is exactly as old as the instinct that draws the mother to her child; and that dates back to the period when the young first needed care,—among the later reptiles, perhaps. This tie has lasted unbroken through the whole line of progression, and is stronger with us than with any other creature, because in our social evolution the parent is of advantage to the child not only through its entire life, but even after death, by our laws of inheritance. So early, so radically important, so long accumulated an animal instinct, added to by social law, is a great force. Besides this, we must reckon with our long period of ancestor worship. This finally changed the hideous concepts of early idolaters into the idea of parental divinity; for, having first made a god of their father, they then made a father of God, and this deep religious feeling has added much to the heavy weight of instinct. Parental government, too, absolute in the patriarchal period, has added further to our devout, blind faith in parenthood until it is *lèse-majesté*[2] to question its right fulfilment. Two most interesting developments are to be noted along this line. One is that the height of filial devotion was reached in the patriarchal age; when the father was the sole governor and feeder of the family, and could slay or sell his child at will; and that this relic of ancestor worship has steadily declined with the extension of government, until, in our democracy, with the fullest development of individual liberty and responsibility, is found the lowest degree of filial reverence and submission. Its place is taken, to our great gain, by such familiar, loving intercourse between parent and child as was utterly incompatible with the grovelling attitude of children in earlier times.

The other is the gradual swing from supreme devotion to the father, "the author of my being," as the child used to consider him, to our modern mother-worship. The dying soldier on the

---

1 Excessive reverence for motherhood, especially to the extent of idolatrous worship.
2 French: crime against a sovereign; offense against a divine ruler.

battlefield thinks of his mother, longs for her, not for his father. The traveller and exile dreams of his mother's care, his mother's doughnuts. The pathos of the popular tale to-day is in bringing the prodigal back to his mother, not to his father. If the original prodigal[1] had a mother, she was probably busy in cooking the fatted calf. If to-day's prodigal has a father, he is merely engaged in paying for the veal. Our tenderest love, our deepest reverence, our fiercest resentment of insult, all centre about the mother to-day rather than about the father; and this is a strong proof that the recognition of woman's real power and place in life grow upon us just as our minds grow able to perceive it. Nothing can ever exceed the truth as to the value of the mother. Our instinct is a right one, as all deep-seated social instincts are; but about it has grown up a mass of falsehoods and absurdities such as always tend to confuse and impede the progress of great truths.

As the main agent in reproduction, the mother is most to be venerated on basic physiological grounds. As the main agent in developing love, the great human condition, she is the fountain of all our growth. As the beginner of industry, she is again a source of progress. As the first and final educator, she outwardly moulds what she has inwardly made; and, as she is the visible, tangible, lovable, living type of all this, the being in whose person is expressed the very sum of good to the individual, it is no wonder that our strongest, deepest, tenderest feelings cluster about the great word "mother."

Fully recognizing all this, it yet remains open to us to turn the light of science and the honest labor of thought upon this phase of human life as upon any other; to lay aside our feelings, and use our reason; to discover if even here we are justified in leaving the most important work of individual life to the methods of primitive instinct. Motherhood is but a process of life, and open to study as all processes of life are open. Among unconscious, early forms it fulfils its mission by a simple instinct. In the consciousness and complexity of human life it demands far more numerous and varied forces for its right fulfilment. It is with us a conscious process,—a process rife with consequences for good or evil. With this voluntary power come new responsibility and a need for new methods,—a need not merely to consider whether or not we will enter upon the duties of maternity, but how best we can fulfil them.

---

1 Luke 15.11–32, in which Jesus tells a parable of a wasteful (prodigal) son who squanders his inheritance but is nonetheless welcomed back into the family by his forgiving father.

Motherhood, like every other natural process, is to be measured by its results. It is good or evil as it serves its purpose. Human motherhood must be judged as it serves its purpose to the human race. Primarily, its purpose is to reproduce the race by reproducing the individual; secondarily, to improve the race by improving the individual. The mere office of reproduction is as well performed by the laying of eggs to be posthumously hatched as by many years of exquisite devotion; but in the improvement of the species we come to other requirements. The functions of motherhood have been evolved as naturally as the functions of nutrition, and each stage of development has brought new duties to the mother. The mother bird must brood her young, the mother cow must suckle them, the mother cat must hunt for them; and, in every varied service which the mother gives, its value is to be measured by its effect upon the young. To perform that which is most good for the young of the species is the measure of right motherhood, and that which is most good for the young is what will help them to a better maturity than that of their parents. To leave in the world a creature better than its parent, this is the purpose of right motherhood.

In the human race this purpose is served by two processes: first, by the simple individual function of reproduction, of which all care and nursing are but an extension; and, second, by the complex social function of education. This was primarily a maternal process, and therefore individual; but it has long since become a racial rather than an individual function, and bears no relation to sex or other personal limitation. The young of the human race require for their best development not only the love and care of the mother, but the care and instruction of many besides their mother. So largely is this true that it may be said in extreme terms that it would be better for a child to-day to be left absolutely without mother or family of any sort, in the city of Boston, for instance, than to be supplied with a large and affectionate family and be planted with them in Darkest Africa.

Human functions are race-functions, social functions; and education is one of them. The duty of the human mother, and the measure of its right or wrong fulfilment, are to be judged along these two main lines, reproduction and education. As we have no species above us with which to compare our motherhood, we must measure by those below us. We must show improvement upon them in this function which we all hold in common.

Does the human mother succeed better than others of her order, mammalia, in the reproduction of the species? Does she bring forth and rear her young more perfectly than lower mothers? They, being less conscious, act simply under instinct, mating in their season, bringing forth young in their season, nursing, guarding, defending as best they may; and they leave in the world behind them creatures as good, or better, than their mothers. Of wild animals we have few reliable statistics, and of tame ones it is difficult to detach their natural processes from our interference therewith. But in both the simple maintenance of species shows that motherhood at least reproduces fairly well; and in those we breed for our advantage the wonderful possibilities of race-development through this process are made apparent. How do we, with the human brain and the human conscience, rich in the power and wisdom of our dominant race,—how do we, as mothers, compare with our forerunners?

Human motherhood is more pathological than any other, more morbid, defective, irregular, diseased. Human childhood is similarly pathological. We, as animals, are very inferior animals in this particular. When we take credit to ourselves for the sublime devotion with which we face "the perils of maternity," and boast of "going down to the gates of death" for our children, we should rather take shame to ourselves for bringing these perils upon both mother and child. The gates of death? They are the gates of life to the unborn; and there is no death there save what we, the mothers, by our unnatural lives, have brought upon our own children. Gates of death, indeed, to the thousands of babies late-born, prematurely born, misborn, and stillborn for lack of right motherhood. In the primal physical functions of maternity the human female cannot show that her supposed specialization to these uses has improved her fulfilment of them, rather the opposite. The more freely the human mother mingles in the natural industries of a human creature, as in the case of the savage woman, the peasant woman, the working-woman everywhere who is not overworked, the more rightly she fulfils these functions.

The more absolutely woman is segregated to sex-functions only, cut off from all economic use and made wholly dependent on the sex-relation as means of livelihood, the more pathological does her motherhood become. The over-development of sex caused by her economic dependence on the male reacts unfavorably upon her essential duties. She is too female for perfect motherhood! Her excessive specialization in the secondary sexual characteristics is a detrimental element in heredity. Small, weak, soft, ill-proportioned women do not tend to produce large, strong, sturdy, well-made men or women. When Frederic the Great[1] wanted grenadiers of great size, he married big men to big women,—not to little ones. The female segregated to the uses of sex alone naturally deteriorates in racial development, and naturally transmits that deterioration to her offspring. The human mother, in the processes of reproduction, shows no gain in efficiency over the lower animals, but rather a loss, and so far presents no evidence to prove that her specialization to sex is of any advantage to her young. The mother of a dead baby or the baby of a dead mother; the sick baby, the crooked baby, the idiot baby;[2] the exhausted, nervous, prematurely aged mother,—these are not uncommon among us; and they do not show much progress in our motherhood.

Since we cannot justify the human method of maternity in the physical processes of reproduction, can we prove its advantages in the other branch, education? Though the mother be sickly and the child the same, will not her loving care more than make up for it? Will not the tender devotion of the mother, and her unflagging attendance upon the child, render human motherhood sufficiently successful in comparison with that of other species to justify our peculiar method? We must now show that our motherhood, in its usually accepted sense, the "care" of the child (more accurately described as education), is of a superior nature.

Here, again, we lack the benefit of comparison. No other animal species is required to care for its young so long, to teach it so much. So far as they have it to do, they do it well. The hen with her brood is an accepted model of motherhood in this respect. She not only lays eggs and hatches them, but educates and protects her young so far as it is necessary. But beyond such simple uses as this we have no standard of comparison for educative motherhood. We can only study it among ourselves, comparing the child left motherless with the child mothered, the child with a mother and nothing else with the child whose mother is helped by servants and teachers, the child with what we recognize as a superior mother to the child with an inferior mother. This last distinction, a comparison between mothers, is of great value. We have tacitly formulated a certain vague standard of human motherhood, and loosely apply it, especially in the epithets "natural" and "unnatural" mother.

---

1 Frederick II, King of Prussia (r. 1740–86).
2 During Gilman's lifetime, such terms as "idiot" and "feeble-minded" were widely used to describe people who had intellectual disabilities.

But these terms again show how prone we still are to consider the whole field of maternal action as one of instinct rather than of reason, as a function rather than a service. We do have a standard, however, loose and vague as it is; and even by that standard it is painful to see how many human mothers fail. Ask yourselves honestly how many of the mothers whose action toward their children confronts you in street and shop and car and boat, in hotel and boarding-house and neighboring yard,—how many call forth favorable comment compared with those you judge unfavorably? Consider not the rosy ideal of motherhood you have in your mind, but the coarse, hard facts of motherhood as you see them, and hear them, in daily life.

Motherhood in its fulfilment of educational duty can be measured only by its effects. If we take for a standard the noble men and women whose fine physique and character we so fondly attribute to "a devoted mother," what are we to say of the motherhood which has filled the world with the ignoble men and women, of depraved physique and character? If the good mother makes the good man, how about the bad ones? When we see great men and women, we give credit to their mothers. When we see inferior men and women,—and that is a common circumstance,—no one presumes to question the motherhood which has produced them. When it comes to congenital criminality, we are beginning to murmur something about "heredity"; and, to meet gross national ignorance, we do demand a better system of education. But no one presumes to suggest that the mothering of mankind could be improved upon; and yet there is where the responsibility really lies. If our human method of reproduction is defective, let the mother answer. She is the main factor in reproduction. If our human method of education is defective, let the mother answer. She is the main factor in education.

To this it is bitterly objected that such a claim omits the father and his responsibility. When the mother of the world is in her right place and doing her full duty, she will have no ground of complaint against the father. In the first place, she will make better men. In the second, she will hold herself socially responsible for the choice of a right father for her children. In the third place, as an economic free agent, she will do half duty in providing for the child. Men who are not equal to good fatherhood under such conditions will have no chance to become fathers, and will die with general pity instead of living with general condemnation. In his position, doing all the world's work, all the father's, and half the mother's, man has made better shift to achieve the impossible than woman has in hers. She has been supposed to have no work or care on earth save as mother. She has really had the work of the mother and that of the world's house service besides. But she has surely had as much time and strength to give to motherhood as man to fatherhood; and not until she can show that the children of the world are as well mothered as they are well fed can she cast on him the blame for our general deficiency.

There is no personal blame to be laid on either party. The sexuo-economic relation has its inevitable ill-effects on both motherhood and fatherhood. But it is to the mother that the appeal must be made to change this injurious relation. Having the deeper sense of duty to the young, the larger love, she must come to feel how her false position hurts her motherhood, and for her children's sake break away from it. Of man and his fatherhood she can make what she will.

The duty of the mother is first to produce children as good as or better than herself; to hand down the constitution and character of those behind her the better for her stewardship; to build up and improve the human race through her enormous power as mother; to make better people. This being done, it is then the duty of the mother, the human mother so to educate her children as to complete what bearing and nursing have only begun. She carries the child nine months in her body, two years in her arms, and as long as she lives in her heart and mind. The education of the young is a tremendous factor in human reproduction. A right motherhood should be able to fulfil this great function perfectly. It should understand with an ever growing power the best methods of developing, strengthening, and directing the child's faculties of body and mind, so that each generation, reaching maturity, would start clear of the last, and show a finer, fuller growth, both physically and mentally, than the preceding. That humanity does slowly improve is not here denied; but, granting our gradual improvement, is it all that we could make? And is the gain due to a commensurate improvement in motherhood?

To both we must say no. When we see how some families improve, while others deteriorate, and how uncertain and irregular is such improvement as appears, we know that we could make better progress if all children had the same rich endowment and wise care that some receive. And, when we see how much of our improvement is due to gains made in hygienic knowledge, in public provision for education and sanitary regulation, none of which has been accomplished by mothers, we are forced to see that whatever advance the race has made is not exclusively attributable to motherhood. The human mother does less for her young, both absolutely and proportionately, than any kind of mother on earth. She does not obtain food for them, nor covering, nor shelter, nor protection, nor defence. She does not educate them beyond the personal habits required in the family circle and in her limited range of social life. The necessary knowledge of the world, so indispensable to every human being, she cannot give, because she does not possess it. All this provision and education are given by other hands and brains than hers. Neither does the amount of physical care and labor bestowed on the child by its mother warrant her claims to superiority in motherhood; this is but a part of our idealism of the subject.

The poor man's wife has far too much of other work to do to spend all her time in waiting on her children. The rich man's wife could do it, but does not, partly because she hires some one to do it for her, and partly because she, too, has other duties to occupy her time. Only in isolated cases do we find a mother deputing[1] all other service to others, and concentrating her energies on feeding, clothing, washing, dressing, and, as far as may be, educating her own child. When such cases are found, it remains to be shown that the child so reared is proportionately benefited by this unremitting devotion of its mother. On the contrary, the best service and education a child can receive involve the accumulated knowledge and exchanged activities of thousands upon thousands besides his mother,—the fathers of the race.

There does not appear, in the care and education of the child as given by the mother, any special superiority in human maternity. Measuring woman first in direct comparison of her reproductive processes with those of other animals, she does not fulfil this function so easily or so well as they. Measuring her educative processes by inter-personal comparison, the few admittedly able mothers with the many painfully unable ones, she seems more lacking, if possible, than in the other branch. The gain in human education thus far has not been acquired or distributed through the mother, but through men and single women; and there is nothing in the achievements of human motherhood to prove that it is for the advantage of the race to have women give all their time to it. Giving all their time to it does not improve it either in quantity or quality. The woman

---

[1] Appointing or instructing another person to perform a task for which one is responsible.

who works is usually a better reproducer than the woman who does not. And the woman who does not work is not proportionately a better educator.

An extra-terrestrial sociologist, studying human life and hearing for the first time of our so-called "maternal sacrifice" as a means of benefiting the species, might be touched and impressed by the idea. "How beautiful!" he would say. "How exquisitely pathetic and tender! One-half of humanity surrendering all other human interests and activities to concentrate its time, strength, and devotion upon the functions of maternity! To bear and rear the majestic race to which they can never fully belong! To live vicariously forever, through their sons, the daughters being only another vicarious link! What a supreme and magnificent martyrdom!" And he would direct his researches toward discovering what system was used to develope and perfect this sublime consecration of half the race to the perpetuation of the other half. He would view with intense and pathetic interest the endless procession of girls, born human as their brothers were, but marked down at once as "female—abortive type—only use to produce males." He would expect to see this "sex sacrificed to reproductive necessities," yet gifted with human consciousness and intelligence, rise grandly to the occasion, and strive to fit itself in every way for its high office. He would expect to find society commiserating the sacrifice, and honoring above all the glorious creature whose life was to be sunk utterly in the lives of others, and using every force properly to rear and fully to fit these functionaries for their noble office. Alas for the extra-terrestrial sociologist and his natural expectations! After exhaustive study, finding nothing of these things, he would return to Mars or Saturn or wherever he came from, marvelling within himself at the vastness of the human paradox.

If the position of woman is to be justified by the doctrine of maternal sacrifice, surely society, or the individual, or both, would make some preparation for it. No such preparation is made. Society recognizes no such function. Premiums have been sometimes paid for large numbers of children, but they were paid to the fathers of them. The elaborate social machinery which constitutes our universal marriage market has no department to assist or advance motherhood. On the contrary, it is directly inimical to it, so that in our society life motherhood means direct loss, and is avoided by the social devotee. And the individual? Surely here right provision will be made. Young women, glorying in their prospective duties, their sacred and inalienable[1] office, their great sex-martyrdom to race-advantage, will be found solemnly preparing for this work. What do we find? We find our young women reared in an attitude which is absolutely unconscious of and often injurious to their coming motherhood,—an irresponsible, indifferent, ignorant class of beings, so far as motherhood is concerned. They are fitted to attract the other sex for economic uses or, at most, for mutual gratification, but not for motherhood. They are reared in unbroken ignorance of their supposed principal duties, knowing nothing of these duties till they enter upon them.

This is as though all men were to be soldiers with the fate of nations in their hands; and no man told or taught a word of war or military service until he entered the battlefield!

The education of young women has no department of maternity. It is considered indelicate to give this consecrated functionary any previous knowledge of her sacred duties. This most important and wonderful of human functions is left from age to age in the hands of absolutely untaught women. It is tacitly supposed to be fulfilled by the mysterious working of what we call "the divine instinct of maternity." Maternal instinct is a very respectable and useful instinct common to most animals. It is "divine" and "holy" only as all the laws of nature are divine and holy; and it is such only when it works to the right fulfilment of its use. If the race-preservative processes are to be held more sacred than the self-preservative processes, we must admit all the functions and faculties of reproduction to the same degree of reverence,—the passion of the male for the female as well as the passion of the mother for her young. And if, still further, we are to honor the race-preservative processes most in their highest and latest development, which is the only comparison to be made on a natural basis, we should place the great, disinterested, social function of education far above the second-selfishness of individual maternal functions. Maternal instinct, merely as an instinct, is unworthy of our superstitious reverence. It should be measured only as a means to an end, and valued in proportion to its efficacy.

Among animals, which have but a low degree of intelligence, instinct is at its height, and works well. Among savages, still incapable of much intellectual development, instinct holds large place. The mother beast can and does take all the care of her young by instinct; the mother savage, nearly all, supplemented by

---

1 A right or prerogative that cannot be taken away or transferred to another person.

the tribal traditions, the educative influences of association, and some direct instruction. As humanity advances, growing more complex and varied, and as human intelligence advances to keep pace with new functions and new needs, instinct decreases in value. The human creature prospers and progresses not by virtue of his animal instinct, but by the wisdom and force of a cultivated intelligence and will, with which to guide his action and to control and modify the very instincts which used to govern him.

The human female, denied the enlarged activities which have developed intelligence in man, denied the education of the will which only comes by freedom and power, has maintained the rudimentary forces of instinct to the present day. With her extreme modification to sex, this faculty of instinct runs mainly along sex-lines, and finds fullest vent in the processes of maternity, where it has held unbroken sway. So the children of humanity are born into the arms of an endless succession of untrained mothers, who bring to the care and teaching of their children neither education for that wonderful work nor experience therein: they bring merely the intense accumulated force of a brute instinct,—the blind devoted passion of the mother for the child. Maternal love is an enormous force, but force needs direction. Simply to love the child does not serve him unless specific acts of service express this love. What these acts of service are and how they are performed make or mar his life forever.

Observe the futility of unaided maternal love and instinct in the simple act of feeding the child. Belonging to order mammalia, the human mother has an instinctive desire to suckle her young. (Some ultra civilized have lost even that.) But this instinct has not taught her such habits of life as insure her ability to fulfil this natural function. Failing in the natural method, of what further use is instinct in the nourishment of the child? Can maternal instinct discriminate between Marrow's Food and Bridge's Food, Hayrick's Food and Pestle's Food, Pennywhistle's Sterilized Milk, and all the other infants' foods which are prepared and put upon the market by—men! These are not prepared by instinct, maternal or paternal, but by chemical analysis and physiological study; and their effect is observed and the diet varied by physicians, who do not do their work by instinct, either.

If the bottle-baby survive the loss of mother's milk, when he comes to the table, does maternal instinct suffice then to administer a proper diet for young children? Let the doctor and the undertaker answer. The wide and varied field of masculine activity in the interests of little children, from the peculiar human phenomenon of masculine assistance in parturition[1] (there is one animal, the obstetric frog, where it also appears) to the manufacture of articles for feeding, clothing, protecting, amusing, and educating the baby, goes to show the utter inadequacy of maternal instinct in the human female. Another thing it shows also,—the criminal failure of that human female to supply by intelligent effort what instinct can no longer accomplish. For a reasoning, conscious being deliberately to undertake the responsibility of maintaining human life without making due preparation for the task is more than carelessness.

Before a man enters a trade, art, or profession, he studies it. He qualifies himself for the duties he is to undertake. He would be held a presuming impostor if he engaged in work he was not fitted to do, and his failure would mark him instantly with ridicule and reproach. In the more important professions, especially in those dealing with what we call "matters of life and death," the shipmaster or pilot, doctor or druggist, is required not only to study his business, but to pass an examination under those who have already become past masters, and obtain a certificate or a diploma or some credential to show that he is fit to be intrusted with the direct responsibility for human life.

Women enter a position which gives into their hands direct responsibility for the life or death of the whole human race with neither study nor experience, with no shadow of preparation or guarantee of capability. So far as they give it a thought, they fondly imagine that this mysterious "maternal instinct" will see them through. Instruction, if needed, they will pick up when the time comes: experience they will acquire as the children appear. "I guess I know how to bring up children!" cried the resentful old lady who was being advised: "I've buried seven!" The record of untrained instinct as a maternal faculty in the human race is to be read on the rows and rows of little gravestones which crowd our cemeteries. The experience gained by practising on the child is frequently buried with it.

No, the maternal sacrifice theory will not bear examination. As a sex specialized to reproduction, giving up all personal activity, all honest independence, all useful and progressive economic service for her glorious consecration to the uses of maternity, the human female has little to show in the way of results which can justify her position. Neither the enormous percentage of children lost by death nor the low average health of those who survive,

---

1 The act of giving birth.

neither physical nor mental progress, give any proof of race advantage from the maternal sacrifice.

X.

Although the superior maternity of the human female is so difficult to prove, so open to heavy charges of inadequacy, so erratic and pathological, there remain intact our devout belief in it, our reverence, our unshaken conviction that it is the one perfect thing. The facts as to our carelessness and ignorance in the fulfilment of this function are undeniable: the rate of infant mortality and children's diseases,—those classed by physicians as "preventable diseases," namely,—these mortal errors and failures confront us everywhere; but we ignore them all, or attribute them to any and every reason save deficient motherhood.

One of the most frequent excuses, among those who have gone far enough to admit that excuse is needed, is that the father is to blame for these conditions. His vices, it is alleged, weaken the constitution of the race. His failure to provide prevents the mother from giving the proper care. He is held responsible for what evil we see in our children; and still we worship the mother for the physical process of bearing a child,—now considered an act of heroism,—and for the "devotion" with which she clings to it afterward, irrespective of the wisdom or effectiveness of this devotion. A healthy and independent motherhood would no more think of taking credit to itself for the right fulfilment of its natural functions than would a cat for bringing forth her kittens or a sheep her lambs. The common fact that the women of the lower social grades bear more children and bear them more easily than the women of higher classes ought to give pause to this ridiculous assumption, but it does not. The more women weaken themselves and their offspring, and imperil their very lives by anti-maternal habits, the more difficulty, danger, and expense are associated with this natural process, the more do women solemnly take credit to themselves and receive it from others for the glorious self-sacrifice with which they risk their lives (and their babies' lives!) for the preservation of humanity. As to the father and his share in the evil results, nothing that he has ever done or can do removes from motherhood its primal responsibility.

Suppose the female of some other species, ignoring her racial duty of right selection, should mate with mangy, toothless cripples,—if there were such among her kind,—and so produce weak, malformed young, and help exterminate her race. Should she then blame him for the result? An entire sex, sacredly set apart for maternal functions so superior as to justify their lack of economic usefulness, should in the course of ages have learned how to select proper fathers. If the only way in which the human mother can feed and guard her children is through another person, a provider and protector on whom their lives and safety must depend, what natural, social, or moral excuse has she for not choosing a good one?

But how can a young girl know a good prospective father, we ask. That she is not so educated as to know proves her unfitness for her great task. That she does not think or care proves her dishonorable indifference to her great duty. She can in no way shirk the responsibility for criminal carelessness in choosing a father for her children, unless indeed there were no choice,—no good men left on earth.[1] Moreover, we are not obliged to leave this crucial choice in the hands of young girls. Motherhood is the work of grown women, not of half-children; and, when we honestly care as much for motherhood as we pretend, we shall train the woman for her duty, not the girl for her guileless manœuvres to secure a husband. We talk about the noble duties of the mother, but our maidens are educated for economically successful marriage.

Leaving this field of maternal duty through sex-selection, there remains the far larger ground to which the popular mind flees in triumph: that the later work of the mother proves the success of our racial division of labor on sex-lines, that in the care of the child, the education of the child, the beautiful life of the home and family, it is shown how well our system works. This is the last stronghold. Solidly intrenched herein sits popular thought, safe in the sacred precincts of the home. "Every man's home is his castle,"[2] is the common saying. The windows are shut to keep out the air. The curtains are down to keep out the light. The doors are barred to keep out the stranger. Within are the hearth fire and its gentle priestess, the initial combination of human life,—the family in the home.

Our thrones have been emptied, and turned into mere chairs for passing presidents. Our churches have been opened to the light of modern life, and the odor of sanctity has been freshened

---

1 Micah 7.2: The good man is perished out of the earth: and there is none upright among men.
2 This maxim has roots in British common law and conveys the idea of the right to privacy.

with sweet sunny air. We can see room for change in these old sanctuaries, but none in the sanctuary of the home. And this temple, with its rights, is so closely interwound with the services of subject woman, its altar so demands her ceaseless sacrifices, that we find it impossible to conceive of any other basis of human living. We are chilled to the heart's core by the fear of losing any of these ancient and hallowed associations. Without this blessed background of all our memories and foreground of all our hopes, life seems empty indeed. In homes we were all born. In homes we all die or hope to die. In homes we all live or want to live. For homes we all labor, in them or out of them. The home is the centre and circumference, the start and the finish, of most of our lives. We love it with a love older than the human race. We reverence it with the blind obeisance of those crouching centuries when its cult began. We cling to it with the tenacity of every inmost, oldest instinct of our animal natures, and with the enthusiasm of every latest word in the unbroken chant of adoration which we have sung to it since first we learned to praise.

And since we hold that our home life, just as we have it, is the best thing on earth, and that our home life plainly demands one whole woman at the least to each home, and usually more, it follows that anything which offers to change the position of woman threatens to "undermine the home," "strikes at the root of the family," and we will none of it. If, in honest endeavor to keep up to the modern standard of free thought and free speech, we do listen,—turning from our idol for a moment, and saying to the daring iconoclast, "Come, show us anything better!"—with what unlimited derision do we greet his proposed substitute! Yet everywhere about us to-day this inner tower, this castle keep of vanishing tradition, is becoming more difficult to defend or even to keep in repair. We buttress it anew with every generation; we love its very cracks and crumbling corners; we hang and drape it with endless decorations; we hide the looming dangers overhead with fresh clouds of incense; and we demand of the would-be repairers and rebuilders that they prove to us the desirability of their wild plans before they lift a hammer. But, when they show their plans, we laugh them to scorn.

It is a difficult case to meet. To call attention to existing conditions and to establish the relation between them and existing phenomena is one thing. To point out how a change of condition will produce new phenomena, and how these phenomena will benefit us, is quite another. Yet this is the task that is always involved in the conscious progress of the human race. While that progress was unconscious, it was enough that certain individuals and classes gradually entered into new relations in process of social evolution, and that they forced their conditions upon the reluctant conservatives who failed so to evolve.

In the quite recent passage from the feudal to the monarchical system, no time was wasted in the endeavor to persuade and convince the headstrong barons of their national duty. The growing power of the king struggled with and survived the lessening power of the barons,—that was all. Had a book been written then to urge the change, it could have proved clearly enough the evils of the feudal system; but, when it tried to portray the glories of national peace and power under a single monarch, it would have had small weight. National peace and power, which had been hitherto non-existent, would have failed to appeal to the sturdy lords of the soil, whose only idea of peace and power was to sit down and rest on their prostrate neighbors. Had their strength run in the line of argument, they would have scouted the "should be's" and "will be's" of the author, and defied him to prove that the new condition would be developed by the new processes; and, indeed, he would have found it hard.

So to-day, in questioning the economic status of woman and her position in the home and in the family, it is far easier to prove present evil than future good. Yet this is what is most exactingly demanded. It is required of the advocate of social reform not only that he convince the contented followers of the present system of its wrong, but that he prove to their satisfaction the superiority of some other system. This, in the nature of the case, is impossible. When people are contented, you cannot make them feel that what is is wrong, or that something else might be better. Even the discontented are far more willing to refer their troubles to some personal factor than to admit that their condition as a whole inevitably produces the general trouble in which they share. Even if convinced that a change of condition will remove the source of injury, they, like the fox with the swarm of flies, fear to be disturbed, lest their last state be worse than their first.[1] In the face of this inevitable difficulty, however, the task must be undertaken.

Two things let us premise and agree upon before starting. First, that the duty of human life is progress, development; that we are here, not merely to live, but to grow,—not to be content

---

1 From Aesop's *Fables* (recorded between the tenth and sixteenth centuries CE), "The Fox and the Hedgehog" is a lesson about the dangers of replacing one evil with another.

with lean savagery or fat barbarism or sordid semi-civilization, but to toil on through the centuries, and build up the ever-nobler forms of life toward which social evolution tends. If this is not believed, if any hold that to keep alive and reproduce the species is the limit of our human duty, then they need look no farther here. That aim can be attained, and has been attained, for irrefutable centuries, through many forms of sex-relation and of economic relation. Human beings have lived and brought up children as good as their parents in free promiscuity and laziness, in forced polygamy and slavery, in willing polyandry and industry,[1] and in monogamy *plus* prostitution and manufactures. Just to live and bear children does not prove the relative superiority of any system, either in sex or economics. But, when we believe that life means progress, then each succeeding form of sex-relation or economic relation is to be measured by its effect on that progress.

It may be necessary here to agree on a definition of human progress. According to the general law of organic evolution, it may be defined as follows: such progress in the individual and in his social relations as shall maintain him in health and happiness and increase the organic development of society.

If we accept such a definition of human progress, if we agree that progress is the duty of society, and that all social institutions are to be measured by it, we may proceed to our second premise. This is not to be ranked with the first in importance: it should be too commonly understood and accepted to be dragged into such a prominent position. But it is not commonly understood and accepted. In fact, it is misunderstood and denied to so general a degree that no apology is needed for insisting on it here.

The second premise is this: our enjoyment of a thing does not prove that it is right. Even our love, admiration, and reverence for a thing does not prove that it is right; and, even from an evolutionary point of view, our belief that a thing is "natural" does not prove that it is right. A thing may be right in one stage of evolution which becomes wrong in another. For instance, promiscuity is "natural"; the human animal, like many others, is quite easily inclined thereto. Monogamy is proven right by social evolution: it is the best way to carry on the human race in social relation; but it is not yet as "natural" as could be desired.

---

1 Polygamy: having more than one spouse at the same time; polyandry: a form of polygamy in which a woman has two or more husbands or sexual partners at the same time.

So, to return to our second premise, which is admittedly rather a large one, to show that any custom or status of ours is "natural" and enjoyable does not prove that it is right. It does not of course prevent its being right. Right things may be enjoyed, may be loved, admired, and reverenced, may even be "natural"; but so may wrong things. Even that subhuman faculty called instinct is only a true guide to conduct when the conditions are present which originally developed that instinct. The instinct that makes a modern house-dog turn around three times before he lies down is not worthy of much admiration to-day, though it served its purpose on the grassy plains and in the leafy hollows where it was formed. If these two premises are granted, that the duty of human life is progress, and that a given condition is not necessarily right because we like it, we may go on.

Is our present method of home life, based on the economic dependence of woman in the sex-relation, the best calculated to maintain the individual in health and happiness, and develope in him the higher social faculties? The individual is not maintained in health and happiness,—that is visible to all; and how little he is developed in social relation is shown in the jarring irregularity and wastefulness of our present economic system.

Economic independence for women necessarily involves a change in the home and family relation. But, if that change is for the advantage of individual and race, we need not fear it. It does not involve a change in the marriage relation except in withdrawing the element of economic dependence, nor in the relation of mother to child save to improve it. But it does involve the exercise of human faculty in women, in social service and exchange rather than in domestic service solely. This will of course require the introduction of some other form of living than that which now obtains. It will render impossible the present method of feeding the world by means of millions of private servants, and bringing up children by the same hand.

It is a melancholy fact that the vast majority of our children are reared and trained by domestic servants,—generally their mothers, to be sure, but domestic servants by trade. To become a producer, a factor in the economic activities of the world, must perforce interfere with woman's present status as a private servant. House mistress she may still be, in the sense of owning and ordering her home, but housekeeper or house-servant she may not be—and be anything else. Her position as mother will alter, too. Mother in the sense of bearer and rearer of noble children she will be, as the closest and dearest, the one most honored and best loved; but mother in the sense of exclusive individual nursery-maid and nursery-governess she may not be—and be anything else.

It is precisely here that the world calls a halt. Nothing, it says, can be better than our homes with their fair priestesses. Nothing can be better for children than the hourly care of their own mothers. It is the position of the feudal baron over again. We can perhaps be made to see the evils of existing conditions: we cannot be made to see any possibility of improving on them. Nevertheless, it may be tried.

Let us deliberately set ourselves to imagine, by sheer muscular effort as it were, a better kind of motherhood than that of the private nursery governess, a better way to feed and clean and clothe the world than by the private house servant.

Here is felt the need of our second premise; for we enjoy things as they are (that is, some of us do, sometimes, and the rest of us think that we do). We love, admire, and reverence them; and it is "natural" to have them so. If it can be shown that human progress is better served by other methods, then other methods will be proven right; and we must grow to enjoy and honor them as fast as we can, and in due course of time we shall find them natural. If it can be shown that our babies would be better off if part of their time was passed in other care than their mothers', then such other care would be right; and it would be the duty of motherhood to provide it. If it can be shown that we could all be better provided for in our personal needs of nutrition, cleanliness, warmth, shelter, privacy, by some other method than that which requires the labor of one woman or more to each family, then it would be the duty of womanhood to find such method and to practise it.

Perhaps it is worth while to examine the nature of our feeling toward that social institution called "the family," and the probable effect upon it of the change in woman's economic status.

Marriage and "the family" are two institutions, not one, as is commonly supposed. We confuse the natural result of marriage in children, common to all forms of sex-union, with the family,—a purely social phenomenon. Marriage is a form of sex-union recognized and sanctioned by society. It is a relation between two or more persons, according to the custom of the country, and involves mutual obligations. Although made by us an economic relation, it is not essentially so, and will exist in much higher fulfilment after the economic phase is outgrown.

The family is a social group, an entity, a little state. It holds an important place in the evolution of society quite aside from its connection with marriage. There was a time when the family was the highest form of social relation,—indeed, the only form of social relation,—when to the minds of pastoral, patriarchal tribes there was no conception so large as "my country," no State, no nation. There was only a great land spotted with families, each family its own little world, of which Grandpa was priest and king. The family was a social unit. Its interests were common to its members, and inimical to those of other families. It moved over the earth, following its food supply, and fighting occasionally with stranger families for the grass or water on which it depended. Indissoluble common interests are what make organic union, and those interests long rested on blood relationship.

While the human individual was best fed and guarded by the family, and so required the prompt, correlative[1] action of all the members of that family, naturally the family must have a head; and that form of government known as the patriarchal was produced. The natural family relation, as seen in parents and young of other species, or in ourselves in later forms, involves no such governmental development: that is a feature of the family as a social entity alone.

One of the essentials of the patriarchal family life was polygamy, and not only polygamy, but open concubinage,[2] and a woman slavery which was almost the same thing. The highest period of the family as a social institution was a very low period for marriage as a social institution,—a period, in fact, when marriage was but partially evolved from the early promiscuity of the primitive savage. The family seems indeed to be a gradually disappearing survival of the still looser unit of the horde, which again is more closely allied to the band or pack of gregarious carnivora than to an organic social relation. A loose, promiscuous group of animals is not a tribe; and the most primitive savage groups seem to have been no more than this.

The tribe in its true form follows the family,—is a natural extension of it, and derives its essential ties from the same relationship. These social forms, too, are closely related to economic conditions. The horde was the hunting unit; the family, and later the tribe, the pastoral unit. Agriculture and its resultant, commerce and manufacture, gradually weaken these crude blood ties, and establish the social relationship which constitutes the State. Before the pastoral era the family held no important posi-

---

[1] Mutually interdependent or naturally related.
[2] The practice of having or being a concubine.

tion, and since that era it has gradually declined. With social progress we find human relations resting less and less on a personal and sex basis, and more and more on general economic independence. As individuals have become more highly specialized, they have made possible a higher form of marriage.

The family is a decreasing survival of the earliest grouping known to man. Marriage is an increasing development of high social life, not fully evolved. So far from being identical with the family, it improves and strengthens in inverse ratio to the family, as is easily seen by the broad contrast between the marriage relations of Jacob[1] and the unquenchable demand for lifelong single mating that grows in our hearts to-day. There was no conception of marriage as a personal union for life of two well-matched individuals during the patriarchal era. Wives were valued merely for child-bearing. The family needed numbers of its own blood, especially males; and the man-child was the price of favor to women then. It was but a few degrees beyond the horde, not yet become a tribe in the full sense. Its bonds of union were of the loosest,—merely common paternity, with a miscellaneous maternity of inimical interests. Such a basis forever forbade any high individualization, and high individualization with its demands for a higher marriage forbids any numerical importance to the family. Marriage has risen and developed in social importance as the family has sunk and decreased.

It is most interesting to note that, under the comparatively similar conditions of the settlement of Utah, the numerical strength and easily handled common interests of many people under one head, which distinguish the polygamous family, were found useful factors in that great pioneering enterprise.[2] In the further development of society a relation of individuals more fluent, subtle, and extensive was needed. The family as a social unit makes a ponderous body of somewhat irreconcilable constituents, requiring a sort of military rule to make it work at all; and it is only useful while the ends to be attained are of a simple nature, and allow of the slowest accomplishment. It is easy to see

---

1 Old Testament Hebrew patriarch who married sisters Leah and Rachel and bore children by the two maidservants Zilpah and Bilhah (Genesis 25–50).

2 The Latter-day Saints, or Mormons, a Euro-American settler population, colonized the Utah valley in the second half of the nineteenth century. A substantial minority of Mormon families practiced polygamy until 1890, when the Mormon Church announced it would no longer sanction the practice of husbands marrying multiple wives.

the family extending to the tribe by its own physical increase; and, similarly, the father hardening into the chief, under the necessities of larger growth. Then, as the steadily enlarging forces of national unity make the chief an outgrown name and the tribe an outgrown form, the family dwindles to a monogamic basis, as the higher needs of the sex-relation become differentiated from the more primitive economic necessities of the family.

And now, further, when our still developing social needs call for an ever-increasing delicacy and freedom in the inter-service and common service of individuals, we find that even what economic unity remains to the family is being rapidly eliminated. As the economic relation becomes rudimentary and disappears, the sex-relation asserts itself more purely; and the demand in the world to-day for a higher and nobler sex-union is as sharply defined as the growing objection to the existing economic union. Strange as it may seem to us, so long accustomed to confound the two, it is precisely the outgrown relics of a previously valuable family relation which so painfully retard the higher development of the monogamic marriage relation.

Each generation of young men and women comes to the formation of sex-union with higher and higher demands for a true marriage, with ever-growing needs for companionship. Each generation of men and women need and ask more of each other. A woman is no longer content and grateful to have "a kind husband": a man is no longer content with a patient Griselda;[1] and, as all men and women, in marrying, revert to the economic status of the earlier family, they come under conditions which steadily tend to lower the standard of their mutual love, and make of the average marriage only a sort of compromise, borne with varying ease or difficulty according to the good breeding and loving-kindness of the parties concerned. This is not necessarily, to their conscious knowledge, an "unhappy marriage." It is as happy as those they see about them, as happy perhaps as we resignedly expect "on earth"; and in heaven we do not expect marriages. But it is not what they looked forward to when they were young.

When two young people love each other, in the long hours which are never long enough for them to be together in, do they dwell in ecstatic forecast on the duties of housekeeping? They do not. They dwell on the pleasure of having a home, in which they can be "at last alone"; on the opportunity of enjoying each other's

---

1 A literary character noted for her obedience and patience.

society; and, always, on what they will *do* together. To act with those we love,—to walk together, work together, read together, paint, write, sing, anything you please, so that it be together,— that is what love looks forward to.

Human love, as it rises to an ever higher grade, looks more and more for such companionship. But the economic status of marriage rudely breaks in upon love's young dream.[1] On the economic side, apart from all the sweetness and truth of the sex-relation, the woman in marrying becomes the house-servant, or at least the housekeeper, of the man. Of the world we may say that the intimate personal necessities of the human animal are ministered to by woman. Married lovers do not work together. They may, if they have time, rest together: they may, if they can, play together; but they do not make beds and sweep and cook together, and they do not go down town to the office together. They are economically on entirely different social planes, and these constitute a bar to any higher, truer union than such as we see about us. Marriage is not perfect unless it is between class equals. There is no equality in class between those who do their share in the world's work in the largest, newest, highest ways and those who do theirs in the smallest, oldest, lowest ways.

Granting squarely that it is the business of women to make the home life of the world true, healthful, and beautiful, the economically dependent woman does not do this, and never can. The economically independent woman can and will. As the family is by no means identical with marriage, so is the home by no means identical with either.

A home is a permanent dwelling-place, whether for one, two, forty, or a thousand, for a pair, a flock, or a swarm. The hive is the home of the bees as literally and absolutely as the nest is the home of mating birds in their season. Home and the love of it may dwindle to the one chamber of the bachelor or spread to the span of a continent, when the returning traveller sees land and calls it "home." There is no sweeter word, there is no dearer fact, no feeling closer to the human heart than this.

On close analysis, what are the bases of our feelings in this connection? and what are their supporting facts? Far down below humanity, where "the foxes have holes, and the birds of the air have nests,"[2] there begins the deep home feeling. Maternal instinct seeks a place to shelter the defenceless young, while the

---

1 An idyllic romantic relationship between young lovers.
2 Luke 9.58.

mother goes abroad to search for food. The first sharp impressions of infancy are associated with the sheltering walls of home, be it the swinging cradle in the branches, the soft dark hollow in the trunk of a tree, or the cave with its hidden lair. A place to be safe in; a place to be warm and dry in; a place to eat in peace and sleep in quiet; a place whose close, familiar limits rest the nerves from the continuous hail of impressions in the changing world outside; the same place over and over,—the restful repetition, rousing no keen response, but healing and soothing each weary sense,—that "feels like home." All this from our first consciousness. All this for millions and millions of years. No wonder we love it.

Then comes the gradual addition of tenderer associations, family ties of the earliest. Then, still primitive, but not yet outgrown, the groping religious sentiment of early ancestor-worship, adding sanctity to safety, and driving deep our sentiment for home. It was the place in which to pray, to keep alight the sacred fire, and pour libations to departed grandfathers. Following this, the slow-dying era of paternal government gave a new sense of honor to the place of comfort and the place of prayer. It became the seat of government also,—the palace and the throne. Upon this deep foundation we have built a towering superstructure of habit, custom, law; and in it dwell together every deepest, oldest, closest, and tenderest emotion of the human individual. No wonder we are blind and deaf to any suggested improvement in our lordly pleasure-house.

But look farther. Without contradicting any word of the above, it is equally true that the highest emotions of humanity arise and live outside the home and apart from it. While religion stayed at home, in dogma and ceremony, in spirit and expression, it was a low and narrow religion. It could never rise till it found a new spirit and a new expression in human life outside the home, until it found a common place of worship, a ceremonial and a morality on a human basis, not a family basis. Science, art, government, education, industry,—the home is the cradle of them all, and their grave, if they stay in it. Only as we live, think, feel, and work outside the home, do we become humanly developed, civilized, socialized.

The exquisite development of modern home life is made possible only as an accompaniment and result of modern social life. If the reverse were true, as is popularly supposed, all nations that have homes would continue to evolve a noble civilization. But they do not. On the contrary, those nations in which home and family worship most prevail, as in China, present a melancholy proof of the result of the domestic virtues without the social. A noble home life is the product of a noble social life. The home does not produce the virtues needed in society. But society does produce the virtues needed in such homes as we desire to-day. The members of the freest, most highly civilized and individualized nations, make the most delightful members of the home and family. The members of the closest and most highly venerated homes do not necessarily make the most delightful members of society.

In social evolution as in all evolution the tendency is from "indefinite, incoherent homogeneity to definite, coherent heterogeneity";[1] and the home, in its rigid maintenance of a permanent homogeneity, constitutes a definite limit to social progress. What we need is not less home, but more; not a lessening of the love of human beings for a home, but its extension through new and more effective expression. And, above all, we need the complete disentanglement in our thoughts of the varied and often radically opposed interests and industries so long supposed to be component parts of the home and family.

The change in the economic position of woman from dependence to independence must bring with it a rearrangement of these home interests and industries, to our great gain.

XI.

As a natural consequence of our division of labor on sex-lines, giving to woman the home and to man the world in which to work, we have come to have a dense prejudice in favor of the essential womanliness of the home duties, as opposed to the essential manliness of every other kind of work. We have assumed that the preparation and serving of food and the removal of dirt, the nutritive and excretive processes of the family, are feminine functions; and we have also assumed that these processes must go on in what we call the home, which is the external expression of the family. In the home the human individual is fed, cleaned, warmed, and generally cared for, while not engaged in working in the world.

---

1 "Evolution is an integration of matter and concomitant dissipation of motion during which the matter passes from an indefinite, incoherent homogeneity to definite, coherent heterogeneity, and during which the retained motion undergoes a parallel transformation" (Spencer 407).

Human nutrition is a long process. There's many a ship 'twixt the cup and the lip, to paraphrase an old proverb.[1] Food is produced by the human race collectively,—not by individuals for their own consumption, but by interrelated groups of individuals, all over the world, for the world's consumption. This collectively produced food circulates over the earth's surface through elaborate processes of transportation, exchange, and preparation, before it reaches the mouths of the consumers; and the final processes of selection and preparation are in the hands of woman. She is the final purchaser: she is the final handler in that process of human nutrition known as cooking, which is a sort of extra-organic digestion proven advantageous to our species. This department of human digestion has become a sex-function, supposed to pertain to women by nature.

If it is to the advantage of the human race that its food supply should be thus handled by a special sex, this advantage should be shown in superior health and purity of habit. But no such advantage is visible. In spite of all our power and skill in the production and preparation of food we remain "the sickest beast alive" in the matter of eating. Our impotent outcries against adulteration prove that part of the trouble is in the food products as offered for purchase, the pathetic reiteration of our numerous cookbooks proves that part of the trouble is in the preparation of those products, and the futile exhortations of physicians and mothers prove that part of the trouble is in our morbid tastes and appetites. It would really seem as if the human race after all its long centuries had not learned how to prepare good food, nor how to cook it, nor how to eat it,—which is painfully true.

This great function of human nutrition is confounded with the sex-relation, and is considered a sex-function: it is in the helpless hands of that amiable but abortive[2] agent, the economically dependent women; and the essential incapacity of such an agent is not hard to show. In her position as private house-steward she is the last purchaser of the food of the world, and here we reach the governing factor in our incredible adulteration of food products.

All kinds of deceit and imposition in human service are due to that desire to get without giving, which, as has been shown in previous chapters, is largely due to the training of women as non-productive consumers. But the particular form of deceit and imposition practised by a given dealer is governed by the intelligence and power of the buyer. The dilution and adulteration of food products is a particularly easy path to profit, because the

---

1 A paraphrase of "There's many a slip 'twixt the cup and the lip."
2 Unsuccessful; fruitless; useless.

ultimate purchaser has almost no power and very little intelligence. The individual housewife must buy at short intervals and in small quantities. This operates to her pecuniary disadvantage, as is well known; but its effect on the quality of her purchases is not so commonly observed. Not unless she becomes the head of a wealthy household, and so purchases in quantity for family, servants, and guests, is her trade of sufficient value to have force in the market. The dealer who sells to a hundred poor women can and does sell a much lower quality of food than he who sells an equal amount to one purchaser. Therefore, the home, as a food agency, holds an essentially and permanently unfavorable position as a purchaser; and it is thereby the principal factor in maintaining the low standard of food products against which we struggle with the cumbrous machinery of legislation.

Most housekeepers will innocently prove their ignorance of these matters by denying that the standard of food products is so low. Let such offended ladies but examine the statutes and ordinances of their own cities,—of any civilized city,—and see how the bread, the milk, the meat, the fruit, are under a steady legislative inspection which endeavors to protect the ignorance and helplessness of the individual purchaser. If the private housekeeper had the technical intelligence as purchaser which is needed to discriminate in the selection of foods, if she were prepared to test her milk, to detect the foreign substance in her coffee and spices, rightly to estimate the quality of her meat and the age of her fruit and vegetables, she would then be able at least to protest against her supply, and to seek, as far as time, distance, and funds allowed, a better market. This technical intelligence, however, is only to be obtained by special study and experience; and its attainment only involves added misery and difficulty to the private purchaser, unless accompanied by the power to enforce what the intelligence demands.

As it is, woman brings to her selection from the world's food only the empirical experience gained by practising upon her helpless family, and this during the very time when her growing children need the wise care which she is only able to give them in later years. This experience, with its pitiful limitation and its practical check by the personal taste and pecuniary standing of the family, is lost where it was found. Each mother slowly acquires some knowledge of her business by practising it upon the lives and health of her family and by observing its effect on the survivors; and each daughter begins again as ignorant as her mother was before her. This "rule of thumb" is not transmissible. It is not a genuine education such as all important work demands, but a slow animal process of soaking up experience,—hopelessly ineffectual in protecting the health of society. As the ultimate selecting agent in feeding humanity, the private housewife fails, and this not by reason of any lack of effort on her part, but by the essential defect of her position as individual purchaser. Only organization can oppose such evils as the wholesale adulteration of food; and woman, the house-servant, belongs to the lowest grade of unorganized labor.

Leaving the selection of food, and examining its preparation, one would naturally suppose that the segregation of an entire sex to the fulfilment of this function would insure most remarkable results. It has, but they are not so favorable as might be expected. The art and science of cooking involve a large and thorough knowledge of nutritive value and of the laws of physiology and hygiene. As a science, it verges on preventive medicine. As an art, it is capable of noble expression within its natural bounds. As it stands among us to-day, it is so far from being a science and akin to preventive medicine, that it is the lowest of amateur handicrafts and a prolific source of disease; and, as an art, it has developed under the peculiar stimulus of its position as a sex-function into a voluptuous profusion as false as it is evil. Our innocent proverb, "The way to a man's heart is through his stomach," is a painfully plain comment on the way in which we have come to deprave our bodies and degrade our souls at the table.

On the side of knowledge it is permanently impossible that half the world, acting as amateur cooks for the other half, can attain any high degree of scientific accuracy or technical skill. The development of any human labor requires specialization, and specialization is forbidden to our cook-by-nature system. What progress we have made in the science of cooking has been made through the study and experience of professional men cooks and chemists, not through the Sisyphean labors[1] of our endless generations of isolated women, each beginning again where her mother began before her.

Here, of course, will arise a pained outcry along the "mother's doughnuts" line, in answer to which we refer to our second premise in the last chapter. The fact that we like a thing does not prove it to be right. A Missouri child may regard his mother's sal-

---

[1] In Greek mythology, Sisyphus was forced to roll a boulder up a hill only for it to roll down every time it neared the top, repeating this action for eternity.

eratus biscuit with fond desire, but that does not alter their effect upon his spirits or his complexion. Cooking is a matter of law, not the harmless play of fancy. Architecture might be more sportive and varied if every man built his own house, but it would not be the art and science that we have made it; and, while every woman prepares food for her own family, cooking can never rise beyond the level of the amateur's work.

But, low as is the status of cooking as a science, as an art it is lower. Since the wife-cook's main industry is to please,—that being her chief means of getting what she wants or of expressing affection,—she early learned to cater to the palate instead of faithfully studying and meeting the needs of the stomach. For uncounted generations the grown man and the growing child have been subject to the constant efforts of her who cooked from affection, not from knowledge,—who cooked to please. This is one of the widest pathways of evil that has ever been opened. In every field of life it is an evil to put the incident before the object, the means before the end; and here it has produced that familiar result whereby we live to eat instead of eating to live.

This attitude of the woman has developed the rambling excess called "fancy cookery,"—a thing as far removed from true artistic development as a swinging ice-pitcher from a Greek vase. Through this has come the limitless unhealthy folly of high living, in which human labor and time and skill are wasted in producing what is neither pure food nor pure pleasure, but an artificial performance, to be appreciated only by the virtuoso. Lower living could hardly be imagined than that which results from this unnatural race between artifice and appetite, in which body and soul are both corrupted.

In the man, the subject of all this dining-room devotion, has been developed and maintained that cultivated interest in his personal tastes and their gratification,—that demand for things which he likes rather than for things which he knows to be good, wherein lies one of the most dangerous elements in character known to the psychologist. The sequences of this affectionate catering to physical appetites may be traced far afield to its last result in the unchecked indulgence in personal tastes and desires, in drug habits and all intemperance. The temperament which is unable to resist these temptations is constantly being bred at home.

As the concentration of woman's physical energies on the sex-functions, enforced by her economic dependence, has tended to produce and maintain man's excess in sex-indulgence, to the injury of the race; so the concentration of woman's industrial energies on the close and constant service of personal tastes and appetites has tended to produce and maintain an excess in table indulgence, both in eating and drinking, which is also injurious to the race. It is not here alleged that this is the only cause of our habits of this nature; but it is one of primal importance, and of ceaseless action.

We can perhaps see its working better by a light-minded analogy than by a bold statement. Suppose two large, healthy, nimble apes. Suppose that the male ape did not allow the female ape to skip about and pluck her own cocoanuts, but brought to her what she was to have. Suppose that she was then required to break the shell, pick out the meat, prepare for the male what he wished to consume; and suppose, further, that her share in the dinner, to say nothing of her chance of a little pleasure excursion in the treetops afterward, was dependent on his satisfaction with the food she prepared for him. She, as an ape of intelligence, would seek, by all devices known to her, to add stimulus and variety to the meals she arranged, to select the bits he specially preferred to please his taste and to meet his appetite; and he, developing under this agreeable pressure, would gradually acquire a fine discrimination in foods, and would look forward to his elaborate feasts with increasing complacency. He would have a new force to make him eat,—not only his need of food, with its natural and healthy demands, but her need of—everything, acting through his need of food.

This sounds somewhat absurd in a family of apes, but it is precisely what has occurred in the human family. To gratify her husband has been the woman's way of obtaining her own ends, and she has of necessity learned how to do it; and, as she has been in general an uneducated and unskilled worker, she could only seek to please him through what powers she had,—mainly those of house service. She has been set to serve two appetites, and to profit accordingly. She has served them well, but the profit to either party is questionable.

On lines of social development we are progressing from the gross gorging of the savage on whatever food he could seize, toward the discriminating selection of proper foods, and an increasing delicacy and accuracy in their use. Against this social tendency runs the cross-current of our sexuo-economic relation, making the preparation of food a sex function, and confusing all its processes with the ardor of personal affection and the dragging weight of self-interest. This method is applied, not only to the husband, but, in a certain degree, to the children; for, where maternal love and maternal energy are forced to express themselves mainly in the preparation of food, the desire properly to feed the child becomes confounded with an unwise desire to please, and the mother degrades her high estate by catering steadily to the lower tastes of humanity instead of to the higher.

Our general notion is that we have lifted and ennobled our eating and drinking by combining them with love. On the contrary, we have lowered and degraded our love by combining it with eating and drinking; and, what is more, we have lowered these habits also. Some progress has been made, socially; but this unhappy mingling of sex-interest and self-interest with normal appetites, this Cupid-in-the-kitchen arrangement, has gravely impeded that progress. Professional cooking has taught us much. Commerce and manufacture have added to our range of supplies. Science has shown us what we need, and how and when we need it. But the affectionate labor of wife and mother is little touched by these advances. If she goes to the cooking school, it is to learn how to make the rich delicacies that will please rather than to study the nutritive value of food in order to guard the health of the household. From the constantly enlarging stores opened to her through man's activities she chooses widely, to make "a variety" that shall kindle appetite, knowing nothing of the combination best for physical needs. As to science, chemistry, hygiene,—they are but names to her. "John likes it so." "Willie won't eat it so." "Your father never could bear cabbage." She must consider what he likes, not only because she loves to please him or because she profits by pleasing him, but because he pays for the dinner, and she is a private servant.

Is it not time that the way to a man's heart through his stomach should be relinquished for some higher avenue? The stomach should be left to its natural uses, not made a thoroughfare for stranger passions and purposes; and the heart should be approached through higher channels. We need a new picture of our overworked blind god,—fat, greasy, pampered with sweetmeats by the poor worshippers long forced to pay their devotion through such degraded means.

No, the human race is not well nourished by making the process of feeding it a sex-function. The selection and preparation of food should be in the hands of trained experts. And woman should stand beside man as the comrade of his soul, not the servant of his body.

This will require large changes in our method of living. To feed the world by expert service, bringing to that great function the skill and experience of the trained specialist, the power of science, and the beauty of art, is impossible in the sexuo-economic relation. While we treat cooking as a sex-function common to all women and eating as a family function not otherwise rightly accomplished, we can develop no farther. We are spending much earnest study and hard labor to-day on the problem of teaching and training women in the art of cooking, both the wife and the servant; for, with our usual habit of considering voluntary individual conduct as the cause of conditions, we seek to modify conditions by changing individual conduct.

What we must recognize is that, while the conditions remain, the conduct cannot be altered. Any trade or profession, the development of which depended upon the labor of isolated individuals, assisted only by hired servants more ignorant than themselves, would remain at a similarly low level.

So far as health can be promoted by public means, we are steadily improving by sanitary regulations and medical inspection, by professionally prepared "health foods" and by the literature of hygiene, by special legislation as to contagious diseases and dangerous trades; but the health that lies in the hands of the housewife is not reached by these measures. The nine-tenths of our women who do their own work cannot be turned into proficient purchasers and cooks any more than nine-tenths of our men could be turned into proficient tailors with no better training or opportunity than would be furnished by clothing their own families. The alternative remaining to the women who comprise the other tenth is that peculiar survival of earlier labor methods known as "domestic service."

As a method of feeding humanity, hired domestic service is inferior even to the service of the wife and mother, and brings to the art of cooking an even lower degree of training and a narrower experience. The majority of domestic servants are young girls who leave this form of service for marriage as soon as they are able; and we thus intrust the physical health of human beings, so far as cooking affects it, to the hands of untrained, immature women, of the lowest social grade, who are actuated by no higher impulse than that of pecuniary necessity. The love of the wife and mother stimulates at least her desire to feed her family well. The servant has no such motive. The only cases in which domestic cooking reaches anything like proficiency are those in which the wife and mother is "a natural-born cook," and regales her family with the products of genius, or those in which the households of the rich are able to command the service of professionals.

There was a time when kings and lords retained their private poets to praise and entertain them; but the poet is not truly great until he sings for the world. So the art of cooking can never be lifted to its true place as a human need and a social function by private service. Such an arrangement of our lives and of our houses as will allow cooking to become a profession is the only way in which to free this great art from its present limitations. It should be a reputable, well-paid profession, wherein those women or those men who were adapted to this form of labor could become cooks, as they would become composers or carpenters. Natural distinctions would be developed between the mere craftsman and the artist; and we should have large, new avenues of lucrative and honorable industry, and a new basis for human health and happiness.

This does not involve what is known as "co-operation." Co-operation, in the usual sense, is the union of families for the better performance of their supposed functions. The process fails because the principle is wrong. Cooking and cleaning are not family functions. We do not have a family mouth, a family stomach, a family face to be washed. Individuals require to be fed and cleaned from birth to death, quite irrespective of their family relations. The orphan, the bachelor, the childless widower, have as much need of these nutritive and excretive processes as any patriarchal parent. Eating is an individual function. Cooking is a social function. Neither is in the faintest degree a family function. That we have found it convenient in early stages of civilization to do our cooking at home proves no more than the allied fact that we have also found it convenient in such stages to do our weaving and spinning at home, our soap and candle making, our butchering and pickling, our baking and washing.

As society develops, its functions specialize; and the reason why this great race-function of cooking has been so retarded in its natural growth is that the economic dependence of women has kept them back from their share in human progress. When women stand free as economic agents, they will lift and free their arrested functions, to the much better fulfilment of their duties as wives and mothers and to the vast improvement in health and happiness of the human race.

Co-operation is not what is required for this, but trained professional service and such arrangement of our methods of living as shall allow us to benefit by such service. When numbers of people patronize the same tailor or baker or confectioner, they do not co-operate. Neither would they co-operate in patronizing the same cook. The change must come from the side of the cook, not from the side of the family. It must come through natural functional development in society, and it is so coming. Woman, recognizing that her duty as feeder and cleaner is a social duty, not a sexual one, must face the requirements of the situation, and prepare herself to meet them. A hundred years ago this could not have been done. Now it is being done, because the time is ripe for it.

If there should be built and opened in any of our large cities to-day a commodious and well-served apartment house for professional women with families, it would be filled at once. The apartments would be without kitchens; but there would be a kitchen belonging to the house from which meals could be served to the families in their rooms or in a common dining-room, as preferred. It would be a home where the cleaning was done by efficient workers, not hired separately by the families, but engaged by the manager of the establishment; and a roof-garden, day nursery, and kindergarten, under well-trained professional nurses and teachers, would insure proper care of the children. The demand for such provision is increasing daily, and must soon be met, not by a boarding-house or a lodging-house, a hotel, a restaurant, or any makeshift patching together of these; but by a permanent provision for the needs of women and children, of family privacy with collective advantage. This must be offered on a business basis to prove a substantial business success; and it will so prove, for it is a growing social need.

There are hundreds of thousands of women in New York City alone who are wage-earners, and who also have families; and the number increases. This is true not only among the poor and unskilled, but more and more among business women, professional women, scientific, artistic, literary women. Our schoolteachers, who form a numerous class, are not entirely without relatives. To board does not satisfy the needs of a human soul. These women want homes, but they do not want the clumsy tangle of rudimentary industries that are supposed to accompany the home. The strain under which such women labor is no longer necessary. The privacy of the home could be as well maintained in such a building as described as in any house in a block, any room, flat, or apartment, under present methods. The food would be better, and would cost less; and this would be true of the service and of all common necessities.

In suburban homes this purpose could be accomplished much better by a grouping of adjacent houses, each distinct and having its own yard, but all kitchenless, and connected by covered ways with the eating-house. No detailed prophecy can be made of the precise forms which would ultimately prove most useful and pleasant; but the growing social need is for the specializing of the industries practised in the home and for the proper mechanical provision for them.

The cleaning required in each house would be much reduced by the removal of the two chief elements of household dirt,—grease and ashes.

Meals could of course be served in the house as long as desired; but, when people become accustomed to pure, clean homes, where no steaming industry is carried on, they will gradually prefer to go to their food instead of having it brought to them. It is a perfectly natural process, and a healthful one, to go to one's food. And, after all, the changes between living in one room, and so having the cooking most absolutely convenient; going as far as the limits of a large house permit, to one's own dining-room; and going a little further to a dining-room not in one's own house, but near by,—these differ but in degree. Families could go to eat together, just as they can go to bathe together or to listen to music together; but, if it fell out that different individuals presumed to develope an appetite at different hours, they could meet it without interfering with other people's comfort or sacrificing their own. Any housewife knows the difficulty of always getting a family together at meals. Why try? Then arises sentiment, and asserts that family affection, family unity, the very existence of the family, depend on their being together at meals. A family unity which is only bound together with a table-cloth is of questionable value.

There are several professions involved in our clumsy method of housekeeping. A good cook is not necessarily a good manager, nor a good manager an accurate and thorough cleaner, nor a good cleaner a wise purchaser. Under the free development of these branches a woman could choose her position, train for it, and become a most valuable functionary in her special branch, all the while living in her own home; that is, she would live in it as a man lives in his home, spending certain hours of the day at work and others at home.

This division of the labor of housekeeping would require the service of fewer women for fewer hours a day. Where now twenty women in twenty homes work all the time, and insufficiently accomplish their varied duties, the same work in the hands of specialists could be done in less time by fewer people; and the others would be left free to do other work for which they were better fitted, thus increasing the productive power of the world. Attempts at co-operation so far have endeavored to lessen the existing labors of women without recognizing their need for other occupation, and this is one reason for their repeated failure.

It seems almost unnecessary to suggest that women as economic producers will naturally choose those professions which are compatible with motherhood, and there are many professions much more in harmony with that function than the household service. Motherhood is not a remote contingency, but the common duty and the common glory of womanhood. If women did choose professions unsuitable to maternity, Nature would quietly extinguish them by her unvarying process. Those mothers who persisted in being acrobats, horse-breakers, or sailors before the mast, would probably not produce vigorous and numerous children. If they did, it would simply prove that such work did not hurt them. There is no fear to be wasted on the danger of women's choosing wrong professions, when they are free to choose. Many women would continue to prefer the very kinds of work which they are doing now, in the new and higher methods of execution. Even cleaning, rightly understood and practised, is a useful, and therefore honorable, profession. It has been amusing heretofore to see how this least desirable of labors has been so innocently held to be woman's natural duty. It is woman, the dainty, the beautiful, the beloved wife and revered mother, who has by common consent been expected to do the chamber-work and scullery work of the world. All that is basest and foulest she in the last instance must handle and remove. Grease, ashes, dust, foul linen, and sooty ironware,—among these her days must pass. As we socialize our functions, this passes from her hands into those of man. The city's cleaning is his work. And even in our houses the professional cleaner is more and more frequently a man.

The organization of household industries will simplify and centralize its cleaning processes, allowing of many mechanical conveniences and the application of scientific skill and thoroughness. We shall be cleaner than we ever were before. There will be less work to do, and far better means of doing it. The daily needs of a well-plumbed house could be met easily by each individual in his or her own room or by one who liked to do such work; and the labor less frequently required would be furnished by an expert, who would clean one home after another with the swift skill of training and experience. The home would cease to be to us a workshop or a museum, and would become far more the personal expression of its occupants—the place of peace and rest, of love and privacy—than it can be in its present condition of arrested industrial development. And woman will fill her place in those industries with far better results than are now provided by her ceaseless struggles, her conscientious devotion, her pathetic ignorance and inefficiency.

XII.

As self-conscious creatures, to whom is always open the easy error of mistaking feeling for fact, to whose consciousness indeed the feeling is the fact,—a further process of reasoning being required to infer the fact from the feeling,—we are not greatly to be blamed for laying such stress on sentiment and emotion. We may perhaps admit, in the light of cold reasoning, that the home is not the best place in which to do so much work in, nor the wife and mother the best person to do it. But this intellectual conviction by no means alters our feeling on the subject. Feeling, deep, long established, and over-stimulated, lies thick over the whole field of home life. Not what we think about it (for we never have thought about it very much), but what we feel about it, constitutes the sum of our opinion. Many of our feelings are true, right, legitimate. Some are fatuous absurdities, mere dangling relics of outgrown tradition, slowly moulting from us as we grow.

Consider, for instance, that long-standing popular myth known as "the privacy of the home." There is something repugnant in the idea of food cooked outside the home, even though served within it; still more in the going out of the family to eat, and more yet in the going out of separate individuals to eat. The limitless personal taste developed by "home cooking" fears that it will lose its own particular shade of brown on the bacon, its own hottest of hot cakes, its own corner biscuit.

This objection must be honestly faced, and admitted in some degree. A *menu*, however liberally planned by professional cooks, would not allow so much play for personal idiosyncrasy as do those prepared by the numerous individual cooks now serving us. There would be a far larger range of choice in materials, but not so much in methods of preparation and service. The difference would be like that between every man's making his own coat or having his women servants make it for him, on the one hand, and his selecting one from many ready made or ordering it of his tailor, on the other.

In the regular professional service of food there would be a good general standard, and the work of specialists for special occasions. We have long seen this process going on in the steady increase of professionally prepared food, from the cheap eating-house to the fashionable caterer, from the common "cracker" to the delicate "wafer." "Home cooking," robbed of its professional adjuncts, would fall a long way. We do not realize how far we have already progressed in this line, nor how fast we are going.

One of the most important effects of a steady general standard of good food will be the elevation of the popular taste. We should acquire a cultivated appreciation of what *is* good food, far removed from the erratic and whimsical self-indulgence of the private table. Our only standard of taste in cooking is personal appetite and caprice. That we "like" a dish is enough to warrant full approval. But liking is only adaptation. Nature is forever seeking to modify the organism to the environment; and, when it becomes so modified, so adapted, the organism "likes" the environment. In the earlier form, "it likes me," this derivation is plainer.

Each nation, each locality, each family, each individual, "likes," in large measure, those things to which it has been accustomed. What else it might have liked, if it had had it, can never be known; but the slow penetration of new tastes and habits, the reluctant adoption of the potato, the tomato, maize, and other new vegetables by old countries, show that it is quite possible to change a liking.

In the narrow range of family capacity to supply and of family ability to prepare our food, and in our exaggerated intensity of personal preference, we have grown very rigid in our little field of choice. We insist on the superiority of our own methods, and despise the methods of our neighbors, with a sublime ignorance of any higher standard of criticism than our own uneducated tastes. When we become accustomed from childhood to scientifically and artistically prepared foods, we shall grow to know what is good and to enjoy it, as we learn to know good music by hearing it.

As we learn to appreciate a wider and higher range of cooking, we shall also learn to care for simplicity in this art. Neither is attainable under our present system by the average person. As cooking becomes dissociated from the home, we shall gradually cease to attach emotions to it; and we shall learn to judge it impersonally upon a scientific and artistic basis. This will not, of course, prevent some persons' having peculiar tastes; but these will know that they are peculiar, and so will their neighbors. It will not prevent, either, the woman who has a dilettante fondness for some branch of cookery, wherewith she loves to delight herself and her friends, from keeping a small cooking plant within reach, as she might a sewing-machine or a turning-lathe.

In regard to the eating of food we are still more opposed by the "privacy of the home" idea, and a marked—indeed, a pained—disinclination to dissociate that function from family life. To eat together does, of course, form a temporary bond. To establish a medium of communication between dissimilar persons, some common ground must be found,—some rite, some game, some entertainment,—something that they can *do* together. And, if the persons desiring to associate have no other common ground than this physical function,—which is so common, indeed, that it includes not only all humanity, but all the animal kingdom,—then by all means let them seek that. On occasions of general social rejoicing to celebrate some event of universal importance, the feast will always be a natural and satisfying institution.

To the primitive husband with fighting for his industry, the primitive wife with domestic service for hers, the primitive children with no relation to their parents but the physical,—to such a common table was the only common tie; and the simplicity of their food furnished a medium that hurt no one. But in the higher individualization of modern life the process of eating is by no means the only common interest among members of a family, and by no means the best. The sweetest, tenderest, holiest memories of family life are not connected with the table, though many jovial and pleasant ones may be so associated. And on many an occasion of deep feeling, whether of joy or of pain, the ruthless averaging of the whole group three times a day at table becomes an unbearable strain. If good food suited to a wide range of needs were always attainable, a family could go and feast together when it chose or simply eat together when it chose; and each individual could go alone when he chose. This is not to be forced or hurried; but, with a steady supply of food, easy of access to all, the stomach need no longer be compelled to serve as a family tie.

We have so far held that the lower animals ate alone in their brutality, and that man has made eating a social function, and so elevated it. The elevation is the difficult part to prove, when we look at humanity's gross habits, morbid tastes, and deadly diseases, its artifice, and its unutterable depravity of gluttony and intemperance. The animals may be lower than we in their simple habit of eating what is good for them when they are hungry, but it serves their purpose well.

One result of our making eating a social function is that, the more elaborately we socialize it, the more we require at our feasts the service of a number of strangers absolutely shut out from social intercourse,—functionaries who do not eat with us, who do not talk with us, who must not by the twinkling of an eyelash show any interest in this performance, save to minister to the grosser needs of the occasion on a strictly commercial basis. Such extraneous presence must and does keep the conversation at one level. In the family without a servant both mother and father are too hard worked to make the meal a social success; and, as soon as servants are introduced, a limit is set to the range of conversation. The effect of our social eating, either in families or in larger groups, is not wholly good. It is well open to question whether we cannot, in this particular, improve our system of living.

When the cooking of the world is open to full development by those whose natural talent and patient study lead them to learn how better and better to meet the needs of the body by delicate and delicious combinations of the elements of nutrition, we shall begin to understand what food means to us, and how to build up the human body in sweet health and full vigor. A world of pure, strong, beautiful men and women, knowing what they ought to eat and drink, and taking it when they need it, will be capable of much higher and subtler forms of association than this much-prized common table furnishes. The contented grossness of to-day, the persistent self-indulgence of otherwise intelligent adults, the fatness and leanness and feebleness, the whole train of food-made disorders, together with all drug habits,—these morbid phenomena are largely traceable to the abnormal attention given to both eating and cooking, which must accompany them as family functions. When we detach them from this false position by untangling the knot of our sexuo-economic relation, we shall give natural forces a chance to work their own pure way in us, and make us better.

Our domestic privacy is held to be further threatened by the invasion of professional cleaners. We should see that a kitchenless home will require far less cleaning than is now needed, and that the daily ordering of one's own room could be easily accomplished by the individual, when desired. Many would so desire, keeping their own rooms, their personal inner chambers, inviolate from other presence than that of their nearest and dearest. Such an ideal of privacy may seem ridiculous to those who accept contentedly the gross publicity of our present method. Of all popular paradoxes, none is more nakedly absurd than to hear us prate of privacy in a place where we cheerfully admit to our table-talk and to our door service—yes, and to the making of our beds and to the handling of our clothing—a complete stranger, a stranger not only by reason of new acquaintance and of the false view inevitable to new eyes let in upon our secrets, but a stranger by birth, almost always an alien in race, and, more hopeless still, a stranger by breeding, one who can never truly understand.

This stranger all of us who can afford it summon to our homes,—one or more at once, and many in succession. If, like barbaric kings of old or bloody pirates of the main, we cut their tongues out that they might not tell, it would still remain an irreconcilable intrusion. But, as it is, with eyes to see, ears to hear, and tongues to speak, with no other interests to occupy their minds, and with the retaliatory fling that follows the enforced silence of those who must not "answer back,"—with this observing and repeating army lodged in the very bosom of the family, may we not smile a little bitterly at our fond ideal of "the privacy of the home"? The swift progress of professional sweepers, dusters, and scrubbers, through rooms where they were wanted, and when they were wanted, would be at least no more injurious to privacy than the present method. Indeed, the exclusion of the domestic servant, and the entrance of woman on a plane of interest at once more social and more personal, would bring into the world a new conception of the sacredness of privacy, a feeling for the rights of the individual as yet unknown.

Closely connected with the question of cleaning is that of household decoration and furnishing. The economically dependent woman, spending the accumulating energies of the race in her small cage, has thrown out a tangled mass of expression, as a large plant throws out roots in a small pot. She has crowded her limited habitat with unlimited things,—things useful and unuseful, ornamental and unornamental, comfortable and uncomfortable; and the labor of her life is to wait upon these things, and keep them clean.

The free woman, having room for full individual expression in her economic activities and in her social relation, will not be forced so to pour out her soul in tidies and photograph holders. The home will be her place of rest, not of uneasy activity; and she will learn to love simplicity at last. This will mean better sanitary conditions in the home, more beauty and less work. And the trend of the new conditions, enhancing the value of real privacy and developing the sense of beauty, will be toward a delicate loveliness in the interiors of our houses, which the owners can keep in order without undue exertion.

Besides these comparatively external conditions, there are psychic effects produced upon the family by the sexuo-economic relation not altogether favorable to our best growth. One is the levelling effect of the group upon its members, under pressure of this relation. Such privacy as we do have in our homes is family privacy, an aggregate privacy; and this does not insure—indeed, it prevents—individual privacy. This is another of the lingering rudiments of methods of living belonging to ages long since outgrown, and maintained among us by the careful preservation of primitive customs in the unchanged position of women. In very early times a crude and undifferentiated people could flock in family groups in one small tent without serious inconvenience or injury. The effects of such grouping on modern people is known in the tenement districts of large cities, where families live in single rooms; and these effects are of a distinctly degrading nature.

The progressive individuation of human beings requires a personal home, one room at least for each person. This need forces some recognition for itself in family life, and is met so far as private purses in private houses can meet it; but for the vast majority of the population no such provision is possible. To women, especially, a private room is the luxury of the rich alone. Even where a partial provision for personal needs is made under pressure of social development, the other pressure of undeveloped family life is constantly against it. The home is the one place on earth where no one of the component individuals can have any privacy. A family is a crude aggregate of persons of different ages, sizes, sexes, and temperaments, held together by sex-ties and economic necessity; and the affection which should exist between the members of a family is not increased in the least by the economic pressure, rather it is lessened. Such affection as is maintained by economic forces is not the kind which humanity most needs.

At present any tendency to withdraw and live one's own life on any plane of separate interest or industry is naturally resented, or at least regretted, by the other members of the family. This affects women more than men, because men live very little in the family and very much in the world. The man has his individual life, his personal expression and its rights, his office, studio, shop: the women and children live in the home—because they must. For a woman to wish to spend much time elsewhere is considered wrong, and the children have no choice. The historic tendency of women to "gad abroad," of children to run away, to be forever teasing for permission to go and play somewhere else; the ceaseless, futile, well-meant efforts to "keep the boys at home,"—these facts, together with the definite absence of the man of the home for so much of the time, constitute a curious commentary upon our patient belief that we live at home, and like it. Yet the home ties bind us with a gentle dragging hold that few can resist. Those who do resist, and who insist upon living their individual lives, find that this costs them loneliness and privation; and they lose so much in daily comfort and affection that others are deterred from following them.

There is no reason why this painful choice should be forced upon us, no reason why the home life of the human race should not be such as to allow—yes, to promote—the highest development of personality. We need the society of those dear to us, their love and their companionship. These will endure. But the common cook-shops of our industrially undeveloped homes, and all the allied evils, are not essential, and need not endure.

To our general thought the home just as it stands is held to be what is best for us. We imagine that it is at home that we learn the higher traits, the nobler emotions,—that the home teaches us how to live. The truth beneath this popular concept is this: the love of the mother for the child is at the base of all our higher love for one another. Indeed, even behind that lies the generous giving impulse of sex-love, the outgoing force of sex-energy. The family relations ensuing do underlie our higher, wider social relations. The "home comforts" are essential to the preservation of individual life. And the bearing and forbearing of home life, with the dominant, ceaseless influence of conservative femininity, is a most useful check to the irregular flying impulses of masculine energy. While the world lasts, we shall need not only the individual home, but the family home, the common sheath for the budded leaflets of each new branch, held close to the parent stem before they finally diverge.

Granting all this, there remains the steadily increasing ill effect, not of home life *per se*, but of the kind of home life based on the sexuo-economic relation. A home in which the rightly dominant feminine force is held at a primitive plane of development, and denied free participation in the swift, wide, upward movement of the world, reacts upon those who hold it down by holding them down in turn. A home in which the inordinate love of receiving things, so long bred into one sex, and the fierce hunger for procuring things, so carefully trained into the other, continually act upon the child, keeps ever before his eyes the fact that life consists in getting dinner and in getting the money to pay for it, getting the food from the market, working forever and ever to cook and serve it. These are the prominent facts of the home as we have made it. The kind of care in which our lives are spent, the things that wear and worry us, are things that should have been outgrown long, long ago if the human race had advanced evenly. Man has advanced, but woman has been kept behind. By inheritance she advances, by experience she is retarded, being always forced back to the economic grade of many thousand years ago.

If a modern man, with all his intellect and energy and resource, were forced to spend all his days hunting with a bow and arrow, fishing with a bone-pointed spear, waiting hungrily on his traps and snares in hope of prey, he could not bring to his children or to his wife the uplifting influences of the true manhood of our time. Even if he started with a college education, even if he had large books to read (when he had time to read them) and improving conversation, still the economic efforts of his life, the steady daily pressure of what he had to do for his living, would check the growth of higher powers. If all men had to be hunters from day to day, the world would be savage still. While all women have to be house servants from day to day, we are still a servile world.

A home life with a dependent mother, a servant-wife, is not an ennobling influence. We all feel this at times. The man, spreading and growing with the world's great growth, comes home, and settles into the tiny talk and fret, or the alluring animal comfort of the place, with a distinct sense of coming down. It is pleasant, it is gratifying to every sense, it is kept warm and soft and pretty to suit the needs of the feebler and smaller creature who is forced to stay in it. It is even considered a virtue for the man to stay in it and to prize it, to value his slippers and his newspaper, his hearth fire and his supper table, his spring bed, and his clean clothes above any other interests.

The harm does not lie in loving home and in staying there as one can, but in the kind of a home and in the kind of womanhood that it fosters, in the grade of industrial development on which it rests. And here, without prophesying, it is easy to look along the line of present progress, and see whither our home life tends. From the cave and tent and hovel up to a graded, differentiated home, with as much room for the individual as the family can afford; from the surly dominance of the absolute patriarch, with his silent servile women and chattel children, to the comparative freedom, equality, and finely diversified lives of a well-bred family of to-day; from the bottom grade of industry in the savage camp, where all things are cooked together by the same person in the same pot,—without neatness, without delicacy, without specialization,—to the million widely separated hands that serve the home to-day in a thousand wide-spread industries,—the man and the mill have achieved it all; the woman has but gone shopping outside, and stayed at the base of the pyramid within.

And, more important and suggestive yet, mark this: whereas, in historic beginnings, nothing but the home of the family existed; slowly, as we have grown, has developed the home of the individual. The first wider movement of social life meant a freer flux of population,—trade, commerce, exchange, communication. Along river courses and sea margins, from canoe to steamship, along paths and roads as they made them, from "shank's mare to the iron horse,"[1] faster and freer, wider and oftener, the individual human beings have flowed and mingled in the life that is humanity. At first the traveller's only help was hospitality,—the right of the stranger; but his increasing functional use brought with it, of necessity, the organic structure which made it easy, the transitory individual home. From the most primitive caravansary[2] up to the square miles of floor-space in our grand hotels, the public house has met the needs of social evolution as no private house could have done.

To man, so far the only fully human being of his age, the bachelor apartment of some sort has been a temporary home for that part of his life wherein he had escaped from one family and not yet entered another. To woman this possibility is opening to-day. More and more we see women presuming to live and have a home, even though they have not a family. The family home itself is more and more yielding to the influence of progress. Once it was stationary and permanent, occupied from generation to generation. Now we move, even in families,—move with reluctance and painful objection and with bitter sacrifice of household gods; but move we must under the increasing irritation of irreconcilable conditions. And so has sprung up and grown to vast proportions that startling portent of our times, the "family hotel."

---

1 Shank's mare: walking; iron horse: steam train.
2 Inn or resting place for a travelling group of people (caravan).

Consider it. Here is the inn, once a mere makeshift stopping-place for weary travellers. Yet even so the weary traveller long since noted the difference between his individual freedom there and his home restrictions, and cheerfully remarked, "I take mine ease in mine inn."[1] Here is this temporary stopping-place for single men become a permanent dwelling-place for families! Not from financial necessity. These are inhabited by people who could well afford to "keep house." But they do not want to keep house. They are tired of keeping house. It is so difficult to keep house, the servant problem is so trying. The health of their wives is not equal to keeping house. These are the things they say.

But under these vague perceptions and expressions is heaving and stirring a slow, uprising social tide. The primitive home, based on the economic dependence of woman, with its unorganized industries, its servile labors, its smothering drag on individual development, is becoming increasingly unsuitable to the men and women of to-day. Of course, they hark back to it, of necessity, so long as marriage and child-bearing are supposed to require it, so long as our fondest sentiments and our earliest memories so closely cling to it. But in its practical results, as shown by the ever-rising draught upon the man's purse and the woman's strength, it is fast wearing out.

We have watched the approach of this condition, and have laid it to every cause but the real one. We have blamed men for not staying at home as they once did. We have blamed women for not being as good housekeepers as they once were. We have blamed the children for their discontent, the servants for their inefficiency, the very brick and mortar for their poor construction. But we have never thought to blame the institution itself, and see whether it could not be improved upon.

On wide Western prairies, or anywhere in lonely farm houses, the women of to-day, confined absolutely to this strangling cradle of the race, go mad by scores and hundreds. Our asylums show a greater proportion of insane women among farmers' wives than in any other class.[2] In the cities, where there is less "home life," people seem to stand it better. There are more distractions, the men say, and seek them. There is more excitement, amusement, variety, the women say, and seek them. What is really felt is the larger social interests and the pressure of forces newer than those of the home circle.

---

1 Shakespeare, *Henry IV.I*, 3.3.86–87.
2 In the nineteenth century, so-called "prairie madness" affected settlers in the western states who experienced periods of prolonged isolation.

Many fear this movement, and vainly strive to check it. There is no cause for alarm. We are not going to lose our homes nor our families, nor any of the sweetness and happiness that go with them. But we are going to lose our kitchens, as we have lost our laundries and bakeries. The cook-stove will follow the loom and wheel, the wool-carder and shears. We shall have homes that are places to live in and love in, to rest in and play in, to be alone in and to be together in; and they will not be confused and declassed by admixture with any industry whatever.

In homes like these the family life will have all its finer, truer spirit well maintained; and the cares and labors that now mar its beauty will have passed out into fields of higher fulfilment. The relation of wife to husband and mother to child is changing for the better with this outward alteration. All the personal relations of the family will be open to a far purer and fuller growth.

Nothing in the exquisite pathos of woman's long subjection goes deeper to the heart than the degradation of motherhood by the very conditions we supposed were essential to it. To see the mother's heart and mind longing to go with the child, to help it all the way, and yet to see it year by year pass farther from her, learn things she never was allowed to know, do things she never was allowed to do, go out into "the world"—their world, not hers—alone, and

"To bear, to nurse, to rear, to love, and then to lose!"[1]

this not by the natural separation of growth and personal divergence, but by the unnatural separation of falsely divided classes,—rudimentary women and more highly developed men. It is the fissure that opens before the boy is ten years old, and it widens with each year.

A mother economically free, a world-servant instead of a house-servant; a mother knowing the world and living in it,—can be to her children far more than has ever been possible before. Motherhood in the world will make that world a different place for her child.

---

1 Jean Ingelow, *Song of Seven* (1866), "Seven Times Six—Giving in Marriage" 1–2.

XIII.

In reconstructing in our minds the position of woman under conditions of economic independence, it is most difficult to think of her as a mother.

We are so unbrokenly accustomed to the old methods of motherhood, so convinced that all its processes are inter-relative and indispensable, and that to alter one of them is to endanger the whole relation, that we cannot conceive of any desirable change.

When definite plans for such change are suggested,—ways in which babies might be better cared for than at present,—we either deny the advantages of the change proposed or insist that these advantages can be reached under our present system. Just as in cooking we seek to train the private cook and to exalt and purify the private taste, so in baby-culture we seek to train the individual mother, and to call for better conditions in the private home; in both cases ignoring the relation between our general system and its particular phenomena. Though it may be shown, with clearness, that in physical conditions the private house, as a place in which to raise children, may be improved upon, yet all the more stoutly do we protest that the mental life, the emotional life, of the home is the best possible environment for the young.

There was a time in human history when this was true. While progress derived its main impetus from the sex-passion, and the highest emotions were those that held us together in the family relation, such education and such surroundings as fostered and intensified these emotions were naturally the best. But in the stage into which we are now growing, when the family relation is only a part of life, and our highest duties lie between individuals in social relation, the child has new needs.

This does not mean, as the scared rush of the unreasoning mind to an immediate opposite would suggest, a disruption of the family circle or the destruction of the home. It does not mean the separation of mother and child,—that instant dread of the crude instinct of animal maternity. But it does mean a change of basis in the family relation by the removal of its previous economic foundation, and a change of method in our child-culture. We are no more bound to maintain forever our early methods in baby-raising than we are bound to maintain them in the education of older children, or in floriculture. All human life is in its very nature open to improvement, and motherhood is not excepted. The relation between men and women, between husband and wife, between parent and child, changes inevitably with social advance; but we are loath to admit it. We think a change here must be wrong, because we are so convinced that the present condition is right.

On examination, however, we find that the existing relation between parents and children in the home is by no means what we unquestioningly assume. We all hold certain ideals of home life, of family life. When we see around us, or read of, scores and hundreds of cases of family unhappiness and open revolt, we lay it to the individual misbehavior of the parties concerned, and go on implicitly believing in the intrinsic perfection of the institution. When, on the other hand, we find people living together in this relation, in peace and love and courtesy, we do not conversely attribute this to individual superiority and virtue; but we point to it as instancing the innate beauty of the relation.

To the careful sociological observer what really appears is this: when individual and racial progress was best served by the close associations of family life, people were very largely developed in capacity for family affection. They were insensitive to the essential limitations and incessant friction of the relation. They assented to the absolute authority of the head of the family and to the minor despotism of lower functionaries, manifesting none of those sharply defined individual characteristics which are so inimical to the family relation.

But we have reached a stage where individual and racial progress is best served by the higher specialization of individuals and by a far wider sense of love and duty. This change renders the psychic condition of home life increasingly disadvantageous. We constantly hear of the inferior manners of the children of to-day, of the restlessness of the young, of the flat treason of deserting parents. It is visibly not so easy to live at home as it used to be. Our children are not more perversely constituted than the children of earlier ages, but the conditions in which they are reared are not suited to develop the qualities now needed in human beings.

This increasing friction between members of families should not be viewed with condemnation from a moral point of view, but studied with scientific interest. If our families are so relatively uncomfortable under present conditions, are there not conditions wherein the same families could be far more comfortable? No: we are afraid not. We think it is right to have things as they are, wrong to wish to change them. We think that virtue lies largely in being uncomfortable, and that there is special virtue in the existing family relation.

Virtue is a relative term. Human virtues change from age to age with the change in conditions. Consider the great virtue of loyalty,—our highest name for duty. This is a quality that became valuable in human life the moment we began to do things which were not instantly and visibly profitable to ourselves. The permanent application of the individual to a task not directly attractive was an indispensable social quality, and therefore a virtue. Steadfastness, faithfulness, loyalty, duty, that conscious, voluntary attitude of the individual which holds him to a previously assumed relation, even to his extreme personal injury,—to death itself,—from this results the cohesion of the social body: it is a first principle of social existence.

To the personal conscience a social necessity must express itself in a recognized and accepted pressure,—a force to which we bow, a duty, a virtue. So the virtue of loyalty came into early and lasting esteem, whether in the form of loyalty to one's own spoken word or vow—"He that sweareth to his hurt, and doeth it"[1]—to a friend or group of friends in temporary union for some common purpose, or to a larger and more permanent relation. The highest form is, of course, loyalty to the largest common interest; and here we can plainly trace the growth of this quality.

First, we see it in the vague, nebulous, coherence of the horde of savages, then in the tense devotion of families,—that absolute duty to the highest known social group. It was in this period that obedience to parents was writ so large in our scale of virtues. The family feud, the *vendetta*[2] of the Corsicans, is an over-development of this force of family devotion. Next came loyalty to the chief, passing even that due the father. And with the king—that dramatic personification of a nation, "Lo! royal England comes!"—loyalty became a very passion. It took precedence of every virtue, with good reason; for it was not, as was supposed, the person of the king which was so revered: it was the embodied nation, the far-reaching, collective interests of every citizen, the common good, which called for the willing sacrifice of every individual. We still exhibit all these phases of loyalty, in differently diminishing degrees; but we show, also, a larger form of this great virtue peculiar to our age.

The lines of social relation to-day are mainly industrial. Our individual lives, our social peace and progress, depend more

---

1 It is righteous to keep one's promise, even when it is not to one's advantage to do so (see Psalm 15.11).
2 A family blood feud.

upon our economic relations than upon any other. For a long time society was organized only on a sex-basis, a religious basis, or a military basis, each of such organizations being comparatively transient; and its component individuals labored alone on an economic basis of helpless individualism.

Duty is a social sense, and developes only with social organization. As our civil organization has become national, we have developed the sense of duty to the State. As our industrial organization has grown to the world-encircling intricacies of to-day, as we have come to hold our place on earth by reason of our vast and elaborate economic relation with its throbbing and sensitive machinery of communication and universal interservice, the unerring response of the soul to social needs has given us a new kind of loyalty,—loyalty to our work. The engineer who sticks to his engine till he dies, that his trainload of passengers may live; the cashier who submits to torture rather than disclose the secret of the safe,—these are loyal exactly as was the servitor[1] of feudal times, who followed his master to the death, or the subject who gave up all for his king. Professional honor, duty to one's employers, duty to the work itself, at any cost,—this is loyalty, faithfulness, the power to stay put in a relation necessary to the social good, though it may be directly against personal interest.

It is in the training of children for this stage of human life that the private home has ceased to be sufficient, or the isolated, primitive, dependent woman capable. Not that the mother does not have an intense and overpowering sense of loyalty and of duty; but it is duty to individuals, just as it was in the year one. What she is unable to follow, in her enforced industrial restriction, is the higher specialization of labor, and the honorable devotion of human lives to the development of their work. She is most slavishly bound to her daily duty, it is true; but it does not occur to her as a duty to raise the grade of her own labor for the sake of humanity, nor as a sin so to keep back the progress of the world by her contented immobility.

She cannot teach what she does not know. She cannot in any sincerity uphold as a duty what she does not practise. The child learns more of the virtues needed in modern life—of fairness, of justice, of comradeship, of collective interest and action—in a common school than can be taught in the most perfect family circle. We may preach to our children as we will of the great duty of loving and serving one's neighbor; but what the baby is born

---

1 A domestic servant.

into, what the child grows up to see and feel, is the concentration of one entire life—his mother's—upon the personal aggrandizement of one family, and the human service of another entire life—his father's—so warped and strained by the necessity of "supporting his family" that treason to society is the common price of comfort in the home. For a man to do any base, false work for which he is hired, work that injures producer and consumer alike; to prostitute what power and talent he possesses to whatever purchaser may use them,—this is justified among men by what they call duty to the family, and is unblamed by the moral sense of dependent women.

And this is the atmosphere in which the wholly home-bred, mother-taught child grows up. Why should not food and clothes and the comforts of his own people stand first in his young mind? Does he not see his mother, the all-loved, all-perfect one, peacefully spending her days in the arrangement of these things which his father's ceaseless labor has procured? Why should he not grow up to care for his own, to the neglect and willing injury of all the rest, when his earliest, deepest impressions are formed under such exclusive devotion?

It is not the home as a place of family life and love that injures the child, but as the centre of a tangled heap of industries, low in their ungraded condition, and lower still because they are wholly personal. Work the object of which is merely to serve one's self is the lowest. Work the object of which is merely to serve one's family is the next lowest. Work the object of which is to serve more and more people, in widening range, till it approximates the divine spirit that cares for all the world, is social service in the fullest sense, and the highest form of service that we can reach.

It is this personality in home industry that keeps it hopelessly down. The short range between effort and attainment, the constant attention given to personal needs, is bad for the man, worse for the woman, and worst for the child. It belittles his impressions of life at the start. It accustoms him to magnify the personal duties and minify the social ones, and it greatly retards his adjustment to larger life. This servant-motherhood, with all its unavoidable limitation and ill results, is the concomitant of the economic dependence of woman upon man, the direct and inevitable effect of the sexuo-economic relation.

The child is affected by it during his most impressionable years, and feels the effect throughout life. The woman is permanently retarded by it; the man, less so, because of his normal social activities, wherein he is under more developing influence.

But he is injured in great degree, and our whole civilization is checked and perverted.

We suffer also, our lives long, from an intense self-consciousness, from a sensitiveness beyond all need; we demand measureless personal attention and devotion, because we have been born and reared in a very hotbed of these qualities. A baby who spent certain hours of every day among other babies, being cared for because he was a baby, and not because he was "my baby," would grow to have a very different opinion of himself from that which is forced upon each new soul that comes among us by the ceaseless adoration of his own immediate family. What he needs to learn at once and for all, to learn softly and easily, but inexorably, is that he is one of many. We all dimly recognize this in our praise of large families, and in our saying that "an only child is apt to be selfish." So is an only family. The earlier and more easily a child can learn that human life means many people, and their behavior to one another, the happier and stronger and more useful his life will be.

This could be taught him with no difficulty whatever, under certain conditions, just as he is taught his present sensitiveness and egotism by the present conditions. It is not only temperature and diet and rest and exercise which affect the baby. "He does love to be noticed," we say. "He is never so happy as when he has a dozen worshippers around him." But what is the young soul learning all the while? What does he gather, as he sees and hears and slowly absorbs impressions? With the inflexible inferences of a clear, young brain, unsupplied with any counter-evidence until later in life, he learns that women are meant to wait on people, to get dinner, and sweep and pick up things; that men are made to bring home things, and are to be begged of according to circumstances; that babies are the object of concentrated admiration; that their hair, hands, feet, are specially attractive; that they are the heated focus of attention, to be passed from hand to hand, swung and danced and amused most violently, and also be laid aside and have nothing done to them, with no regard to their preference in either case.

And then, in the midst of all this tingling self-consciousness and desire for loving praise, he learns that he is "naughty"! The grief, the shame, the anger at injustice, the hopeless bewilderment, the morbid sensitiveness of conscience or the stolid dulling of it, the gradual retirement of the baffled brain from all these premature sensations to a contentment with mere personal gratification and a growing ingenuity in obtaining it,—all these experiences are the common lot of the child among us, our common lot when we were children. Of course, we don't remember. Of course, we loved our mother, and thought her perfect. Comparisons among mothers are difficult for a baby. Of course, we loved our homes, and never dreamed of any other way of being "brought up." And, of course, when we have children of our own, we bring them up in the same way. What other way is there? What is there to be said on the subject? Children always were brought up at home. Isn't that enough?

And yet, insidiously, slowly, irresistibly, while we flatter ourselves that things remain the same, they are changing under our very eyes from year to year, from day to day. Education, hiding itself behind a wall of books, but consisting more and more fully in the grouping of children and in the training of faculties never mentioned in the curriculum,—education, which is our human motherhood, has crept nearer and nearer to its true place, its best work,—the care and training of the little child. Some women there are, and some men, whose highest service to humanity is the care of children. Such should not concentrate their powers upon their own children alone,—a most questionable advantage,—but should be so placed that their talent and skill, their knowledge and experience, would benefit the largest number of children. Many women there are, and many men, who, though able to bring forth fine children, are unable to educate them properly. Simply to bear children is a personal matter,—an animal function. Education is collective, human, a social function.

As we now arrange life, our children must take their chances while babies, and live or die, improve or deteriorate, according to the mother to whom they chance to be born. An inefficient mother does not prevent a child from having a good school education or a good college education; but the education of babyhood, the most important of all, is wholly in her hands. It is futile to say that mothers should be taught how to fulfil their duties. You cannot teach every mother to be a good school educator or a good college educator. Why should you expect every mother to be a good nursery educator? Whatever our expectations, she is not; and our mistrained babies, such of them as survive the maternal handling, grow to be such people as we see about us.

The growth and change in home and family life goes steadily on under and over and through our prejudices and convictions; and the education of the child has changed and become a social function, while we still imagine the mother to be doing it all.

In its earliest and most rudimentary manifestations, education was but part of the individual maternal function of the female animal. But no sooner did the human mind begin to show capacity for giving and receiving its impressions through language (thus attaining the power of acquiring information through sources other than its own experience) than the individual mother ceased to be the sole educator. The young savage receives not only guidance from his anxious mother, but from the chiefs and elders of his tribe. For a long time the aged were considered the only suitable teachers, because the major part of knowledge was still derived from personal experience; and, of course, the older the person, the greater his experience, other things being equal, and they were rather equal then. This primitive notion still holds among us. People still assume superior wisdom because of superior age, putting mere number of experiences against a more essential and better arranged variety, and quite forgetting that the needed wisdom of to-day is not the accumulation of facts, but the power to think about them to some purpose.

With our increased power to preserve and transmit individual experience through literature, and to disseminate such information through systematic education, we see younger and younger people, more rich in, say, chemical or electrical experience than "the oldest inhabitant" could have been in earlier times. Therefore, the teacher of to-day is not the graybeard and beldame, but the man and woman most newly filled with the gathered experience of the world. As this change from age to youth has taken place in the teacher, it has also shown itself in the taught. Grown men frequented the academic groves of Greece. Youths filled the universities of the Middle Ages. Boys and, later, girls were given the increasing school advantages of progressive centuries.

To-day the beautiful development of the kindergarten has brought education to the nursery door. Even our purblind[1] motherhood is beginning to open that door; and we have at last entered upon the study of babyhood, its needs and powers, and are seeing that education begins with life itself. It is no new and daring heresy to suggest that babies need better education than the individual mother now gives them. It is simply a little further extension of the steadily expanding system of human education which is coming upon us, as civilization grows. And it no more infringes upon the mother's rights, the mother's duties, the mother's pleasures, than does the college or the school.

---

1 Visually impaired or partially sighted.

We think no harm of motherhood because our darlings go out each day to spend long hours in school. The mother is not held neglectful, nor the child bereft. It is not called a "separation of mother and child." There would be no further harm or risk or loss in a babyhood passed among such changed surroundings and skilled service as should meet its needs more perfectly than it is possible for the mother to meet them alone at home.

Better surroundings and care for babies, better education, do not mean, as some mothers may imagine, that the tiny monthling is to be taught to read, or even that it is to be exposed to cabalistical[1] arrangements of color and form and sound which shall mysteriously force the young intelligence to flower. It would mean, mainly, a far quieter and more peaceful life than is possible for the heavily loved and violently cared for baby in the busy household; and the impressions which it did meet would be planned and maintained with an intelligent appreciation of its mental powers. The mother would not be excluded, but supplemented, as she is now, by the teacher and the school.

Try and imagine for yourself, if you like, a new kind of coming alive,—the mother breast and mother arms there, of course, fulfilling the service which no other, however tender, could supervene; but there would be other service also. The long, bright hours of the still widening days would find one in sunny, soft-colored rooms, or among the grass and flowers, or by the warm sand and waters. There would be about one more of one's self, others of the same size and age, in restful, helpful companionship. A year means an enormous difference in the ages of babies. Think what a passion little children have for playmates of exactly their own age, because in them alone is perfect equality; and then think that the home-kept baby never has such companionship, unless, indeed, there are twins!

In this larger grouping, in full companionship, the child would unconsciously absorb the knowledge that "we" were humanity, that "we" were creatures to be so fed, so watched, so laid to sleep, so kissed and cuddled and set free to roll and play. The motherhours would be sweetest of all, perhaps. Here would be something wholly one's own, and the better appreciated for the contrast. But the long, steady days would bring their peaceful lessons of equality and common interest instead of the feverish personality of the isolated one-baby household, or the innumerable tyrannies and exactions, the forced submissions and exclusions, of the

---

1 Mysterious or cultish.

nursery full of brothers and sisters of widely differing ages and powers. Mothers accustomed to consider many babies besides their own would begin, on the one hand, to learn something of mere general babyness, and so understand that stage of life far better, and, on the other, to outgrow the pathetic idolatry of the fabled crow,—to recognize a difference in babies, and so to learn a new ideal in their great work of motherhood.

This alone is reason good for a wider maternity. As long as each mother dotes and gloats upon her own children, knowing no others, so long this animal passion overestimates or underestimates real human qualities in the child. So long as this endures, we must grow up with the false, unbalanced opinion of ourselves forced upon us in our infancy. We may think too well of ourselves or we may think too ill of ourselves; but we think always too much of ourselves, because of this untrained and unmodified concentration of maternal feeling. Our whole attitude toward the child is too intensely personal. Through all our aching later life we labor to outgrow the false perspective taught by primitive motherhood.

A baby, brought up with other babies, would never have that labor or that pain. However much his mother might love him, and he might enjoy her love, he would still find that for most of the time he was treated precisely like other people of the same age. Such a change would not involve any greater loss to home and family life than does the school or kindergarten. It would not rob the baby of his mother nor the mother of her baby. And such a change would give the mother certain free hours as a human being, as a member of a civilized community, as an economic producer, as a growing, self-realizing individual. This freedom, growth, and power will make her a wiser, stronger, and nobler mother.

After all is said of loving gratitude to our unfailing mother-nurse, we must have a most exalted sense of our own personal importance so to canonize the service of ourselves. The mother as a social servant instead of a home servant will not lack in true mother duty. She will love her child as well, perhaps better, when she is not in hourly contact with it, when she goes from its life to her own life, and back from her own life to its life, with ever new delight and power. She can keep the deep, thrilling joy of motherhood far fresher in her heart, far more vivid and open in voice and eyes and tender hands, when the hours of individual work give her mind another channel for her own part of the day. From her work, loved and honored though it is, she will return to the home life, the child life, with an eager, ceaseless pleasure, cleansed of all the fret and friction and weariness that so mar it now.

The child, also, will feel this beneficent effect. It is a mistake to suppose that the baby, more than the older child, needs the direct care and presence of the mother. Careful experiment has shown that a new-born baby does not know its own mother, and that a new-made mother does not know her own baby. They have been changed without the faintest recognition on either side.

The services of a foster-mother, a nurse, a grandma, are often liked by a baby as well as, and perhaps better than, those of its own mother. The mere bodily care of a young infant is as well given by one wise, loving hand as another. It is that trained hand that the baby needs, not mere blood-relationship. While the mother keeps her beautiful prerogative of nursing,[1] she need never fear that any other will be dearer to the little heart than she who is the blessed provider of his highest known good. A healthy, happy, rightly occupied motherhood should be able to keep up this function longer than is now customary,—to the child's great gain. Aside from this special relationship, however, the baby would grow easily into the sense of other and wider relationship.

In the freedom and peace of his baby bedroom and baby parlor, in his easy association with others of his own age, he would absorb a sense of right human relation with his mother's milk, as it were,—a sense of others' rights and of his own. Instead of finding life a place in which all the fun was in being carried round and "done to" by others, and a place also in which these others were a tyranny and a weariness unutterable; he would find life a place in which to spread out, unhindered, getting acquainted with his own unfolding powers of body and mind in an atmosphere of physical warmth and ease and of quiet peace of mind.

Direct, concentrated, unvarying personal love is too hot an atmosphere for a young soul. Variations of loneliness, anger, and injustice, are not changes to be desired. A steady, diffused love, lighted with wisdom, based always on justice, and varied with rapturous draughts of our own mother's depth of devotion, would make us into a new people in a few generations. The bent and reach of our whole lives are largely modified by the surroundings of infancy; and those surroundings are capable of betterment, though not to be attained by the individual mother in the individual home.

---

1 I.e., breastfeeding.

There are three reasons why the individual mother can never be fit to take all the care of her children. The first two are so commonly true as to have much weight, the last so absolutely and finally true as to be sufficient in itself alone.

First, not every woman is born with the special qualities and powers needed to take right care of children: she has not the talent for it. Second, not every woman can have the instruction and training needed to fit her for the right care of children: she has not the education for it. Third, while each woman takes all the care of her own children herself, no woman can ever have the requisite experience for it. That is the final bar. That is what keeps back our human motherhood. No mother knows more than her mother knew: no mother has ever learned her business; and our children pass under the well-meaning experiments of an endless succession of amateurs.

We try to get "an experienced nurse." We insist on "an experienced physician." But our idea of an experienced mother is simply one who has borne many children, as if parturition was an educative process!

To experience the pangs of child-birth, or the further pangs of a baby's funeral, adds nothing whatever to the mother's knowledge of the proper care, clothing, feeding, and teaching of the child. The educative department of maternity is not a personal function: it is in its very nature a social function; and we fail grievously in its fulfilment.

The economically independent mother, widened and freed, strengthened and developed, by her social service, will do better service as mother than it has been possible to her before. No one thing could do more to advance the interests of humanity than the wiser care and wider love of organized human motherhood around our babies. This nobler mother, bearing nobler children, and rearing them in nobler ways, would go far toward making possible the world which we want to see. And this change is coming upon us overpoweringly in spite of our foolish fears.

XIV.

The changes in our conception and expression of home life, so rapidly and steadily going on about us, involve many far-reaching effects, all helpful to human advancement. Not the least of these is the improvement in our machinery of social intercourse.

This necessity of civilization was unknown in those primitive ages when family intercourse was sufficient for all, and when any further contact between individuals meant war. Trade and its travel, the specialization of labor and the distribution of its products, with their ensuing development, have produced a wider, freer, and more frequent movement and interchange among the innumerable individuals whose interaction makes society. Only recently, and as yet but partially, have women as individuals come to their share of this fluent social intercourse which is the essential condition of civilization. It is not merely a pleasure or an indulgence: it is the human necessity.

For women as individuals to meet men and other women as individuals, with no regard whatever to the family relation, is a growing demand of our time. As a social necessity, it is perforce[1] being met in some fashion; but its right development is greatly impeded by the clinging folds of domestic and social customs derived from the sexuo-economic relation. The demand for a wider and freer social intercourse between the sexes rests, primarily, on the needs of their respective natures, but is developed in modern life to a far subtler and higher range of emotion than existed in the primitive state, where they had but one need and but one way of meeting it; and this demand, too, calls for a better arrangement of our machinery of living.

Always in social evolution, as in other evolution, the external form suited to earlier needs is but slowly outgrown; and the period of transition, while the new functions are fumbling through the old organs, and slowly forcing mechanical expression for themselves, is necessarily painful. So far in our development, acting on a deep-seated conviction that the world consisted only of families and the necessary business arrangements involved in providing for those families, we have conscientiously striven to build and plan for family advantage, and either unconsciously or grudgingly have been forced to make transient provision for individuals. Whatever did not tend to promote family life, and did tend to provide for the needs of individuals not at the time in family relation, we have deprecated in principle, though reluctantly forced to admit it in practice.

To this day articles are written, seriously and humorously, protesting against the increasing luxury and comfort of bachelor apartments for men, as well as against the pecuniary independence of women, on the ground that these conditions militate against marriage and family life. Most men, even now, pass through a period of perhaps ten years, when they are individuals,

---

1 Necessarily.

business calling them away from their parental family, and business not allowing them to start new families of their own. Women, also, more and more each year, are entering upon a similar period of individual life. And there is a certain permanent percentage of individuals, "odd numbers" and "broken sets," who fall short of family life or who are left over from it; and these need to live.

The residence hotel, the boarding-house, club, lodging-house, and restaurant are our present provision for this large and constantly increasing class. It is not a travelling class. These are people who want to live somewhere for years at a time, but who are not married or otherwise provided with a family. Home life being in our minds inextricably connected with married life, a home being held to imply a family, and a family implying a head, these detached persons are unable to achieve any home life, and are thereby subjected to the inconvenience, deprivation, and expense, the often inhygienic, and sometimes immoral influences, of our makeshift substitutes.

What the human race requires is permanent provision for the needs of individuals, disconnected from the sex-relation. Our assumption that only married people and their immediate relatives have any right to live in comfort and health is erroneous. Every human being needs a home,—bachelor, husband, or widower, girl, wife, or widow, young or old. They need it from the cradle to the grave, and without regard to sex-connections. We should so build and arrange for the shelter and comfort of humanity as not to interfere with marriage, and yet not to make that comfort dependent upon marriage. With the industries of home life managed professionally, with rooms and suites of rooms and houses obtainable by any person or persons desiring them, we could live singly without losing home comfort and general companionship, we could meet bereavement without being robbed of the common conveniences of living as well as of the heart's love, and we could marry in ease and freedom without involving any change in the economic base of either party concerned.

Married people will always prefer a home together, and can have it; but groups of women or groups of men can also have a home together if they like, or contiguous rooms. And individuals even could have a house to themselves, without having, also, the business of a home upon their shoulders.

Take the kitchens out of the houses, and you leave rooms which are open to any form of arrangement and extension; and the occupancy of them does not mean "housekeeping." In such living, personal character and taste would flower as never before; the home of each individual would be at last a true personal expression; and the union of individuals in marriage would not compel the jumbling together of all the external machinery of their lives,—a process in which much of the delicacy and freshness of love, to say nothing of the power of mutual rest and refreshment, is constantly lost. The sense of lifelong freedom and self-respect and of the peace and permanence of one's own home will do much to purify and uplift the personal relations of life, and more to strengthen and extend the social relations. The individual will learn to feel himself an integral part of the social structure, in close, direct, permanent connection with the needs and uses of society.

This is especially needed for women, who are generally considered, and who consider themselves, mere fractions of families, and incapable of any wholesome life of their own. The knowledge that peace and comfort may be theirs for life, even if they do not marry,—and may be still theirs for life, even if they do,—will develop a serenity and strength in women most beneficial to them and to the world. It is a glaring proof of the insufficient and irritating character of our existing form of marriage that women must be forced to it by the need of food and clothes, and men by the need of cooks and housekeepers. We are absurdly afraid that, if men or women can meet these needs of life by other means, they will cheerfully renounce the marriage relation. And yet we sing adoringly of the power of love!

In reality, we may hope that the most valuable effect of this change in the basis of living will be the cleansing of love and marriage from this base admixture of pecuniary interest and creature comfort, and that men and women, eternally drawn together by the deepest force in nature, will be able at last to meet on a plane of pure and perfect love. We shame our own ideals, our deepest instincts, our highest knowledge, by this gross assumption that the noblest race on earth will not mate, or, at least, not mate monogamously, unless bought and bribed through the common animal necessities of food and shelter, and chained by law and custom.

The depth and purity and permanence of the marriage relation rest on the necessity for the prolonged care of children by both parents,—a law of racial development which we can never escape. When parents are less occupied in getting food and cooking it, in getting furniture and dusting it, they may find time to give new thought and new effort to the care of their children. The necessities of the child are far deeper than for bread and bed: those are his mere racial needs, held in common with all his kind. What he needs far more and receives far less is the companionship, the association, the personal touch, of his father and mother. When the common labors of life are removed from the home, we shall have the time, and perhaps the inclination, to make the personal acquaintance of our children. They will seem to us not so much creatures to be waited on as people to be understood. As the civil and military protection of society has long since superseded the tooth-and-claw defence of the fierce parent, without in the least endangering the truth and intensity of the family relation, so the economic provision of society will in time supersede the bringing home of prey by the parent, without evil effects to the love or prosperity of the family. These primitive needs and primitive methods of meeting them are unquestionably at the base of the family relation; but we have long passed them by, and the ties between parent and child are not weakened, but strengthened, by the change.

The more we grow away from these basic conditions, the more fully we realize the deeper and higher forms of relation which are the strength and the delight of human life. Full and permanent provision for individual life and comfort will not cut off the forces that draw men and women together or hold children to their parents; but it will purify and intensify these relations to a degree which we can somewhat foretell by observing the effect of such changes as are already accomplished in this direction. And, in freeing the individual, old and young, from enforced association on family lines, and allowing this emergence into free association on social lines, we shall healthfully assist the development of true social intercourse.

The present economic basis of family life holds our friendly and familiar intercourse in narrow grooves. Such visiting and mingling as is possible to us is between families rather than between individuals; and the growing specialization of individuals renders it increasingly unlikely that all the members of a given family shall please a given visitor or he please them. This, on our present basis, either checks the intercourse or painfully strains the family relation. The change of economic relation in families from a sex-basis to a social basis will make possible wide individual intercourse without this accompanying strain on the family ties.

This outgoing impulse among members of families, their growing desire for general and personal social intercourse, has been considered as a mere thirst for amusement, and deprecated by the moralist. He has so far maintained that the highest form of association was association with one's own family, and that a desire for a wider and more fluent relationship was distinctly unworthy. "He is a good family man," we say admiringly of him who asks only for his newspaper and slippers in the evening; and for the woman who dares admit that she wishes further society than that of her husband we have but one name. With the children, too, our constant effort is to "keep the boys at home," to "make home attractive," so that our ancient ideal, the patriarchal ideal, of a world of families and nothing else, may be maintained.

But this is a world of persons as well as of families. We are persons as soon as we are born, though born into families. We are persons when we step out of families, and persons still, even when we step into new families of our own. As persons, we need more and more, in each generation, to associate with other persons. It is most interesting to watch this need making itself felt, and getting itself supplied, by fair means or foul, through all these stupid centuries. In our besotted exaggeration of the sex-relation, we have crudely supposed that a wish for wider human relationship was a wish for wider sex-relationship, and was therefore to be discouraged, as in Spain it was held unwise to teach women to write, lest they become better able to communicate with their lovers, and so shake the foundations of society.

But, when our sex-relation is made pure and orderly by the economic independence of women, when sex-attraction is no longer a consuming fever, forever convulsing the social surface, under all its bars and chains, we shall not be content to sit down forever with half a dozen blood relations for our whole social arena. We shall need each other more, not less, and shall recognize that social need of one another as the highest faculty of this the highest race on earth.

The force which draws friends together is a higher one than that which draws the sexes together,—higher in the sense of belonging to a later race-development. "Passing the love of women"[1] is no unmeaning phrase. Children need one another: young people need one another. Middle-aged people need one another: old people need one another. We all need one another, much and often. Just as every human creature needs a place to be alone in, a sacred, private "home" of his own, so all human crea-

---

1 An intimate form of friendship beyond physical love (from 2 Samuel 1.26).

tures need a place to be together in, from the two who can show each other their souls uninterruptedly, to the largest throng that can throb and stir in unison.

Humanity means being together, and our unutterably outgrown way of living keeps us apart. How many people, if they dare face the fact, have often hopelessly longed for some better way of seeing their friends, their own true friends, relatives by soul, if not by body!

Acting always under the heated misconceptions of our over-sexed minds, we have pictured mankind as a race of beasts whose only desire to be together was based on one great, overworked passion, and who were only kept from universal orgies of promiscuity by being confined in homes. This is not true. It is not true even now in our over-sexed condition. It will be still less true when we are released from the artificial pressure of the sexuo-economic relation and grow natural again.

Men, women, and children need freedom to mingle on a human basis; and that means to mingle in their daily lives and occupations, not to go laboriously to see each other, with no common purpose. We all know the pleasant acquaintance and deep friendship that springs up when people are thrown together naturally, at school, at college, on shipboard, in the cars, in a camping trip, in business. The social need of one another rests at bottom on a common, functional development; and the common, functional service is its natural opportunity.

The reason why friendship means more to men than to women, and why they associate so much more easily and freely, is that they are further developed in race-functions, and that they *work together*. In the natural association of common effort and common relaxation is the true opening for human companionship. Just to put a number of human beings in the same room, to relate their bodies as to cubic space, does not relate their souls. Our present methods of association, especially for women, are most unsatisfactory. They arise, and go to "call" on one another. They solemnly "return" these calls. They prepare much food, and invite many people to come and eat it; or some dance, music, or entertainment is made the temporary ground of union. But these people do not really meet one another. They pass whole lifetimes in going through the steps of these elaborate games, and never become acquainted. There is a constant thirst among us for fuller and truer social intercourse; but our social machinery provides no means for quenching it.

Men have satisfied this desire in large measure; but between women, or between men and women, it is yet far from accomplishment. Men meet one another freely in their work, while women work alone. But the difference is sharpest in their play. "Girls don't have any fun!" say boys, scornfully; and they don't have very much. What they do have must come, like their bread and butter, on lines of sex. Some man must give them what amusement they have, as he must give them everything else. Men have filled the world with games and sports, from the noble contests of the Olympic plain to the brain and body training sports of to-day, good, bad, and indifferent. Through all the ages the men have played; and the women have looked on, when they were asked. Even the amusing occupation of seeing other people do things was denied them, unless they were invited by the real participants. The "queen of the ball-room" is but a wall-flower, unless she is asked to dance by the real king.

Even to-day, when athletics are fast opening to women, when tennis and golf and all the rest are possible to them, the two sexes are far from even in chances to play. To want a good time is not the same thing as to want the society of the other sex, and to make a girl's desire for a good time hang so largely on her power of sex-attraction is another of the grievous strains we put upon that faculty. That people want to see each other is construed by us to mean that "he" wants to see "her," and "she" wants to see "him." The fun and pleasure of the world are so interwound with the sex-dependence of women upon men that women are forced to court "attentions," when not really desirous of anything but amusement; and, as we force the association of the sexes on this plane, so we restrict it on a more wholesome one.

Even our little children in their play are carefully trained to accentuate sex; and a line of conduct for boys, differing from that for girls, is constantly insisted upon long before either would think of a necessity for such difference. Girls and boys, as they associate, are so commented on and teased as to destroy all wholesome friendliness, and induce a premature sex-consciousness. Young men and women are allowed to associate more or less freely, but always on a strictly sex-basis, friendship between man and woman being a common laughing-stock. Every healthy boy and girl resents this, and tries to hold free, natural relation; but such social pressure is hard to resist. She may have as many "beaux" as she can compass, he may "pay attention" to as many girls as he pleases; but that is their only way to meet.

The general discontinuance of all friendly visiting, upon the engagement of either party, proves the nature of the bond. Having chosen the girl he is to marry, why care to call upon any others? having chosen the man she is to marry, why receive attention from any others? these "calls" and "attentions" being all in the nature of tentative preliminaries to possible matrimony. And, after marriage, the wife is never supposed to wish to see any other man than her husband, or the husband any other woman than his wife. In some countries, we vary this arrangement by increasing the social freedom of married people; but the custom is accompanied by a commensurate lack of freedom before marriage, which causes questionable results, both in married life and in social life. In the higher classes of society there is always more freedom of social intercourse between the sexes after marriage; but, speaking generally of America, there is very little natural and serious acquaintance between men and women after the period of pre-matrimonial visiting.

Even the friendship which may have existed between husband and wife before marriage is often destroyed by that relation and its economic complications. They have not time to talk about things as they used: they are too near together, and too deeply involved in the industrial and financial concern of their new business. This works steadily against the development of higher and purer relations between men and women, and tends to keep them forever to the one primitive bond of sex-union.

A young man goes to a city to live and work. He needs the society of women as well as of men. Formerly he had his mother, his sisters, and his sisters' friends, his schoolmates. Now he must face our constrained social conditions. He may visit two kinds of women,—those whom we call "good," and those whom we call "bad." (This classification rests on but one moral quality, and that a sexual one.) He naturally prefers the good. The good are divided, again, into two kinds,—married and single. If he visit a married woman frequently, it is remarked upon: it becomes unpleasant, he does not do it. If he visit an unmarried woman frequently, it is also remarked upon; and he is considered to have "intentions." His best alternative is to visit a number of unmarried women, and distribute his attentions so cautiously that no one can claim them as personal.

Here he enters on the first phase of our sexuo-economic relation: he cannot even visit girls freely without paying for it. Simply to see the girl by calling on her in the family circle is hardly what either wants of the other. One does not meet half a dozen people of various ages and of both sexes as one meets a friend alone. To seek to see her alone is an "attention." To "take her out" costs money, and he cheerfully pays it. But he cannot do this too often, or he will become involved in what is naturally considered a "serious" affair; and every step of the acquaintance is watched and commented upon from a sexual point of view.

There is no natural, simple medium of social intercourse between men and women. The young man can but learn that his popularity depends largely on his pocket-book. The money that he might be saving for marriage is wasted on these miscellaneous preliminaries. As he sees what women like and how much it costs to please them, his hope of marriage recedes farther and farther. The period during which he must live as an individual grows longer; and he becomes accustomed to superficial acquaintance with many women, on the shallowest side of life, with no opportunity for genuine association and true friendship. What wonder that the other kind of woman, who also costs money, it is true, but who does not involve permanent obligation, has come to be so steady a factor in our social life? The sexuo-economic relation promotes vice in more ways than one.

The economic independence of woman will change all these conditions as naturally and inevitably as her dependence has introduced them. In her specialization in industry, she will develope more personality and less sexuality; and this will lower the pressure on this one relation in both women and men. And, in our social intercourse, the new character and new method of living will allow of broad and beautiful developments in human association. As the private home becomes a private home indeed, and no longer the woman's social and industrial horizon; as the workshops of the world—woman's sphere as well as man's—become homelike and beautiful under her influence; and as men and women move freely together in the exercise of common racial functions,—we shall have new channels for the flow of human life.

We shall not move from the isolated home to the sordid shop and back again, in a world torn and dissevered by the selfish production of one sex and the selfish consumption of the other; but we shall live in a world of men and women humanly related, as well as sexually related, working together, as they were meant to do, for the common good of all. The home will be no longer an economic entity, with its cumbrous industrial machinery huddled vulgarly behind it, but a peaceful and permanent expression of personal life as withdrawn from social contact; and that social contact will be provided for by the many common meeting-places necessitated by the organization of domestic industries.

The assembling-room is as deep a need of human life as the retiring-room,—not some ball-room or theatre, to which one must be invited of set purpose, but great common libraries and parlors, baths and gymnasia, work-rooms and play-rooms, to which both sexes have the same access for the same needs, and where they may mingle freely in common human expression. The kind of buildings essential to the carrying out of the organization of home industry will provide such places. There will be the separate rooms for individuals and the separate houses for families; but there will be, also, the common rooms for all. These must include a place for the children, planned and built for the happy occupancy of many children for many years,—a home such as no children have ever had. This, as well as rooms everywhere for young people and old people, in which they can be together as naturally as they can be alone, without effort, question, or remark.

Such an environment would allow of free association among us, on lines of common interest; and, in its natural, easy flow, we should develope far higher qualities than are brought out by the uneasy struggles of our present "society" to see each other without wanting to. It would make an enormous difference to woman's power of choosing the right man. Cut off from the purchasing power which is now his easiest way to compass his desires, freely seen and known in his daily work and amusements, a woman could know and judge a man as she is wholly unable to do now. Her personality developed by a free and useful life, clear-headed and open-eyed,—a woman still, but a personality as well as a woman,—the girl trained to economic independence, and associating freely with young men in their common work and play, would learn a new estimate of what constitutes noble manhood.

The young man, no longer able to cover all his shortcomings with a dress-coat, and to obtain absolution for every offence by the simple penance of paying for it, unable really to do much that was wrong for lack of the old opportunity and the old incentive, constantly helped and inspired by the friendly presence of honest and earnest womanhood, would have all the force of natural law to lift him up instead of pulling him heavily downward, as it does now.

With the pressure of our over-developed sex-instinct lifted off the world, born clean and strong, of noble-hearted, noble-minded, noble-bodied mothers, trained in the large wisdom of the new motherhood, and living freely in daily association with the best womanhood, a new kind of man can and will grow on earth. What this will mean to the race in power and peace and happiness no eye can foresee. But this much we can see:—that our once useful sexuo-economic relation is being outgrown, that it now produces many evil phenomena, and that its displacement by the economic freedom of woman will of itself set free new forces, to develope in us, by their natural working, the very virtues for which we have striven and agonized so long.

This change is not a thing to prophesy and plead for. It is a change already instituted, and gaining ground among us these many years with marvellous rapidity. Neither men nor women wish the change. Neither men nor women have sought it. But the same great force of social evolution which brought us into the old relation—to our great sorrow and pain—is bringing us out, with equal difficulty and distress. The time has come when it is better for the world that women be economically independent, and therefore they are becoming so.

It is worth while for us to consider the case fully and fairly, that we may see what it is that is happening to us, and welcome with open arms the happiest change in human condition that ever came into the world. To free an entire half of humanity from an artificial position; to release vast natural forces from a strained and clumsy combination, and set them free to work smoothly and easily as they were intended to work; to introduce conditions that will change humanity from within, making for better motherhood and fatherhood, better babyhood and childhood, better food, better homes, better society,—this is to work for human improvement along natural lines. It means enormous racial advance, and that with great swiftness; for this change does not wait to create new forces, but sets free those already potentially strong, so that humanity will fly up like a released spring. And it is already happening. All we need do is to understand and help.

XV.

As we learn to see how close is the connection of that which we call the soul with our external conditions, how the moral sense and the behavior of man are modified by the environment, we must of course look for marked results in psychic development arising from so important a condition as our sexuo-economic relation.

The relation of the sexes, in whatever form, has always been observed to affect strongly the moral nature of mankind; and this is one reason why we have placed such disproportionate stress upon the special virtues of that relation. The word "moral" in common use means "chaste"; and, in the case of women, the word "virtue" itself simply implies the one virtue of chastity. Large, popular conceptions are never baseless. They are rooted in deep truths, felt rather than seen, and, however false and silly in external interpretation, may be trusted in their general trend. It is not that the virtue of chastity is so much more important to the race than the virtue of honesty, the virtue of courage, the virtues of cheerfulness, of courtesy, of kindness, but that upon the sex-relation in which we live depends so much of the further development and arrangement of our whole moral nature.

What we call the moral sense is an intellectual recognition of the relative importance of certain acts and their consequences. This appears vaguely and weakly among early savages, and was for long mainly applied to a few clearly defined and arbitrary rites and ceremonies, set rules in a game of priest-and-people. But the habit of associating a sense of worthiness with certain acts by which came praise and profit grew in the childish soul, and the range of moral deeds widened. It has been widening ever since, growing deeper and higher and far more subtle, developing with the other social qualities.

No human distinction is more absolutely and exclusively social than the moral sense. Ethics is a social science. There is no ethics for the individual. Taken by himself, man is but an animal; and his conduct bears relation only to the needs of the animal,—self-preservation and race-preservation. Every virtue, and the power to see and strive for it, is a social quality. The highest virtues are those wherein we best serve the most people, and their development in us keeps pace with the development of society. It is the social relation which calls for our virtues, and which maintains them.

A simple instance of this is in the prompt lapse to barbarism of a man cut off from his kind, and forced to live in conditions of savagery. Even a brief and partial change in condition changes conduct at once, as is shown by the behavior of the most pious New Englanders when in mining camps. It is shown, also, by the different scale of virtue in the different classes and industries.

Every social relation has its ethics; and the general needs of society, as a whole, are the basis of ethics. In every age and race this may be studied, and a clear connection established always between the virtues and vices of a given people and their local conditions. The principal governing condition in the development of ethics is the economic environment. This may seem strange to one accustomed to consider moral laws as not of this world, and to see how often virtue costs its possessor dear. The relative behavior of a given number of people depends, first, upon the existence of those people. Such conduct as should tend to exterminate them would exterminate their ethics. Such conduct as should tend to preserve and increase them is the only conduct of which ethical value can be predicated. Ethics is, therefore, absolutely conditioned upon life and the maintenance thereof. From the lowest and narrowest view which calls an act right or wrong, according to its immediate effects upon one's present life, to the clear vision of ultimate results which calls a course of conduct right or wrong, according to its final effects upon one's eternal life, our ethics, small and great, is the science of human conduct measured by its results.

It is inevitable, then, that in all races we should find those acts whereby men live considered right, and should see a high degree of approval awarded to him who best performs them. In the hunting and fighting period the best hunter and fighter was the best man, praised and honored by his tribe. The virtues cultivated were such as enabled the possessor to hunt and kill most successfully, to maintain himself and be a credit and a help to his friends. Savage virtues are the simple reflection of savage conditions. To be patient and self-controlled was an economic necessity to the hunter: to bear pain and arduous exertion easily was a necessity to the fighter. Therefore, the savage, by precept and example, cultivated these virtues.

In the long agricultural and military periods we see the same thing. In the peasant the virtues of industry and patience were extolled: it takes industry and patience to raise corn. In the soldier the virtues of courage and obedience were extolled, and in every one the virtue of faith was the prime requisite of the existing religion. It took a great deal of faith to accept the religions of those times. The importance of faith as a virtue declines as religion grows more intelligible and applicable to life. It requires no effort to believe what you can understand and do. Slowly the industrial era dawned and grew, from the weak, sporadic efforts of the cringing packman[1] and craftsman, the common prey of the dominant fighting class, to our colossal industrial organization, in

---

1 A pedlar; a traveller who sells their wares.

which the soldier is ruthlessly exploited to some financial interests. With this change in economic conditions has changed the scale of virtues.

Physical courage has sunk: obedience, patience, faith, and the rest do not stand as they did. We praise and value to-day, as always, the virtues whereby we live. Every animal developes the virtues of his conditions: our human distinction is that we add the power of conscious perception and personal volition to the action of natural force. Not only in our own race, but in others, do we call "good" and "bad" those qualities which profit us; and the beasts that we train and use develope, of necessity, the qualities that profit them,—as, for instance, in our well-known friend, the dog.

The dog is an animal long since cut off from his natural means of support, and depending absolutely on man for food. As a free, wild dog, he was profited by a daring initiative, courage, ferocity. As a tame, slave dog, he is profited by abject submission, by a crawling will-lessness that grovels at a blow, and licks the foot that kicks it. We have quite made over the original dog; and his moral nature, his spirit, shows the change even more than his body. The force which has accomplished this is economic,—a change of base in the source of supplies and the processes of obtaining them.

Let us briefly examine the distinctive virtues of humanity, their order of introduction and development, and see how this one peculiar relation has affected them.

The main distinction of human virtue is in what we roughly describe as altruism,—"otherness." To love and serve one another, to care for one another, to feel for and with one another,—our racial adjective, "humane," implies these qualities. The very existence of humanity implies these qualities in some degree, and the development of humanity is commensurate with their development.

Our one great blunder in studying these things lies in our failure to appreciate the organic necessity of such moral qualities in human life. We have assumed that the practice of these social virtues involved a personal effort and sacrifice, and that there is an irreconcilable contest between the cosmic process of development and the ethical process, as Huxley[1] puts it. Social evolution brings with it the essential qualities of social relation, and these are our much boasted virtues. The natural processes of human

---

1 English naturalist and biologist Thomas Henry Huxley (1825–95).

intercourse and interrelation develope the qualities without which such intercourse would be impossible; and this development is as orderly, as natural, as "cosmic," as the processes of organic activity within the individual body. It is as natural for an industrial society to live in peace as for a hunting society to live in war; and this peace is not the result of heroic and self-sacrificing effort on the part of the industrial society; it is the necessity of their condition.

The course of evolution in human ethics is marked by a gradual extension of our perception of common good and evil as distinct from our initial perception of individual good and evil. This becomes very keen in the more socialized natures among us, as in the far-seeing devotion of statesmanship, patriotism, and philanthropy. Each of these words shows in its construction that the quality described is social,—the statesman, one who thinks and works for the State; the patriot, one who loves and labors for his country; the philanthropist, one who loves mankind. All these qualities, in their extreme and in their first beginnings, are a mere recognition of the equal right of the next man, common "fair play" and courtesy; they are but the natural product of social conditions acting on the individual through primal laws of economic necessity. The individual, in the absolute economic isolation of the beast, is profited by pure egoism, and he developes it. The individual, in the increasing economic interdependence of social relation, is profited by altruism; and he developes it.

All our virtues can be so traced and accounted for. The great main stem of them all, what we call "love," is merely the first condition of social existence. It is cohesion, working among us as the constituent particles of society. Without some attraction to hold us together, we should not be able to hold together; and this attraction, as perceived by our consciousness, we call love. The virtue of obedience consists in the surrender of the individual will, so often necessary to the common good; and it stands highest in military organization, wherein great numbers of men must act together against their personal interests, even to the sacrifice of life, in the service of the community.

As we have grown into fuller social life, we have slowly and experimentally, painfully and expensively, discovered what kind of man was the best social factor. The type of a satisfactory member of society to-day is a man self-controlled, kind, gentle, strong, wise, brave, courteous, cheerful, true. In the Middle Ages, strong, brave, and true would have satisfied the demands of the time. We now require for our common good a larger range of qualities, a more elaborate moral organization. All this is a simple, evolutionary process of social life, and should have involved no more confusion, effort, and pain than any other natural process.

But the moral development of humanity is a most tempestuous and contradictory field of study. Some virtues we have developed in orderly fashion, hardly recognizing that they were virtues, because they came so easily into use. Accuracy and punctuality are qualities which were unknown to the savage, because they were not needed in his business. They have been developed in us, because they were required, and so have been gradually assumed under pressure of economic necessity. Obedience, even in its extreme form of self-sacrifice, has been produced in the soldier; and no quality is more altruistic, more unnatural, or more difficult of adoption by the sturdy individual will. The common, law-abiding citizen does not consider himself a hero; yet he is manifesting a high degree of social virtue, often at great personal sacrifice.

But in other virtues we have not progressed so smoothly. In the ordinary economic relations of life, and in our sex-relations, we are distinguished by peculiar and injurious qualities. Our condition may be described as consisting of a tenacious survival of qualities which we ought, on every ground of social good, to have long since outgrown; and an incessant struggle between these rudimentary survivals and the normal growth. This it is which has so forcibly assailed our consciousness since its awakening, and which we call the contest between good and evil. We have felt within ourselves the pull of diverse tendencies,—the impulse to do what was immediately good for ourselves, but which our growing social sense knew was bad for the community, and therefore wrong; and the impulse to do what might be immediately bad for ourselves, but which the same social sense knew was good for the community, and therefore right. This we felt, and cast about in our minds for an explanation of the way we behaved: we knew it was peculiar. The human brain is an organ that must have an explanation, if it has to make one. We made one.

The belated impulses of the individual beast—good in him because he needed them, bad in us because we were becoming human and had other needs—we lumped together, and, with our facile, dramatic, personifying tendency, called them "the devil." And, as these evil promptings were usually along the lines of physical impulse, we considered our own bodies, and nature in general, as part and parcel of the wrong,—"the world, the flesh, and the devil."[1] We felt, also, within us the mighty stirrings of new powers and strange tendencies, that led us out of ourselves and toward each other, new loves and hopes and wishes, new desires to give instead of to take, to serve instead of to fight; and, realizing, with true social instinct, that this impulse tended to help us most, was really good for us, we called it the will of God, the voice of God, the way to God. The tearing contest between these ill-adjusted impulses and tendencies, with our growing power of self-conscious decision and voluntary adoption of one or another course of action,—this process in psychic evolution has given us the greatest world-drama ever conceived, the struggle between good and evil.

And, fumbling vaguely at the sources of our pain so far as we could trace them, judging always by persons, and not by conditions,—as a child strikes the chair he bumps his head upon,—race after race has located the cause of the trouble in woman. Not that she primarily invented all the evil, and brought it upon us,—our vague devil was the remoter cause,—but that woman let the trouble in. Pandora did not make the mischief-box; but she perversely opened it, even against the wise man's advice. Eve did not plant that apple-tree; but she ate of it, and tempted the superior man. It seems a childish and clumsy guess, but there is something in it. Nothing of the unspeakable blame and shame with which man has blackened the face of his mother through all these centuries, but a sociological truth for all that.

Not woman, but the condition of woman, has always been a doorway of evil. The sexuo-economic relation has debarred her from the social activities in which, and in which alone, are developed the social virtues. She was not allowed to acquire the qualities needed in our racial advance; and, in her position of arrested development, she has maintained the virtues and the vices of the period of human evolution at which she was imprisoned. At a period of isolated economic activity,—mere animal individualism,—at a period when social ties ceased with the ties of blood, woman was cut off from personal activity in social economics, and confined to the functional activities of her sex.

In keeping her on this primitive basis of economic life, we have kept half humanity tied to the starting-post, while the other half ran. We have trained and bred one kind of qualities into one-half the species, and another kind into the other half. And then we

---

1 In Christian theology, the world, the flesh, and the devil are considered anathema to maintaining faith in God.

wonder at the contradictions of human nature! For instance, we have done all we could, in addition to natural forces, to make men brave. We have done all we could, in addition to natural forces, to make women cowards. And, since every human creature is born of two parents, it is not surprising that we are a little mixed.

We have trained in men the large qualities of social usefulness which the pressure of their economic conditions was also developing; and we have done this by means of conscious praise and blame, reward and punishment, and with the aid of law and custom. We have trained in women, by the same means, the small qualities of personal usefulness which the pressure of their economic conditions was also developing. We have made a creature who is not homogeneous, whose life is fed by two currents of inheritance as dissimilar and opposed as could be well imagined. We have bred a race of psychic hybrids, and the moral qualities of hybrids are well known.

Away back in that early beginning, by dividing the economic conditions of women and men, we have divided their psychic development, and built into the constitution of the race the irreconcilable elements of these diverse characters. The incongruous behavior of this cross-bred product is the riddle of human life. We ourselves, by maintaining this artificial diversity between the sexes, have constantly kept before us the enigma which we found so hard to solve, and have preserved in our own characters the confusion and contradiction which is our greatest difficulty in life.

The largest and most radical effect of restoring women to economic independence will be in its result in clarifying and harmonizing the human soul. With a homogeneous nature bred of two parents in the same degree of social development, we shall be able to feel simply, to see clearly, to agree with ourselves, to be one person and master of our own lives, instead of wrestling in such hopeless perplexity with what we have called "man's dual nature." Marry a civilized man to a primitive savage, and their child will naturally have a dual nature. Marry an Anglo-Saxon to an African or Oriental, and their child has a dual nature. Marry any man of a highly developed nation, full of the specialized activities of his race and their accompanying moral qualities, to the carefully preserved, rudimentary female creature he has so religiously maintained by his side, and you have as result what we all know so well,—the human soul in its pitiful, well-meaning efforts, its cross-eyed, purblind errors, its baby fits of passion, and its beautiful and ceaseless upward impulse through all this wavering.

We are quite familiar with this result, but we have not so far accurately located the cause. We have had our glimmering perception that woman had something to do with it; and she has been treated accordingly, by many simple races, to her further injury, and to that of the whole people. What we need to see is that it is not woman as a sex who is responsible for this mismothered world, but the economic position of woman which makes her what she is. If men were so placed, it would have the same effect. Not the sex-relation, but the economic relation of the sexes, has so tangled the skein of human life.

Besides the essential evils of an unbalanced nature, many harmful qualities have been developed in human characters by these conditions. For countless centuries we have sought to develope, by selection and education, a timid submission in woman. When there did appear "a curst shrew," she was left unmarried; and her temper perished with her, or she was "tamed" by some Petruchio.[1] The dependence of women on the personal favor of men has produced an exceeding cleverness in the adaptation of the dependent one to the source of her supplies. Under the necessity of pleasing, whether she wished or no, of interceding for a child's pardon or of suing for new pleasures for herself, "the vices of the slave" have been forever maintained in this housemaid of the world.

Another discord introduced by the condition of servitude is that between will and action. A servant places his time and strength at the disposal of another will. He must hold himself in readiness to do what he is told; and the mere physical law of conservation of energy, to say nothing of his own conscious judgment, forbids wasting nerve-force in planning and undertaking what he may not be able to accomplish. This produces a condition of inactivity, save under compulsion, and, on the other side, a perverse, capricious wilfulness in little things,—the reaction from a forced submission.

A more insidious, disintegrating force to offset the evolution of human character could hardly be imagined than this steady training of the habits of servitude into half the human race,—the mother of all of it. These results have been modified, of course, by the different education and environment of men, developing in them opposite qualities, and transmitting the contradictory traits to the children indiscriminately.

---

1 Character in Shakespeare, *The Taming of the Shrew*.

Heredity has no Salic law. The boy inherits from his mother, as well as from his father; the girl from her father, as well as from her mother. This has prevented the full evil of the results that might have ensued, but has also added to the personal difficulties of each of us, and retarded the general progress of the race.

Worse than the check set upon the physical activities of women has been the restriction of their power to think and judge for themselves. The extended use of the human will and its decisions is conditioned upon free, voluntary action. In her rudimentary position, woman was denied the physical freedom which underlies all knowledge, she was denied the mental freedom which is the path to further wisdom, she was denied the moral freedom of being mistress of her own action and of learning by the merciful law of consequences what was right and what was wrong; and she has remained, perforce, undeveloped in the larger judgment of ethics.

Her moral sense is large enough, morbidly large, because in this tutelage she is always being praised or blamed for her conduct. She lives in a forcing-bed of sensitiveness to moral distinctions, but the broad judgment that alone can guide and govern this sensitiveness she has not. Her contribution to moral progress has added to the anguish of the world the fierce sense of sin and shame, the desperate desire to do right, the fear of wrong; without giving it the essential help of a practical wisdom and a regulated will. Inheriting with each generation the accumulating forces of our social nature, set back in each generation by the conditions of the primitive human female, women have become vividly self conscious centres of moral impulse, but poor guides as to the conduct which alone can make that impulse useful and build the habit of morality into the constitution of the race.

Recognizing her intense feeling on moral lines, and seeing in her the rigidly preserved virtues of faith, submission, and self-sacrifice,—qualities which in the Dark Ages were held to be the first of virtues,—we have agreed of late years to call woman the moral superior of man. But the ceaseless growth of human life, social life, has developed in him new virtues, later, higher, more needful; and the moral nature of woman, as maintained in this rudimentary stage by her economic dependence, is a continual check to the progress of the human soul. The main feature of her life—the restriction of her range of duty to the love and service of her own immediate family—acts upon us continually as a retarding influence, hindering the expansion of the spirit of social love and service on which our very lives depend. It keeps the moral standard of the patriarchal era still before us, and blinds our eyes to the full duty of man.

An intense self-consciousness, born of the ceaseless contact of close personal relation; an inordinate self-interest, bred by the constant personal attention and service of this relation; a feverish, torturing, moral sensitiveness, without the width and clarity of vision of a full-grown moral sense; a thwarted will, used to meek surrender, cunning evasion, or futile rebellion; a childish, wavering, short-range judgment, handicapped by emotion; a measureless devotion to one's own sex relatives, and a maternal passion swollen with the full strength of the great social heart, but denied social expression,—such psychic qualities as these, born in us all, are the inevitable result of the sexuo-economic relation.

It is not alone upon woman, and, through her, upon the race, that the ill-effects may be observed. Man, as master, has suffered from his position also. The lust for power and conquest, natural to the male of any species, has been fostered in him to an enormous degree by this cheap and easy lordship. His dominance is not that of one chosen as best fitted to rule or of one ruling by successful competition with "foemen worthy of his steel";[1] but it is a sovereignty based on the accident of sex, and holding over such helpless and inferior dependants as could not question or oppose. The easy superiority that needs no striving to maintain it; the temptation to cruelty always begotten by irresponsible power; the pride and self-will which surely accompany it,—these qualities have been bred into the souls of men by their side of the relation. When man's place was maintained by brute force, it made him more brutal: when his place was maintained by purchase, by the power of economic necessity, then he grew into the merciless use of such power as distinguishes him to-day.

Another giant evil engendered by this relation is what we call selfishness. Social life tends to reduce this feeling, which is but a belated individualism; but the sexuo-economic relation fosters and developes it. To have a whole human creature consecrated to his direct personal service, to pleasing and satisfying him in every way possible,—this has kept man selfish beyond the degree incidental to our stage of social growth. Even in our artificial society life men are more forbearing and considerate, more polite and kind, than they are at home. Pride, cruelty, and selfishness are the vices of the master; and these have been kept strong in the bosom

---

1 A worthy enemy: paraphrase of Sir Walter Scott, *The Lady of the Lake* (1810) 5.10.12.

of the family through the false position of woman. And every human soul is born, an impressionable child, into the close presence of these conditions. Our men must live in the ethics of a civilized, free, industrial, democratic age; but they are born and trained in the moral atmosphere of a primitive patriarchate. No wonder that we are all somewhat slow to rise to the full powers and privileges of democracy, to feel full social honor and social duty, while every soul of us is reared in this stronghold of ancient and outgrown emotions,—the economically related family.

So we may trace from the sexuo-economic relation of our species not only definite evils in psychic development, bred severally in men and women, and transmitted indifferently to their offspring, but the innate perversion of character resultant from the moral miscegenation of two so diverse souls,—the unfailing shadow and distortion which has darkened and twisted the spirit of man from its beginnings. We have been injured in body and in mind by the too dissimilar traits inherited from our widely separated parents, but nowhere is the injury more apparent than in its ill effects upon the moral nature of the race.

Yet here, as in the other evil results of the sexuo-economic relation, we can see the accompanying good that made the condition necessary in its time; and we can follow the beautiful results of our present changes with comforting assurance. A healthy, normal moral sense will be ours, freed from its exaggerations and contradictions; and, with that clear perception, we shall no longer conceive of the ethical process as something outside of and against nature, but as the most natural thing in the world.

Where now we strive and agonize after impossible virtues, we shall then grow naturally and easily into those very qualities; and we shall not even think of them as especially commendable. Where our progress hitherto has been warped and hindered by the retarding influence of surviving rudimentary forces, it will flow on smoothly and rapidly when both men and women stand equal in economic relation. When the mother of the race is free, we shall have a better world, by the easy right of birth and by the calm, slow, friendly forces of social evolution.

SELECTED POEMS FROM
IN THIS OUR WORLD AND OTHER POEMS

The Rock and the Sea

THE ROCK.

I am the Rock, presumptuous Sea!
I am set to encounter thee.
Angry and loud, or gentle and still,
I am set here to limit thy power, and I will—
      I am the Rock!

I am the Rock. From age to age
I scorn thy fury and dare thy rage.
Scarred by frost and worn by time,
Brown with weed and green with slime,
Thou may'st drench and defile me and spit in my face,
But while I am here thou keep'st thy place!
      I am the Rock!

I am the Rock, beguiling Sea
I know thou art fair as fair can be,
With golden glitter and silver sheen
And bosom of blue and garments of green.
Thou may'st pat my cheek with baby hands,
And lap my feet in diamond sands,
And play before me as children play;
But plead as thou wilt, I bar the way!
      I am the Rock !

I am the Rock. Black midnight falls;
The terrible breakers rise like walls;
With curling lips and gleaming teeth
They plunge and tear at my bones beneath.
Year upon year they grind and beat
In storms of thunder and storms of sleet—
Grind and beat and wrestle and tear,
But the rock they beat on is always there!
      I am the Rock !

THE SEA.

I am the Sea. I hold the land
As one holds an apple in his hand.
Hold it fast with sleepless eyes,
Watching the continents sink and rise.
Out of my bosom the mountains grow,
Back to its depths they crumble slow;
The earth is a helpless child to me—
    I am the Sea!

I am the Sea. When I draw back
Blossom and verdure follow my track,
And the land I leave grows proud and fair,
For the wonderful race of man is there;
And the winds of heaven wail and cry
While the nations rise and reign and die—
Living and dying in folly and pain,
While the laws of the universe thunder in vain.
What is the folly of man to me?
    I am the Sea!

I am the Sea. The earth I sway;
Granite to me is *potter's* clay;
Under the touch of my careless waves
It rises in turrets and sinks in caves;
The iron cliffs that edge the land
I grind to pebbles and sift to sand,
And beach-grass bloweth and children play
In what were the rocks of yesterday;
It is but a moment of sport to me—
    I am the Sea!

I am the Sea. In my bosom deep
Wealth and Wonder and Beauty sleep;
Wealth and Wonder and Beauty rise
In changing splendor of sunset skies
And comfort the earth with rains and snows
Till waves the harvest and laughs the rose.
Flower and forest and child of breath
With me have life—without me, death.
What if the ships go down in me—?
    I am the Sea!

Heaven

Thou bright mirage, that o'er man's arduous way
    Hast hung in the hot sky, with fountains streaming,
    Cool marble domes, and palm-fronds waving, gleaming—
Vision of rest and peace to end the day!
Now he is weariest, alone, astray,
    Spent with long labor, led by thy sweet seeming—
    Faint as the breath of Nature's lightest dreaming,
Thou waverest and vanishest away!

Can Nature dream? Is God's great sky deceiving?
    Where joy like that the clouds above us show
    Be sure the counterpart must lie below,
Sweeter than hope—more blessed than believing!
    We lose the fair reflection of our home
    Because so near its gates our feet have come!

Where Memory Sleeps

RONDEAU.

Where memory sleeps the soul doth rise,
Free of that past where sorrow lies,
    And storeth against future ills
    The courage of the constant hills,
The comfort of the quiet skies.

Fair is this land to tired eyes,
Where summer sunlight never dies,
    And summer's peace the spirit fills,
        Where memory sleeps.

Safe from the season's changing cries
And chill of yearly sacrifice,
    Great roses crowd the window sills—
    Calm roses that no winter kills.
The peaceful heart all pain denies,
        Where memory sleeps.

What Then?

Suppose you write your heart out till the world
    Sobs with one voice—what then?
Small agonies that round your heart-strings curled
    Strung out for choice, that men
May pick a phrase, each for his own pet pain,
    And thank the voice so come,
    They being dumb. What then?

You have no sympathy? O endless claim!
    No one that cares? What then?
Suppose you had the whole world knew your
      name
    And your affairs, and men
Ached with your headache, dreamed your dreadful
      dreams,
    And, with your heart-break due,
    Their hearts broke too. What then?

You think that people do not understand?
    You suffer? Die? What then?
Unhappy child, look here, on either hand,
    Look low or high—all men
Suffer and die, and keep it to themselves!
    They die—they suffer sore—
      You suffer more? What then?

Baby Love

Baby Love came prancing by,
Cap on head and sword on thigh,
Horse to ride and drum to beat—
All the world beneath his feet.

Mother Life was sitting there,
Hard at work and full of care,
Set of mouth and sad of eye—
Baby Love came prancing by.

Baby Love was very proud,
Very lively, very loud—

Mother Life arose in wrath,
Set an arm across his path.

Baby Love wept loud and long,
But his mother's arm was strong.
Mother had to work, she said.
Baby Love was put to bed.

For Us

If we have not learned that God's in man,
        And man in God again
That to love thy God is to love thy brother,
And to serve the Lord is to serve each other—
        Then Christ was born in vain!

If we have not learned that one man's life
        In all men lives again—
That each man's battle, fought alone,
Is won or lost for every one—
        Then Christ hath lived in vain!

If we have not learned that death's no break
        In life's unceasing chain—
That the work in one life well begun
In others is finished, by others is done—
        Then Christ hath died in vain!

If we have not learned of immortal life,
        And a future free from pain
The kingdom of God in the heart of man,
And the living world on Heaven's plan—
        Then Christ arose in vain!

"We, as Women"

There's a cry in the air about us—
We hear it before—behind—
Of the way in which "We, as women,"
Are going to lift mankind!

With our white frocks starched and ruffled,
And our soft hair brushed and curled—
Hats off! for "we, as women,"
Are coming to help the world!

Fair sisters, listen one moment—
And perhaps you'll pause for ten—
The business of women as women
Is only with men as men!

What we do, "we, as women,"
We have done all through our life;
The work that is ours as women
Is the work of mother and wife!

But to elevate public opinion,
And to lift up erring man,
Is the work of the Human Being—
Let us do it—if we can.

But wait, warm-hearted sisters—
Not quite so fast, so far—
Tell me how we are going to lift a thing
Any higher than we are!

We are going to "purify politics,"
And to "elevate the press."
We enter the foul paths of the world
To sweeten and cleanse and bless.

To hear the high things we are going to do,
And the horrors of man we tell,
One would think "we, as women," were angels
And our brothers were fiends of hell.

We, that were born of one mother,
And reared in the selfsame place—
In the school and the church together—
We, of one blood, one race!

Now then, all forward together!
But remember, every one,

That it is not by feminine innocence
The work of the world is done.

The world needs strength and courage,
And wisdom to help and feed—
When "we, as women," bring these to man
We shall lift the world indeed!

To the Young Wife

Are you content, you pretty three-years' wife?
    Are you content and satisfied to live
      On what your loving husband loves to give,
        And give to him your life?

Are you content with work—to toil alone,
    To clean things dirty and to soil things clean,
    To be a kitchen-maid—be called a queen—
        Queen of a cook-stove throne?

Are you content to reign in that small space—
    A wooden palace and a yard-fenced land—
    With other queens abundant on each hand,
        Each fastened in her place?

Are you content to rear your children so?
    Untaught yourself, untrained, perplexed, distressed,
    Are you so sure your way is always best?
        That you can always know ?

Have you forgotten how you used to long
    In days of ardent girlhood, to be great,
    To help the groaning world, to serve the state,
        To be so wise so strong?

And are you quite convinced this is the way,
    The only way a woman's duty lies—
    Knowing all women so have shut their eyes?
        Seeing the world to-day?

Have you no dream of life in fuller store?
    Of growing to be more than that you are?
    Doing the things you now do better far,
        Yet doing others—more?

Losing no love, but finding as you grew
    That as you entered upon nobler life
    You so became a richer sweeter wife,
        A wiser mother too?

What holds you? Ah, my dear, it is your throne,
    Your paltry queenship in that narrow place,
    Your antique labors, your restricted space,
        Your working all alone!

Be not deceived! 'Tis not your wifely bond
    That holds you, nor the mother's royal power,
    But selfish slavish service hour by hour—
        A life with no beyond!

Mother to Child

How best can I serve thee, my child! My child!
Flesh of my flesh and dear heart of my heart!
Once thou wast within me—I held thee—I fed
    thee—
 By the force of my loving and longing I led thee—
        Now we are apart!

I may blind thee with kisses and crush with em-
        bracing,
Thy warm mouth in my neck and our arms inter-
        lacing,
But here in my body my soul lives alone,
And thou answerest me from a house of thine own—
        That house which I builded!

Which we builded together, thy father and I—
In which thou must live, my darling, and die!
Not one stone can I alter, not one atom relay—
Not to save or defend thee or help thee to stay—
        That gift is completed!

How best can I serve thee? child, if they knew
How my heart aches with loving! How deep and
    how true,
How brave and enduring, how patient, how strong,
How longing for good and how fearful of wrong,
        Is the love of thy mother!

Could I crown thee with riches! Surround, over-
    flow thee
With fame and with power till the whole world
    should know thee;
With wisdom and genius to hold the world still,
To bring laughter and tears, joy and pain, at thy will,
        Still—*thou* mightst not be happy!

Such have lived—and in sorrow. The greater the
    mind
The wider and deeper the grief it can find.
The richer, the gladder, the more thou canst feel
The keen stings that a lifetime is sure to reveal.
        O my child! Must thou suffer?

Is there no way my life can save thine from a pain?
Is the love of a mother no possible gain?
No labor of Hercules—search for the Grail—
No way for this wonderful love to avail?
        God in Heaven—O teach me!

My prayer has been answered. The pain thou must
    bear
Is the pain of the world's life which thy life must
    share.
Thou art one with the world—though I love thee
    the best;
And to save thee from pain I must save all the rest—
        Well—with God's help I'll do it!

Thou art one with the rest. I must love thee in them.
Thou wilt sin with the rest—and thy mother must
    stem
The world's sin. Thou wilt weep—and thy mother
    must dry
The tears of the world lest her darling should cry!
        I will do it God helping!

And I stand not alone. I will gather a band
Of all loving mothers from land unto land.
Our children are part of the world! do ye hear?
They are one with the world we must hold them
    all dear!
           Love all for the child's sake!

For the sake of my child I must hasten to save
All the children on earth from the jail and the grave.
For so, and so only, I lighten the share
Of the pain of the world that my darling must bear—
        Even so, and so only!

The Survival of the Fittest[1]

In northern zones the ranging bear
Protects himself with fat and hair.
Where snow is deep, and ice is stark,
And half the year is cold and dark,
He still survives a clime like that
By growing fur, by growing fat.
These traits, Bear, which thou transmittest,
Prove the survival of the fittest!

To polar regions, waste and wan,
Comes the encroaching race of man;
A puny feeble little lubber
He had no fur, he had no blubber.
The scornful bear sat down at ease
To see the stranger starve and freeze;
But lo! the stranger slew the bear,
And ate his fat, and wore his hair!
These deeds, Man, which thou committest,
Prove the survival of the fittest!

In modern times the millionaire
Protects himself as did the bear.
Where Poverty and Hunger are,
He counts his bullion by the car.

---

[1] A phrase coined by Spencer in his book *Principles of Biology* (1864) and later used by Darwin.

Where thousands suffer, still he thrives,
And after death his will survives.
The wealth, Croesus,[1] thou transmittest
Proves the survival of the fittest!

But lo! some people, odd and funny,
Some men without a cent of money,
The simple common Human Race,
Chose to improve their dwelling-place.
They had no use for millionaires;
They calmly said the world was theirs;
They were so wise—so strong—so many—
The millionaire? There wasn't any!
These deeds, O Man, which thou committest,
Prove the survival of the fittest!

An Obstacle

I was climbing up a mountain-path
    With many things to do,
Important business of my own,
    And other people's too,
When I ran against a Prejudice
    That quite cut off the view.

My work was such as could not wait,
    My path quite clearly showed,
My strength and time were limited,
    I carried quite a load,
And there that hulking Prejudice
    Sat all across the road.

So I spoke to him politely,
    For he was huge and high,
And begged that he would move a bit
    And let me travel by—
He smiled, but as for moving!—
    He didn't even try.

---

1 Croesus (died c. 546 BCE) was the last king of Lydia and noted for his extravagant wealth.

And then I reasoned quietly
    With that colossal mule;
My time was short—no other path—
    The mountain winds were cool—
I argued like a Solomon,[1]
    He sat there like a fool.

Then I flew into a passion,
    I danced and howled and swore,
I pelted and belabored him
    Till I was stiff and sore;
He got as mad as I did—
    But he sat there as before.

And then I begged him on my knees—
    I might be kneeling still
If so I hoped to move that mass
    Of obdurate ill-will—
As well invite the monument
    To vacate Bunker Hill![2]

So I sat before him helpless,
    In an ecstasy of woe—
The mountain mists were rising fast,
    The sun was sinking slow—
When a sudden inspiration came,
    As sudden winds do blow.

I took my hat, I took my stick,
    My load I settled fair,
I approached that awful incubus
    With an absent-minded air—
And I walked directly through him,
    As if he wasn't there!

---

1 King Solomon of Israel was noted for his wisdom.
2 A monument erected in Boston, Massachusetts, in commemoration of the American Revolutionary War battle at Bunker Hill.

The Cart before the Horse

Our business system has its base
On one small thought that's out of place;
    The merest trifle nothing much, of course—
The truth is there who says it's not?—
Only—the trouble is—you've got
        The cart before the horse!

You say unless a man shall work
Right earnestly, and never shirk,
    He may not eat. Now look—the change is small,
And yet the truth is plain to see—
Unless man eats, and frequently,
        He cannot work at all!

And which comes first? Why that is plain,
The man comes first. And, look again—
    A baby! with an appetite to fit!
You have to feed him years and years,
And train him up with toil and tears,
        Before he works a bit!

So let us change our old ideas,
And learn with these advancing years
    To give the oats before we ask for speed;
Not set the hungry horse to run,
And tell him when the race is done
        That he shall have his feed!

"The Poor Ye Have Always with You"[1]

The poor ye have always with you, therefore why
    Seek to improve a lot ordained of God—
        Dare to rebel beneath his chastening rod—
           Question the law on high?

The poor ye have always with you—plain to see
    Is this thing so far stated by our Lord—

---

[1] John 12.8: For the poor always ye have with you; but me ye have not always.

Proved by the fact and also by his Word,
    So it must surely be!

Yet wait—"have always"—is the present tense—
    He said they had them always, and they had;
    Must we therefore believe a thing so bad
        Shall always crush us with its weight immense?

"You always have the headache!" I complain—
    'Tis not prediction that you always will,
    Nor yet a lasting curse to say, worse still,
        That you must always bear that pain.

The poor we have had with us in full store
    From senseless age to age. Let man to-day
    Rise up and put this human shame away—
        Let us have poor no more!

Waste

Doth any man consider what we waste?
Here in God's garden? While the sea is full,
The sunlight smiles, and all the blessed earth
Offers her wealth to our intelligence.
We waste our food, enough for half the world,
In helpless luxury among the rich,
In helpless ignorance among the poor,
In spilling what we stop to quarrel for.
We waste our wealth in failing to produce,
In robbing of each other every day
In place of making things—our human crown.
We waste our strength, in endless effort poured
Like water on the sand, still toiling on
To make a million things we do not want.
We waste our lives, those which should still lead on,
Each new one gaining on the age behind,
In doing what we all have done before.
We waste our love—poured up into the sky,
Across the ocean, into desert lands,
Sunk in one narrow circle next ourselves—
While these, our brothers, suffer—are alone.
Ye may not pass the near to love the far;

Ye may not love the near and stop at that;
Love spreads through man, not over or around!
Yea, grievously we waste, and all the time
Humanity is wanting—wanting sore.
Waste not my brothers, and ye shall not want!

Nationalism

The nation is a unit. That which makes
You an American of our to-day
Requires the nation and its history,
Requires the sum of all our citizens,
Requires the product of our common toil,
Requires the freedom of our common laws,
The common heart of our humanity.
Decrease our population, check our growth,
Deprive us of our wealth, our liberty,
Lower the nation's conscience by a hair,
And you are less than that you were before!
You stand here in the world the man you are
Because your country is America.
Our liberty belongs to each of us;
The nation guarantees it; in return
We serve the nation, serving so ourselves.
Our education is a common right;
The state provides it, equally to all,
Each taking what he can, and in return
We serve the state, so serving best ourselves.
Food, clothing, all necessities of life—
These are a right as much as liberty!
The nation feeds its children. In return
We serve the nation, serving still ourselves—
Nay, not ourselves—ourself! We are but parts,
The unit is the state—America.

SELECTIONS FROM *SUFFRAGE SONGS AND VERSES*

The Socialist and the Suffragist

Said the Socialist to the Suffragist:
   "My cause is greater than yours!
      You only work for a Special Class,
      We work for the gain of the General Mass,
   Which every good ensures!"

Said the Suffragist to the Socialist:
   "You underrate my Cause!
      While women remain a Subject Class,
      You never can move the General Mass,
   With your Economic Laws!"

Said the Socialist to the Suffragist:
   "You misinterpret facts!
      There is no room for doubt or schism
      In Economic Determinism—
   It governs all our acts!"

Said the Suffragist to the Socialist:
   "You men will always find
      That this old world will never move
      More swiftly in its ancient groove
   While women stay behind!"

"A lifted world lifts women up,"
   The Socialist explained.
      "You cannot lift the world at all
      While half of it is kept so small,"
   The Suffragist maintained.

The world awoke, and tartly spoke:
   "Your work is all the same:
      Work together or work apart,
      Work, each of you, with all your heart—
   Just get into the game!"

The Malingerer

Exempt! She "does not have to work!"
    So might one talk
Defending long, bedridden ease,
Weak yielding ankles, flaccid knees,
    With "I don't have to walk!"

Not have to work. Why not? Who gave
    Free pass to you?
You're housed and fed and taught and dressed
By age-long labor of the rest—
    Work other people do!

What do you give in honest pay
    For clothes and food?—
Then as a shield, defence, excuse,
She offers her exclusive use—
    Her function–Motherhood!

Is motherhood a trade you make
    A living by?
And does the wealth you so may use,
Squander, accumulate, abuse,
    Show motherhood as high?

Or does the motherhood of those
    Whose toil endures,
The farmers' and mechanics' wives,
Hard working servants all their lives—
    Deserve less price than yours?

We're not exempt! Man's world runs on,
    Motherless, wild;
Our servitude and long duress,
Our shameless, harem idleness,
    Both fail to serve the child.

The Anti-Suffragists

Fashionable women in luxurious homes,
With men to feed them, clothe them, pay their bills,
Bow, doff the hat, and fetch the handkerchief;
Hostess or guest; and always so supplied
With graceful deference and courtesy;
Surrounded by their horses, servants, dogs—
These tell us they have all the rights they want.

Successful women who have won their way
Alone, with strength of their unaided arm,
Or helped by friends, or softly climbing up
By the sweet aid of "woman's influence";
Successful any way, and caring naught
For any other woman's unsuccess—
These tell us they have all the rights they want.

Religious women of the feebler sort—
Not the religion of a righteous world,
A free, enlightened, upward-reaching world,
But the religion that considers life
As something to back out of!—whose ideal
Is to renounce, submit, and sacrifice.
Counting on being patted on the head
And given a high chair when they get to heaven—
These tell us they have all the rights they want.

Ignorant women—college bred sometimes,
But ignorant of life's realities
And principles of righteous government,
And how the privileges they enjoy
Were won with blood and tears by those before—
Those they condemn, whose ways they now oppose;
Saying, "Why not let well enough alone?
Our world is very pleasant as it is"—
These tell us they have all the rights they want.

And selfish women—pigs in petticoats—
Rich, poor, wise, unwise, top or bottom round,
But all sublimely innocent of thought,
And guiltless of ambition, save the one
Deep, voiceless aspiration—to be fed!

These have no use for rights or duties more.
Duties today are more than they can meet,
And law insures their right to clothes and food—
These tell us they have all the rights they want.

And, more's the pity, some good women, too;
Good, conscientious women with ideas;
Who think—or think they think—that woman's cause
Is best advanced by letting it alone;
That she somehow is not a human thing,
And not to be helped on by human means,
Just added to humanity—an "L"—
A wing, a branch, an extra, not mankind—
These tell us they have all the rights they want.

And out of these has come a monstrous thing,
A strange, down-sucking whirlpool of disgrace,
Women uniting against womanhood,
And using that great name to hide their sin!
Vain are their words as that old king's command
Who set his will against the rising tide.
But who shall measure the historic shame
Of these poor traitors—traitors are they all—
To great Democracy and Womanhood!

The "Anti" and the Fly

The fly upon the Cartwheel[1]
    Thought she made all the Sound;
He thought he made the Cart go on—
    And made the wheels go round.

The Fly upon the Cartwheel
    Has won undying fame
For Conceit that was colossal,
    And Ignorance the same.

But today he has a Rival
    As we roll down History's Track—
For the "Anti" on the Cartwheel
    Thinks she makes the Wheels go back!

---

1 Cf. Aesop's fable "The Fly on the Chariot Wheel."

Women Do Not Want It

When the woman suffrage argument first stood upon
　　its legs,
They answered it with cabbages, they answered it
　　with eggs,[1]
They answered it with ridicule, they answered it with
　　scorn,
They thought it a monstrosity that should not have
　　been born.

When the woman suffrage argument grew vigorous
　　and wise,
And was not to be answered by these opposite re-
　　plies,
They turned their opposition into reasoning severe
Upon the limitations of our God-appointed sphere.

We were told of disabilities—a long array of these,
Till one could think that womanhood was merely a
　　disease;
And "the maternal sacrifice" was added to the plan
Of the various sacrifices we have always made-to
　　man.

Religionists and scientists, in amity and bliss,
However else they disagreed, could all agree on this,
And the gist of all their discourse, when you got
　　down in it,
Was—we could not have the ballot because we were
　　not fit!

They would not hear the reason, they would not
　　fairly yield,
They would not own their arguments were beaten in
　　the field;
But time passed on, and someway, we need not ask
　　them how,
Whatever ails those arguments—we do not hear them
　　now!

---

[1] People opposed to extending the suffrage to women threw foodstuffs at pro-suffrage campaigners.

You may talk of suffrage now with an educated man,
And he agrees with all you say, as sweetly as he can:
'T would be better for us all, of course, if womanhood was free;
But "the women do not want it"—and so it must not be!

'T is such a tender thoughtfulness! So exquisite a care!
Not to pile on our frail shoulders what we do not wish to bear!
But, oh, most generous brother! Let us look a little more—
Have we women always wanted what you gave to us before?

Did we ask for veils and harems in the Oriental races?
Did we beseech to be "unclean," shut out of sacred places?
Did we beg for scolding bridles and ducking stools[1] to come?
And clamor for the beating stick no thicker than your thumb?

Did we ask to be forbidden from all the trades that pay?
Did we claim the lower wages for a man's full work today?
Have we petitioned for the laws wherein our shame is shown:
That not a woman's child—nor her own body—is her own?

What women want has never been a strongly acting cause,
When woman has been wronged by man in churches, customs, laws;

---

[1] In the seventeenth and eighteenth centuries, "scold" was a legal term for a loud or insubordinate woman; a scold's bridle was an instrument used to physically silence and humiliate a woman who was regarded as offensive. A ducking stool was a torture device used to punish people accused of witchcraft.

Why should he find this preference so largely in his way,
When he himself admits the right of what we ask today?

Song For Equal Suffrage

Day of hope and day of glory! After slavery and woe,
Comes the dawn of woman's freedom, and the light shall grow and grow
Until every man and woman equal liberty shall know,
    In Freedom marching on!

Woman's right is woman's duty! For our share in life we call!
Our will it is not weakened and our power it is not small.
We are half of every nation! We are mothers of them all!
    In Wisdom marching on!

Not for self but larger service has our cry for freedom grown,
There is crime, disease and warfare in a world of men alone,
In the name of love we're rising now to serve and save our own,
    As Peace comes marching on!

By every sweet and tender tie around our heart-strings curled,
In the cause of nobler motherhood is woman's flag unfurled,
Till every child shall know the joy and peace of Mother's world—
    As Love comes marching on!

We will help to make a pruning hook of every out-grown sword,
We will help to knit the nations in continuing accord,
In humanity made perfect is the glory of the Lord,
    As His world goes marching on!

SOMETHING TO VOTE FOR

A One Act Play

TIME, 50 MINUTES.

PEOPLE IN THE PLAY.

MRS. MAY CARROLL: *A young, beautiful, rich widow; an "Anti"; President of Woman's Club; social leader.*
DR. STRONG: *A woman doctor, from Colorado, interested in Woman Suffrage and pure milk.*
MISS CARRIE TURNER: *Recording Secretary of Club; a social aspirant; agrees with everybody; "Anti."*
MRS. REEDWAY: *Corresponding Secretary of Club; amiable, elderly nonentity; "Anti."*
MRS. WOLVERHAMPTON: *Rich, impressive, middle-aged matron; "Anti."*
MRS. O'SHANE: *A little woman in black; thin, poor.*
LOUISE: *A maid.*
CLUB WOMEN: *Mrs. Black, White, etc.*
MR. HENRY ARNOLD: *A Milk Inspector.*
MR. JAMES BILLINGS: *Head of the Milk Trust.*

PLACE—*A parlor, porch or garden, belonging to Mrs. Carroll.*

PROPERTIES REQUIRED—*Chairs enough, a small table, a small platform covered with a rug, a table bell, two pitchers, a glass, a vase; two milk bottles filled with water, starch and a little black dirt; a yellow-backed bill, some red ink, a small bunch of flowers, two large clean handkerchiefs, a small bottle of iodine, a teacup. Miss Turner has a bag for her papers, and Dr. Strong an instrument bag or something similar, also a large pocket-book.*

SOMETHING TO VOTE FOR.

(Chairs arranged at right, platform, with table and three chairs at left front. Doors at left, right and center.)

(Enter Miss Turner and Mrs. Reedway, l.)

Mrs. Reedway—Dear me! I was so afraid we'd be late!

Miss Turner—*(Looking at watch.)* Oh, no! The meeting begins at three you know, and it's only quarter past!

Mrs. Reedway—*(Drawing scarf about her.)* I wish it would get warmer! I do like warm weather!

Miss Turner—So do I!

Mrs. Reedway—What a lovely place Mrs. Carroll has! I think we are extremely fortunate to have her for our president.

Miss Turner—So do I! She's so sweet!

Mrs. Reedway—I hear she has asked Mr. Billings to this milk discussion.

Miss Turner—Yes—you're not surprised are you?

Mrs. Reedway—Oh, no! Every one is talking about them. He's been conspicuously devoted to her for some time now. I think it's her money he's after.

Miss Turner—So do I! But she's crazy about him!

Mrs. Reedway—I suppose she thinks he's disinterested—being so rich himself. But I've heard that he'd lose a lot if this milk bill goes through.

Miss Turner—So have I!

(Enter Dr. Strong. l.)

Dr. Strong—Sorry to be late. I was detained by a patient.

Miss Turner—Oh, you're not late, Dr. Strong. The ladies are usually a little slow in gathering.

Dr. Strong—I see! And about what time do your meetings really begin?

Miss Turner—About half past three, usually.

Dr. Strong—Next time I'll come then. I could have seen two more patients—I hate to see women so unpunctual.

Miss Turner—So do I! This is Mrs. Reedway, our corresponding secretary, Dr. Strong. *(They shake hands.)*

Mrs. Reedway—You must remember, Dr. Strong, that our members are not—as a whole—professional women.

Dr. Strong—More's the pity!

(Enter Mrs. Wolverhampton, l.)

Mrs. Wolverhampton—Well, well! Not started yet? But you're always on hand, Miss Turner. *(Fans herself.)* Bless me, how hot it is! I do hate hot weather.

Miss Turner—So do I.

Mrs. Reedway—Have you met our new member, Mrs.

Wolverhampton? Dr. Strong, of Colorado. *(Mrs. W. bows. Dr. S. comes forward and shakes hands.)*

MRS. WOLVERHAMPTON—Dear me! From Colorado! And I suppose you have voted!

DR. STRONG—I certainly have. You seem to think I look like it.

MRS. WOLVERHAMPTON—Why, yes; if you'll pardon me, you do.

DR. STRONG—Pardon you? It seems to me a compliment. We're very proud of being voters—in my country.

(Mrs. R. and Mrs. W. draw aside and converse in low tones. Miss T. fussily arranges papers; she has a large flat bag, and is continually diving into it and fumbling about.) (Enter Mrs. Carroll, c.)

MRS. CARROLL—Pardon me, ladies! I'd no idea it was so late. *(Greets them all).*

MISS TURNER—Dear Mrs. Carroll! Would you accept these flowers?

MRS. CARROLL—How charming of you. Miss Turner! They are lovely. *(Sweeps toward Dr. S., both hands out, c.)* My dear Doctor! I feel so glad and proud to have you with us! *(Turns to others.)* You know, Mrs. Wolverhampton, Dr. Strong saved my mother's life! If she had come here sooner I'm sure she would have saved my baby! And she's going to be such a help to our club, aren't you, Doctor?

DR. STRONG—I'm not so sure of that, Mrs. Carroll. I'm afraid this isn't the sort of club I'm used to.

MRS. CARROLL—It's the sort of a club that needs you, Doctor! *(Takes Dr.'s arm and sits down with her.)* Make yourselves quite at home, ladies, the others will be here presently. *(Miss T., Mrs. R. and Mrs. W. go out, c.)* We've got everything arranged, Doctor. I'm going to have a bottle of the Billings Co. milk tested, and Mr. Billings himself is to be here.

DR. STRONG—That may be awkward.

MRS. CARROLL—Oh, no! The milk is all right—I've taken it for years. And I think he's a very fine man.

DR. STRONG—*(Drily.)* So I hear.

MRS. CARROLL—You mustn't believe all you hear, Doctor.

DR. STRONG—I don't. But I hope it isn't true.

MRS. CARROLL—Hope what isn't true?

DR. STRONG—About you and Mr. Billings.

MRS. CARROLL—Never mind about me and Mr. Billings! The question is have you got the new Inspector to come?

DR. STRONG—Yes, he'll be ready on time—but the club won't, I'm afraid.

MRS. CARROLL—Oh, a few moments won't matter, I'm sure. It's a Mr. Arnold you said—do you know his initials?

DR. STRONG—His name's Henry T. Arnold. I believe he's honest and efficient.

MRS. CARROLL—*(Meditatively.)* I used to go to school with a boy named Harry Arnold—he was the very nicest boy in the room. I think he liked me pretty well.

DR. STRONG—And I think you liked him pretty well—eh?

MRS. CARROLL—Oh, well! That was years ago!

DR. STRONG—*(Suddenly.)* By the way, Mrs. Carroll, have you any red ink?

MRS. CARROLL—Red ink?

DR. STRONG—Yes, red ink—can you get me some?

MRS. CARROLL—Why, I'm sure I don't know. Let me see—did have some—it's right here—if there is any. *(Goes out r. and returns with red ink.)*

DR. STRONG—Thank you. *(Takes out a yellow-backed bill, and deliberately marks it.)*

MRS. CARROLL—How exciting! What *do* you do that for, Doctor?

DR. STRONG—Just a habit of mine. Some day I may see that again and then I'd know it.

MRS. CARROLL—Do you mark all your money ?

DR. STRONG—Oh, no. Only some of it. And now will you do me a real favor?

MRS. CARROLL Indeed I will!

DR. STRONG—Please do not make any remark about this bill if you see me change it!!

MRS. CARROLL—How mysterious! I won't say a word.

DR. STRONG—*(Putting away bill.)* You said I might bring along one of my patients, for evidence, and I have. I've got little Mrs. O'Shane here to tell them how it affects the poor people.

MRS. CARROLL—That will be interesting, I'm sure—where is she?

DR. STRONG—Waiting outside—I couldn't induce her to come in.

MRS. CARROLL—I'll bring her in. *(Exit Mrs. C, l., returns with a small shabby women in black, who shrinks into the chair farthest back and sits silent.)*

MRS. CARROLL—It's very good of you to come, Mrs.

O'Shane; we're so much obliged! *(Enter Louise, l.)*

LOUISE—Mr. Arnold, Ma'am.

MRS. CARROLL—Show him in, Louise. *(Exit Louise. Enter Mr. Arnold, l.)*

DR. STRONG—Mrs. Carroll—Mr. Arnold.

MRS. CARROLL—It is Harry Arnold, I do believe! But you don't remember me!

MR. ARNOLD—Don't remember little May Terry! The prettiest girl in school! I've never forgotten her. But I did not expect to find you here.

MRS. CARROLL—I'm glad to welcome you to my home, Mr. Arnold, as well as to our club. And how are you—getting on?

MR. ARNOLD—Nothing to boast of Mrs. Carroll, if you mean in dollars and cents. I like public work you see, and the salaries are not high.

MRS. CARROLL—But some of our officials get very rich, don't they?

MR. ARNOLD—Yes, some of them do,—but not on their salaries.

DR. STRONG—If you knew more about politics, Mrs. Carroll, you would think better of Mr. Arnold for not making much. And he an Inspector, too!

MRS. CARROLL—You don't mean that our public men are bribed, surely!

DR. STRONG—It's been known to occur.

MRS. CARROLL—Oh, I can't believe that such things go on—here! Did any one ever bribe you, Mr. Arnold?

MR. ARNOLD—Some have tried.

MRS. CARROLL—Not in this town, surely.

MR. ARNOLD—Not yet.

DR. STRONG—He's only just appointed, Mrs. Carroll.

MR. ARNOLD—Thanks to you, Dr. Strong.

DR. STRONG—Yes, I guess I did help. *(Enter Louise, l.)*

LOUISE—Mr. Billings.

MRS. CARROLL—Ask him to come in. *(Exit Louise, l. Enter Mr. Billings, l.)* Good afternoon, Mr. Billings. Let me present you to my dear friend, Dr. Strong—our new member. And Mr. Arnold you probably know—the Milk Inspector. *(Mr. Billings approaches Dr. Strong, who bows stiffly. He shakes hands amiably with Mr. Arnold.)*

MR. BILLINGS—Well, Mr. Arnold, I think we're going to

make an impression on these ladies. I trust you'll deal gently with me.

Mr. Arnold—I'll do the best I can, Mr. Billings. I didn't expect to have the head of the Milk Trust in my audience.

Mrs. Carroll—That is all my fault, Mr. Arnold. I have taken milk of Mr. Billings' company for years, and it's always good. And I want the ladies to know it. Mr. Billings can stand the test.

Mr. Arnold—I'm glad to hear it, Mrs. Carroll.

Mr. Billings—*(Genially.)* You'll show up all of us rascally milk-men I don't doubt.

Mr. Arnold—I hope not. *(Mr. Billings goes to Mrs. Carroll. They talk apart. Dr. Strong confers with Mr. Arnold.)*

Dr. Strong—*(To Mr. Arnold.)* Now Mr. Arnold watch me, and be sure you play up. Say you can't make change for this bill! *(Goes to Mr. Billings)* Mr. Billings—can you—and will you—change this bill for me? Mr. Arnold here can't make it.

Mr. Arnold—I'm sorry, Doctor. But I haven't seen a hundred dollar bill in some time.

Mrs. Carroll—Perhaps I can—

Mr. Billings—No indeed, Mrs. Carroll! I shall be delighted. Dr. Strong,—if I have that much about me. *(Brings out bills from pockets and makes up the amount.)*

Dr. Strong—Thank you, Mr. Billings. *(Gives him her marked bill. The club members are seen arriving in background, c. Returning to Mr. A.)* What figures have you brought, Mr. Arnold? I don't want to cross your trail. *(They confer apart.)*

Mr. Billings *(To Mrs. Carroll.)* Isn't it rather a new thing for you to interest yourself in public matters, Mrs. Carroll?

Mrs. Carroll—Oh, but milk is really a domestic matter—don't you think so? So many of our ladies are getting interested in it.

Mr. Billings—I suspect that is because you are! I do not think you realize your influence in this town.

Mrs. Carroll—I'm sure you overestimate it.

Mr. Billings—Not in the least! Look at the way you swing this club! And these are the society lights—all the other women follow. And the men are yours to command anyhow! I tell you such an influence as yours has Woman Suffrage beaten to a standstill!

Mrs. Carroll—Oh!—Woman Suffrage! *(With great scorn. Enter Mrs. Wolverhampton, c.)*

MRS. WOLVERHAMPTON—Pardon me Mrs. Carroll, but it is half past three.

MRS. CARROLL—Dear me! yes, we must come to order. *(Ladies all come in and take seats. Some polite confusion. Mrs. Carroll in the chair. Mrs. O'Shane and Mr. Billings at extreme right, behind others but near front of stage.) (Platform, table, etc., l. front.)*

MRS. CARROLL—*(Rising.)* Ladies, and—gentlemen,—I—er—as you all know, I can't make a speech,—and I'm not in the least fit to be the president of a club—but you would have it you know! *(Murmur of approval; faint applause.)* I am very glad to welcome you to my home, and I'm sure I hope we shall all enjoy meeting here. *(More faint applause.)* I don't suppose it's very business like—but the very first thing I want to do is to introduce our new member, Dr. Strong of Col. *(Mrs. C. sits. Dr. S. rises and bows.)* O do come forward to the platform, Doctor, where we can all see you.

DR. STRONG—*(Coming to platform.)* Madam President—Ladies—and gentlemen! I did not expect to be sprung on you until after the reading of the minutes at least. But I am very glad to meet you and to feel that you have honored me with membership in what I understand is the most influential woman's club in this community. I have heard that this is a very conservative club, but I find that you are interesting yourselves in one of the most vital movements of our time—a question of practical politics—Pure Milk. *(The ladies cool and stiffen at the word "politics.")* It is a great question—a most important question—one that appeals to the mother-heart and housekeeping sense of every woman. It is a matter of saving money and saving life—the lives of little children! I do not know of any single issue now before us which is so sure to make every woman want to vote. The ballot is our best protection. *(Cries of "no!" "no" Much confusion and talking among members. One hiss. Mrs. Wolverhampton rises ponderously.)*

MRS. WOLVERHAMPTON—Madam President! I rise to a point of order! I move you that our new member be informed that all discussion of woman suffrage is forbidden by the by-laws of this club! There is no subject so calculated to disrupt an organization.

MRS. BLACK—Madam President!

MRS. CARROLL—Mrs. Black.

MRS. BLACK—I wish to second the motion! We decided long ago to allow no discussion of woman suffrage! I consider it to be one of the most dangerous movements of our time!

MRS. WHITE—Madam President!

MRS. CARROLL—Mrs. White. Won't you come forward, Mrs. White?

MRS. WHITE—O no, excuse me—no. I'll speak from here. I merely wish to agree with the previous speaker. Woman suffrage breaks up the home.

MRS. GREY—Madam President!

MRS. GREEN—Madam President.

MRS. CARROLL—Mrs. Grey I think spoke first. In a moment, Mrs. Green. Mrs. Grey. I just want to say that I for one should feel obliged to resign if woman suffrage is to be even mentioned in the club!

MRS. GREEN—Madam President!

MRS. BROWN—Madam President!

MRS. &C—Madam President! *(There has been a constant buzz of disapproval.)*

MRS. CARROLL—Ladies! One at a time, please! *(Several ladies are on their feet. All speak together.)*

MRS. GREEN—A woman's place is in the home, Madam President! If she takes good care of the home and brings up her children right—

MRS. BROWN—Women are not fitted for politics, they haven't the mind for it—and my husband says politics is not fit for women, either!

MRS. JONES—This club decided long ago that it was against woman suffrage—et al. Who'd take care of the baby? Our power is through our feminine influence—Yes—a woman's influence.—*(Great confusion.)*

MRS. CARROLL—*(Rapping feebly on the table.)* Ladies, ladies, we will adjourn for some refreshments. Won't you please all come and have some tea? *(All go out, c. and r. still talking. Mrs. C. and Mr. B. last. Dr. S. and Mr. A remain.)*

MR. ARNOLD—*(To Dr. S.)* Well, Dr. Strong, you did put your foot in it!

DR. STRONG—*(Ruefully.)* Yes—that was unfortunate, wasn't it? I'd no idea they'd fly up like that.

MR. ARNOLD—Never mind. I'll only talk milk to 'em—pure milk!

DR. STRONG—*(Walks up and down hands behind her, much perturbed.)* I'm right sorry to have annoyed those women. This is an awfully important occasion. Even if they can't vote, they could do something.

MR. ARNOLD—Don't you fret. Doctor, we'll get them interested.

DR. STRONG—You don't know how important this is. The death rate among the babies here is something shameful—it's mostly owing to bad milk—and the bad milk is mostly owing to this man Billings. If this bill passes he's got the whole thing in his hands! And he's crooked!

MR. ARNOLD—I'd about come to that conclusion, myself.

DR. STRONG—He's got her confidence you see—and she swings this town, socially. What's more, he means to marry her—and he's not a fit man to marry any decent woman. We've got to put a spoke in his wheel, Mr. Arnold!

MR. ARNOLD—I'm willing.

DR. STRONG—You'll never get a better opportunity than right now! He'll try to fix you before you speak—I'll promise you that! and do you stick out for that hundred dollar bill—and take it!

MR. ARNOLD—I guess not! What do you think I am?

DR. STRONG—I think you're man enough to see this game through. It's a marked bill, I tell you! You take that hundred and look at it—if there's a speck of red in the middle on the top—on both sides—you take it, and bring it out in evidence after you've shown up the milk!

MR. ARNOLD—But the milk he sends here'll be all right.

DR. STRONG—Of course! But I've brought in another bottle in my bag—and I'm going to substitute it! It's his milk, all right—the common grocery store kind—you'll be safe with the iodine test. Sh! You take that bill! *(Re-enter Mrs. C. c. bringing tea to Mrs. O'Shane.)*

MRS. CARROLL—*(To Mrs. O.)* We are really much indebted to you for coming, Mrs. O'Shane. I hope you are quite comfortable?

MRS. O'SHANE—Thank you Ma'am, thank you kindly!

MRS. CARROLL—*(Crossing to Dr. S.)* Now Dr. Strong, you musn't be angry because our ladies are not suffragettes.

DR. STRONG—Not a bit—I'm only sorry I mentioned it—I'm here to talk milk—not suffrage.

MRS. CARROLL—That's so nice of you! Now do go out and get some tea, doctor. *(Exit Dr. S. r.)*

MRS. CARROLL—I suppose you're going to be very impressive Mr. Arnold! You were as a boy, you know!

MR. ARNOLD—Was I? I don't remember that.

MRS. CARROLL—Yes, indeed. You used to brush your hair,—when you did brush it—in a way I thought extremely fine.

MR. ARNOLD—And yours was always brushed! Beautiful long soft curls! I used to wish I dared touch them!

MRS. CARROLL—My hair's grown so much darker since then, and I'm getting grey.

MR. ARNOLD—*(Drawing nearer.)* Grey! It's a libel! Not a single one.

MRS. CARROLL—There were—two or three—but, to speak confidentially, I pulled them out.

MR. ARNOLD—It wasn't necessary. You will be still more beautiful with grey hair!

MRS. CARROLL—You didn't make compliments at thirteen.

MR. ARNOLD—No—I didn't dare.

MRS. CARROLL—And how do you dare now.

MR. ARNOLD—The courage of desperation, I suppose. Here you are, still young, more beautiful than ever—the richest woman in the town; the social leader; able to lift and stir all these women—and here am I, a lot older than you are—and nothing but a milk inspector!

MRS. CARROLL—You haven't had much personal ambition, have you?

MR. ARNOLD—No, I haven't. But I might—if I were encouraged.

MRS. CARROLL—Mr. Arnold! I am so glad to find you are my old friend. And to think that you do—perhaps—value my opinion.

MR. ARNOLD—You're right as to that. That's what discouraged me when you married Carroll; and when I heard that you had become a mere society woman—You've got a good mind, always had, but you don't use it.

MRS. CARROLL—You do think I have a mind then?

MR. ARNOLD—Indeed I do! A first-class one!

MRS. CARROLL—Then let me persuade you to speak for this milk bill, Mr. Arnold! And I do hope in your speech—you'll mention the excellent influence—on the milk, you know—of Mr. Billings' company.

MR. ARNOLD—Why—I shall have to tell what I know, Mrs. Carroll; you want the facts.

MRS. CARROLL—Of course we want the facts! But—having Mr. Billings' milk to be tested—and Mr. Billings here—and he being a good friend of mine—I'm particularly anxious to have his reputation thoroughly established.

MR. ARNOLD—I see. And if I said anything against Mr. Billings, we should meet as strangers?

Mrs. Carroll—Not at all, Mr. Arnold! It's the milk we're talking about—not Mr. Billings.

Mr. Arnold—I beg pardon—I understand! *(Re-enter Mr. B. c. Exit Mr. A. r.)*

Mr. Billings—*(Coming to Mrs. C.)* I began to think I shouldn't have a chance to see you at all!

Mrs. Carroll—Why I'm quite conspicuous, I'm sure,—in the chair!

Mr. Billings—Ah! But I like best to see you alone!

Mrs. Carroll—No one sees me when I'm alone!

Mr. Billings—You can joke about it, Mrs. Carroll; it is a very serious matter to me. You must know how much I care for you—how long I have been devoted to you. You know I'm an ambitious man, Mrs. Carroll. I must be to dare hope for you! There are things I can't speak of yet—big chances in politics—if I had you with me—with your beauty and fascinating ways—By Heavens! There's no place I wouldn't try for. *(Walks up and down excitedly.)* I never wanted anything so much in my life—as I want you. When will you give me an answer?

Mrs. Carroll—Certainly not now, Mr. Billings.

Mr. Billings—When the meeting is over?

Mrs. Carroll—Perhaps—when the meeting is over.

(Enter Miss Turner c. with bag and papers.)

Mrs. Carroll *(rises, and goes to her. Mr. B. turns away)*—Well, Miss Turner, are you going to set us to work again?

Miss Turner—I hope I don't interrupt—

Mrs. Carroll—Interrupt! Why this is a club meeting. Miss Turner! Are we ready now?

Miss Turner—Perhaps, if you'd have the maid bring in the sample.

Mrs. Carroll—Oh, yes. *(Rings. Enter maid r.)*

Mrs. Carroll—Bring in the bottle of milk, Louise. *(Exit maid r. Re-enter Dr. S. and Mr. A. c.)*

Mr. Billings *(jocularly)*—I'm to be the scapegoat for the sins of the whole community, I see!

Mrs. Carroll—You are going to clear the good name of our milk supply, Mr. Billings. *(Re-enter maid r. with bottle of milk, sets it on table l. f.)*

Mrs. Carroll—Here it is! The best milk in town. *(They all approach table.)*

Mr. Billings *(takes it up)*—That's mine, all right. Name blown in the bottle, sealed with paraffine, air-tight from cow to customer, Mr. Arnold!

Mr. Arnold *(examining bottle)*—Looks like good milk, Mr. Billings.

Mr. Billings—It *is* good milk, Mr. Arnold; there's none better in the market! We're not afraid of your examination.

Mr. Arnold—Do you send out a uniform quality?

Mr. Billings—Well, hardly that, of course. We have some with less butter fat, comes a cent or two lower—but it's all pure milk.

Dr. Strong *(to A. aside)*—Get 'em to look at your papers—call 'em off!

Mr. Arnold—Have you seen our official cards, Mrs. Carroll? *(Takes out papers. They turn to him. The doctor whips out bottle of milk from her bag and changes it for the one on the table. Billings hears her and turns around. Comes over to table and takes bottle up. Starts. Others turn also.)*

Dr. Strong—What's the matter?

Mr. Billings—Matter? Why—nothing.

Dr. Strong—Name blown in the bottle all right? Paraffine seal all right? *(All come to look.)*

Mr. Billings—Yes, yes, it's all right. *(Moves off evidently perturbed.)*

Mrs. Carroll—What is it? Anything wrong with the milk?

Mr. Billings—No, no, certainly not.

Mrs. Carroll—Well, Miss Turner, I think we must collect our audience. *(They go out. c.)*

Dr. Strong—Can I be of assistance? *(Follows with a meaning glance at Mr. A. who is by the table.)*

(Mr. B. with sudden determination walks swiftly to the table to take milk bottle. Mr. A. seizes it.)

Mr. Billings—Excuse me, Mr. Arnold—but there's a mistake here! This is not the milk I sent Mrs. Carroll—by some error it's a bottle of our second quality. I'd hate to have her find it out. I've got my car here and I'm just going to run off and change this—it won't take but a minute!

Mr. Arnold *(holding the bottle)*—I don't think you'd better, Mr. Billings. It would look badly. There's really no time.

Mr. Billings *(agitated)*—I guess you're right. See here—this is a very important matter to me—more important than you know ... This bottle is not my best milk—but—but I'd be much obliged to you if it tested well—

Mr. Arnold *(drily)*—I hope it will.

MR. BILLINGS—Look here, Arnold, confound it! They'll all be back in a minute! Here! Quick! *(Passes him a bill.)*

MR. ARNOLD *(takes it. Looks at it, both sides)*—I'm not in the habit of taking bribes, Mr. Billings.

MR. BILLINGS—Sh! I can see that—you are so stiff about it! For goodness sake, man, see me through this foolish hen-party and I'll make it well worth your while! Come, put that in your pocket for this one occasion, you understand!

MR. ARNOLD—Well—just for this one occasion! *(Puts bill in pocket.)*

(Ladies all re-enter r. l. c. and take seats. Meeting called to order. Mrs. C. in chair as before; l. f., bustle, talk.)

MRS. CARROLL *(rapping on table)*—Will the meeting please come to order. I think, since it is already so late—and since we have such important—er—such an important—question to discuss, it will be as well to postpone the regular order of business until our next meeting. I'm sure you will be glad to have our discussion opened with a few words from Mr. Billings. Mr. Billings is the head of the milk business here, and knows more about it than any man in town. It is his milk which we are to have tested this afternoon—and he is proud to have it so—aren't you, Mr. Billings? *(Smiles at him.)*

MR. BILLINGS *(rather constrainedly)*—Yes; yes.

MRS. CARROLL—Now, do talk to us a little, Mr. Billings. Won't you please come forward.

MR. BILLINGS *(rising in his place)*—Madam President, and ladies, also Mr. Inspector: I feel it to be an honor to be here to-day to meet so many of the leading ladies of our community; to see so many fair faces—hear so many sweet voices—take the hand of so many I am proud to number among my friends. I wish to congratulate this club on its new president *(bows to Mrs. Carroll)*—a lady whose presence carries a benefaction wherever she goes. *(Applause.)* In these days, when so many misguided and unwomanly women are meeting together for all manner of unnecessary and sometimes utterly mistaken purposes, it is a genuine pleasure to find here so many true women of that innate refinement which always avoids notoriety. *(Takes out large white handkerchief and wipes face.)* The subject upon which I have been asked to address you is one which appeals to the heart of every woman—milk for babes! The favorite food of our children, the mainstay of the invalid, the foundation of all delicate cookery!

It has been my pleasure, ladies, and my pride to have

helped in serving this community with pure and healthful milk for many years past.

Our new organization, of which there is now so much discussion in the public press, is by no means the evil some would have you believe. I speak as one who knows. This is not the place for dry financial statistics, but I assure you that through this combination of milk dealers which has been recently effected you will have cheaper milk than has ever been given here before, and a far more regular and reliable service. For the quality we must trust to the opinion of these experts *(waves his hand to Dr. Strong and Mr. Arnold)*; but for the wish to serve your best interests, and for a capacity in service developed through years of experience, you may always count upon yours truly. *(Bows and sits. Stir and murmurs of approval. Applause.)*

MRS. A.—Isn't he interesting.

MRS. B.—Just what I think.

MRS. CARROLL—I'm sure we are all very grateful to Mr. Billings for giving us so much of his valuable time. It is so interesting, in this study of large general questions, to get information from the fountain head. And now we shall learn the medical side of it from a most competent authority. Ladies, I take pleasure in introducing my dear friend. Dr. Strong, who will speak to us on—what do you call it. Doctor?

DR. STRONG *(coming forward)*—Let us call it The Danger of Impure Milk. *(Stands a moment, looking earnestly at them.)* We all love babies. We love our own babies best of all, naturally. We all want to feed our babies well, and some of us can't do it ourselves. Next to the Mother, the most important food supplier for our children is the Cow. Milk is the most valuable article of food for little children. I suppose you all know that bottle-fed babies die faster than breast-fed—by far; they die mostly in summer, and from enteric and diarrheal diseases. *(Reads from notes.)* 17,437 babies under a year old died in New York in 1907; 1,315 died in Boston between June 1st and November 30th of that same year—in six months. In Fall River, at that time, more than 300 out of 1,000 died—nearly one-third. In New York, in five years, over 23,000 children of all ages died of measles, scarlet fever and diphtheria combined, and in the same time over 26,000 babies under two years died of diarrheal diseases. Out of 1,943 cases of these infantile diseases, in New York, only three per cent were breast-fed.

Now, ladies, this class of diseases comes from bacteria, and the bacteria come, in the vast majority of cases, from the milk. You see, the bottle-fed baby does not get its supply directly from the source, as when fed by its mother; between the Cow and the Baby stands the Milkman. The Milkman is not a mother. I really believe that if mothers ran the milk business they would not be willing to poison other women's babies even to make money for their own!

The producer and distributer of milk has small thought for the consumers' interests. To protect the consumer, the law now provides the Milk Inspector. But the Milk Inspector has on one side a few alert business men, often ready to pay well to protect their interests, and on the other the great mass of apathetic citizens, who do not take the trouble to protect their own.

The discussion to-day is in the hope of rousing this club to see the vital importance of pure milk for our children, and to urge its members to use their influence to secure it. By the kind permission of your president I have brought with me a resident of a less fortunate part of the town, that she may give you a personal experience. Mrs. O'Shane, will you please come to the platform? *(The little woman in black rises, hesitates, sits down again.)*

MRS. CARROLL—Won't you please make room, ladies? *(She comes down and escorts Mrs. O'Shane to platform. Mrs. O'Shane much agitated.)*

DR. STRONG—Brace up, Mrs. O'Shane. It's for little Patsy's sake, you know. He's gone, but there are many more.

MRS. O'SHANE—Indade there are, thank Hiven! It's not too late for the others! The street's full ov thim! If ye please, ladies, did any of you ever lose a child?[1]

MRS. CARROLL *(coming to her and taking her hand)* I have, Mrs. O'Shane. *(Sits again.)*

MRS. O'SHANE—There's many, I don't doubt. But ye have the consolation of knowin' that your children had all done that could be done for thim. An' ours dies on us every summer—such a many of thim dies—an' we can't help it. They used to tell us 'twas the Hand 'o God, and then they said 'twas the hot weather, and now they're preachin' it to us everywhere that 'tis the milk does it! The hot weather is bad, because thim things that's in the milk shwarms thicker and faster—thim little bugs that kills our babies ... If ye could have seen my little Patsy! He was the han'somest child, an' the strongest! Walkin'

---

1 Mrs. O'Shane's name, accent, and obedience to priests identify her as an Irish Catholic immigrant.

he was—and him hardly a year old! An' he was all I had—an' me a widder! An', of course, I took the best milk I could get; but all the milk in our parts comes from the Trust—an' sisteen cents a quart for thim fancy brands I could not pay. An', just think of it—even if I could, there's not enough of that sort to go around! There's so many of us! We have no choice, and we have no money to pay for the extras, an' we must give our babies the milk that is sold to us—an' they die! ...

I know I should care most for the hundreds an' thousands of thim—an' for Mrs. Casey's twins that died in a week last summer, an' three of Mrs. Flaharty's, an' even thim little blackies[1] on Bay street; but I care the most for my Little Patsy—havin' but the wan! Ladies, if you could have seen him! The hair on his head was that soft!—an' all in little rings o' curls! An' his cheeks like roses—before he took sick; an' his little feet was that pretty—an' he'd kick out so strong and bold with them! An' he could stand up, and he was beginning to hold on the chairs like—an' he'd catch me by the skirts an' look up at me with such a smile—an' pull on me he would, an' say Mah! Mah! An' what had I to give him but the milk? And the milk killed him ... I beg your pardon, ladies, but it breaks my heart! *(She cries. Mrs. Carroll comforts her, crying too. Many handkerchiefs out. Mrs. Carroll rises up, repressing emotion.)*

MRS. CARROLL—Ladies, we will now hear from our new Inspector, Mr. Arnold. *(Mr. Arnold comes forward and bows.)*

MR. ARNOLD—I fear cold facts will make but little impression after this moving appeal. Mrs. O'Shane has given you the main points in the case. Most people are poor. Most milk is poor. And the poorest milk goes to the poorest people. The community must protect itself. The Inspector has no power except to point out defects in the supply. Action must be taken to enforce the law, and unless the public does its duty there is often no action taken. *(Reads from paper.)* Dr. Strong has given you some figures as to the mortality among babies. There is also a heavy death rate for adults from contaminated milk, as in the case of the typhoid fever outbreak in Stamford, Conn., in 1895, when 160 cases were reported in nine days, 147 of which had all used milk from one dairyman. In about six weeks 386 cases were reported; of these 352 took milk from that one dealer, and four more got it from him indirectly. His dairy was closed, and in two weeks the outbreak had practically subsided.

---

1 A racist epithet for a Black person.

Typhoid fever, scarlet fever and diptheria, as well as many less common diseases, are spread by infected milk.

The inspection service watches both the producer and distributor; examining the dairy farm as to the health of the cattle, the nature of their surroundings, the care given them, the methods of milking, bottling, and so on; and looking to the milkmen in each step of handling, carriage and delivery.

In judging milk there are three main questions to be considered: Its comparative quality as good milk (the percentage of butter-fats, etc.); its cleanliness (dirty milk is always likely to carry disease); and its freedom from adulteration—from the primative pump-water and starch down to the subtler and more dangerous commercial methods of today.

I have been asked to show you a simple test or two—such as might be used at home. These do not require chemical or bacteriological analysis, a microscope or a lactometer; merely a fine cloth *(produces it)* and a little iodine *(produces that)*.

(The ladies lean forward eagerly. Mr. Billings looks indifferent.)

MR. ARNOLD—Please understand, ladies, that neither of these tests proves anything absolutely harmful. I feel extremely awkward in testing a bottle of the Billings Company milk in the presence of Mr. Billings. Please remember that the Billings Company has many supply dairies. If this one bottle should not prove first-class it is no direct reproach to your guest.

MR. BILLINGS—Ladies, I do not ask any excuses. The Billings Company is reliable.

MRS. CARROLL—We have every confidence in this milk, Mr. Billings; that is why I asked for the test.

MR. ARNOLD—May I ask for another vessel—a pitcher or milk bottle?

(Mrs. Carroll rings. Enter Louise, r.)

MRS. CARROLL—Bring another pitcher, Louise, and an empty milk bottle—clean. *(Exit Louise, r., and returns with them, r., while Mr. Arnold continues.)*

MR. ARNOLD—Only two things are to be decided by this little test—whether the milk is clean, and whether it has starch in it. If it is clean milk, according to our standard, there will be but a slight smear on the cloth when it is strained. *(He puts cloth over top of pitcher, pushing it down inside, and fastens it with string or rubber band; then solemnly pours in most of the milk. Buzz among ladies.)*

MR. ARNOLD—While this is straining, I will apply the iodine test to what remains in the bottle. If there is starch in it, it will turn blue. *(Pours water from a glass into the bottle, adds a few drops of iodine, shakes it, holds it up before them. It is blue.)*

MRS. W., MRS. B., MRS. G. *(together)*—Oh! Look at that! Just think of it!

(Mr. Billings much confused, but unable to escape.)

MR. ARNOLD—I'm afraid one of the supplying dairymen thins his milk and whitens it. Starch is not dangerous. Dirt is. We will now examine our strainer. *(Holds up cloth. A heavy, dark deposit is shown. There is a tense silence.)*

MRS. O'SHANE *(suddenly rising up)* That's what killed my Patsy! *(Points at Mr. Billings.)* An' 'twas him that did it! *(Commotion.)*

MR. BILLINGS *(rising)*—Ladies, I demand to be heard! You have all known me for years. Most of you take my milk. You know it is good. There is some mistake; that is not the milk that should have been delivered here.

MRS. CARROLL—Evidently not.

MRS. O'SHANE—No! 'Tis not the milk for the rich—'tis the milk for the poor!

MR. BILLINGS—Ladies, I protest! My standing in this community—my years of service—ought to give me your confidence long enough to look into this matter. I must find out from which of my suppliers this inferior milk has come. We will have a thorough overhauling, I assure you. I had no idea any such milk was being handled by us.

MR. ARNOLD—Then why did you give me this bill? *(Shows marked bill.)* This was handed to me a few moments ago by Mr. Billings to ensure my giving him a favorable test. It is the first time I ever held a bribe—even for evidence.

DR. STRONG *(coming forward)*—Ladies, I wish to clear Mr. Arnold of even a moment's suspicion. I knew the Milk Trust would not bear inspection, so I urged Mr. Arnold to take the money, if it was offered, and bring it out in evidence. There it is.

MR. BILLINGS—I suspected as much! This is admitted to be a conspiracy between our new doctor and our new inspector. But I trust, ladies, that more than the word of two strangers will be required to condemn an old friend and fellow-citizen.

DR. STRONG—I gave you that bill, Mr. Billings; it's the one you changed for me just now. That much of a conspiracy I admit.

MR. BILLINGS—So you and your accomplice had it all framed up to knife me! And is your word and his—a man whose very admission proves him a venal scoundrel—to stand against mine? Do you think I had but one hundred-dollar bill about me?

DR. STRONG—I doubt if you had more than one with a red mark in the middle of the top—on both sides! *(Mrs. Carroll suddenly takes up bill and examines it. Rises.)*

MRS. CARROLL—It was a painful surprise to find the quality of milk which has been served to me, but it is more painful to see that it was evidently known to be bad. Ladies, I saw Dr. Strong mark that bill. I saw her give it to him in change for smaller ones.

MRS. O'SHANE—Sure, an' I saw him pass it to the man!

MRS. CARROLL—Ladies, if you will kindly move a little I think Mr. Billings would be glad to pass out. *(They make way for him and he goes out, turns at door and shakes fist at Mr. Arnold.)*

MR. BILLINGS—You'll lose your job, young man! I have some power in this town!

MRS. CARROLL—And so have I, Mr. Billings. I'll see that Mr. Arnold keeps his place. We need him. You said this club could carry the town; that we women could do whatever we wanted to here—with our "influence"! Now we see what our "influence" amounts to! Rich or poor, we are all helpless together unless we wake up to the danger and protect ourselves. That's what the ballot is for, ladies—to protect our homes! To protect our children! To protect the children of the poor! I'm willing to vote now! I'm glad to vote now! I've got something to vote for! Friends, sisters, all who are in favor of woman suffrage and pure milk say Aye!

(Clubwomen all rise and wave their handkerchiefs, with cries of "Aye!" "Aye!")

CURTAIN

Appendix A: Socialism, Feminism, Humanism

[In the years immediately prior to publishing *Women and Economics*, Gilman published numerous articles with the radical press, and the selection below demonstrates her efforts to reach Americans across the progressive spectrum. *The Woman's Journal* was founded in 1870 by the prominent woman's rights activist Lucy Stone (1818–93) and her husband Henry Browne Blackwell (1825–1909). Gilman contributed numerous articles to the newspaper from 1884 onwards, and several of these articles sketch out some of the ideas that she developed more extensively in *Women and Economics*. "Masculine, Feminine, and Human" (A1) explores the idea that activities and traits conventionally associated with men should rightly be regarded as human activities and traits, while "Economic Basis of the Woman Question" (A5), published the same year as *Women and Economics*, urges American feminists to recognise the links between female sexual subjugation and an economic system that positions women as the family members of male wage earners, rather than as workers in their own right.

The Impress was the organ of the Pacific Coast Women's Press Association, an organization that encouraged Gilman's public writing and lecturing. Gilman edited the newspaper during her time in California. "Women as a Class" (A2) urges recognition of women's shared experiences with deprivation and inequality—or what second wave feminists of the 1970s would come to call "feminist consciousness"—and it encourages women to engage in collective struggle for change.

While Gilman's essays emphasizing the economic basis of women's inequality established her as an important figure within feminist circles, her writing for *The American Fabian* brought her perspective to American socialists. Fabian socialism originated in Britain in the mid 1880s, and its advocates, including the playwright George Bernard Shaw (1856–1950) and reformers Beatrice (1858–1943) and Sidney (1859–1947) Webb, argued for a gradualist, nonviolent approach to progressive change. Many Americans around this time regarded socialism as a foreign-grown ideology, imported by immigrant radicals from Europe. Gilman drew inspiration from British intellectuals, but she knew that that socialism needed to be made compatible with the American context. "When Socialism Began" (A3) and "Socialism and Patriotism" (A4) have a dual purpose. Addressing socialists, Gilman cautions against narrow sectarianism. To the extent that they appeal to a wider audience, these articles convey Gilman's conviction that all American citizens stand to gain from greater cooperation.]

1. Charlotte Perkins Gilman, "Masculine, Feminine, and Human," *Woman's Journal*, vol. 23, no. 28, 9 July 1892, p. 220

There never was a time when these words were on everyone's tongue as they are to-day.

Between those twin phenomena of the age, the woman's movement and the social movement, even the lightest reader, the shallowest thinker, is used to the sight and sound of the above adjectives. But there is a deep and widespread confusion of ideas respecting the meaning of the first two.

Superficially speaking, we call all things that men are and do, masculine; and all that women are and do, feminine. But, to make the distinction correct, it must follow that all these prevailing characteristics of the two sexes are essential and permanent. As a matter of fact, the great body of these characteristics are neither one nor the other; they are transient habits adopted by the race in its purblind progress; or, at the very most, only what are known to scientists as "secondary sexual characteristics."

Those people who have the deepest feelings about the honor, usefulness, and beauty of sex distinctions, and who entertain such genuine fears for the race should woman perform that unhallowed miracle of "unsexing herself," are precisely those who make sweeping mistakes in their definition of what constitutes the distinction of sex. One would think, to hear them, womanhood was sacredly enwound in a foot or two of hair, or wrapped inalienably in a yard or two of skirt length, or confined exclusively to the four walls of a home. One might as naturally suppose manhood to lie in a smoking car, or to consist mainly in oaths, because, as a rule, women do not smoke or swear.

Neither costume nor custom is true sex distinction. That must lie in something which the one sex is never found without, and the other never found with.

This cuts us down severely to facts. Until the distinction is rightly understood, there can be no clear thought nor just argument on the subject. And the constantly increasing amount of thought and argument on the subject seems amply to justify some discussion of terms.

Reducing the matter to its natural base, the distinction of sex is such organic and structural modification as is conducive to the best reproduction of species—this "best" varying with the race, and with circumstances which make the race. All such physical modifications and their accompanying mental modifications are "primary sexual characteristics."

Then comes an immense series of modifications and developments called "secondary," such as the comb and wattles of the domestic fowl and other birds, the special plumage of the male, special notes of the voice, the antlers of the stag, the mane of a lion, and many another thing. These are not useful primarily, but they are immensely useful secondarily; they serve to attract the attention and command the admiration of the other sex.

Of this nature, it is plain to see, is a large share of those distinctions in the human creature which we are so jealous of preserving. Yet such characteristics are not essential, not permanent, are open to wide alteration and improvement, are frequently interchangeable under certain conditions, may or may not be to the true interest of the sex or the race. They have their use and are entitled to even more consideration than they get; but they should never be confused with the primary distinctions.

In man, whose humanity is so wholly a matter of brain and soul, there have arisen new uses for the great dual relation, and therefore new distinguishing phenomena. And it is these phenomena, complex and manifold, which we now refer to when we say of a thing that it is "masculine" or "feminine." Such derivatives are proper enough when used for descriptive purposes solely; but when the inference exists that these distinctions are radical and necessary, it does much harm.

In the question of costume, for instance, we have a good illustration. Eve was a "woman," having no clothes. So was the primeval savagess. Wherefor it becomes apparent that what a woman wears can in no way alter her sex, unless, indeed, it do so by mechanical injury. A woman was a woman when she rode a horse *à la Amazon*,[1] bareback—two barebacks; she was a woman when she went a-hawking in the middle ages in lovely robes of silken lace; she is a woman riding in the East, astride, but shrouded thick in head to heel; she is a woman in a "habit" and on a side-saddle; she is a woman in bifurcated skirts and cross

---

1 In Greek mythology, Amazons were a race of woman warriors.

saddle; she will be a woman just the same when she wears a Greek kilt and gaiters buttoned to the knee. Her sex not inhering in her clothes she cannot "unsex" herself by changing those clothes.

On the other hand, the habits of modern man are called "masculine," and it is presumed that a woman, in assuming any of those habits assumes masculinity. Only such habits as are acquired through the primary distinction of sex are either masculine or feminine. The business habits of to-day are acquired through racial modification, not sexual; and may be acquired by either sex without injury to manhood or womanhood.

We must remember, in this connection, the power of "associative ideas." When two things have always been seen together the sight of one suggests the other. We have long been accustomed to associate certain habits with man, and certain others with woman, and to see them altered really gives us a bewildered sense that something is wrong. The strong mind, however, rises above this power of association and can consider a detached idea. Let us try to be strong in this respect, and before harshly condemning a thing as "unfeminine," consider if it really be so.

We speak of "feminine" and "unfeminine" occupations; but, if you will notice, we do not often hear of "unmasculine" occupations. Nothing but "rocking the cradle" and "sewing on buttons" has ever been cast up at him. Why? Because the so-called feminine occupations are his also, when he chooses to perform them. The preparation of food was for long a most distinctive "feminine occupation," but no one thinks Cross and Blackwell have unsexed themselves, or Peck and Frear, or Richardson and Robbins.[1] So the teaching of art, science and letters was for long a masculine occupation; but woman, having gradually assumed those functions, is not considered unfeminine in so doing. Indeed, the scales are turning so largely to her side that soon these will be considered as "feminine occupations" *par excellence*.

It will be the same when the encroaching flood of femininity has invaded the business world as it has the school-room.

The male teacher and the female teacher remain male and female in perfect safety. They even continue to love and marry, regardless of the hideous fact that each has the same business. I doubt if it can be shown that two poets who marry, two artists who marry, two lawyers or doctors or teachers or preachers who marry, are any the less male and female, or any the less happy

---

1 A reference to popular British and American food manufacturers.

together than where the male is a "business man" and the female a nurse, seamstress, cook and housekeeper.

It will be noted that among most of the animals the racial existence of the two sexes is identical, and yet they continue to perform their distinctive functions in a highly satisfactory manner. There is no reason to suppose that identity of racial existence will interfere with our distinctive functions.

But here we are met with grieved remonstrances. It is not anything so material and commonplace as functions that these sad prophets speak of. Man will not be so happy, they say, when he is not gratified by the sharp contrast between his life and hers. And how can that be proven? Is man so happy now with the contrast—the dreadful unnecessary disproportionate contrast—that he need fear a change? How does he know he would not be far happier when masculine and feminine were words of narrower range and less use, and human was the adjective to cover both?

There is a combination sometimes seen to-day, where a man's wife is his best friend—where he likes her as well as loves her. It is a happy combination. In the glad days that are coming, there will be more of that happiness, and the equally developed sexes will learn what it is to be human.

2. Charlotte Perkins Gilman, "Women as a Class," *Impress*, vol. 17, 7 November 1894, pp. 2–3

Charles Dudley Warner and Agnes Repplier, Mrs. Lynn Linton, Marion Harland and Ouida,[1] together with various other people, have an objection, a marked and prominent objection, to women being treated as a class. They deprecate, variously, according to their natures and their several vocabularies, the prominence at present given to the progress of woman as apart from the progress of man. They hold that man and woman are, one as it were,—as one dieth, so dieth the other—and that it is illegitimate to so much as discuss them separately.

As to superiority, or inferiority, relative morality or relative intelligence—the very idea of such distinctions is revolting to them. The only distinction to be allowed is that which belongs to

---

[1] Warner (1829–1900) and Repplier (1855–1950) were American essayists; Eliza Lynn Linton (1822–98) was a notable British anti-feminist; Harland (Mary Virginia Terhune, 1830–1922) was an American author; Ouida was the pseudonym of the English novelist Maria Louise Ramé (1839–1908).

the individual,—George Eliot marks the advance of her age in literature as compared to George Meredith and William Black, not the advance of her sex.[1]

And when the other kind of people, who do believe there is a general distinction between men and women as to racial development, make any complaint of the unnecessary limitations of the gentler sex, these fretfully exclaim, as Warner in a recent Harper's Monthly: "Why she has borne the whole race for six thousand years, and she has got to bear it alone in all the ages; she is the great conservative and really controlling force. I wish they would let her alone. I am sick of all this petty talk about her."

Be it observed hereby that those who object to treating women as a class, who deprecate any recognition of her separate achievement, who hold that she is one with man and her progress and his are to be measured always together—that these sensitive spirits are the people who insist most violently on the distinction of sex on its purely physical plane, and who are always holding up to women the inviolable privilege and indisputable power of child-bearing, as if she were parthogenetic![2]

Now woman's relative power as cook, or as seamstress, or as artist, or as author, or as architect, is hers as a class. It is not long since Johnson's brutal comparison with the dog on his hind legs was applied to all woman's work,—as indeed it is yet by the ignorant.[3] But her influence on humanity as a parent is but half an influence—she shares that responsibility with man. No wildest woman suffragist of them all endeavors to set up a class distinction here—a Woman's Building[4] is a mark of progress—a Woman's Baby is not.

Now without sentimentality of any sort, look at the facts of the case. Here is a vast number of people who for uncounted centuries have been denied equal opportunities with other people of the same age and station and who, therefore, have been denied the same development. That the distinction so produced is not more marked is owing to the constant crossing of inheritance between

---

1 Eliot (Mary Anne Evans, 1819–80), Meredith (1828–1909), and Black (1841–98) were nineteenth-century British novelists.
2 Parthenogenesis is the process that allows some creatures to produce offspring without mating.
3 English writer Samuel Johnson (1709–84) reportedly said, "A woman's preaching is like a dog's walking on his hind legs. It is not done well; but you are surprised to find it done at all."
4 The Woman's Building was built for the 1893 World's Columbian Exposition in Chicago.

man and woman—these constantly tending to make even by inheritance what was made uneven by education. That it is marked at all is due, partly to that subtle association which tends to transmit selectively to either sex the characteristics needed, and partly to the endless repetition of the same distinctive education.

This distinction exists and is, to the great good of the race, being rapidly bridged over by the splendid opening of opportunities to woman which marks our age; but while it exists it should be recognized like any other fact.

For a man and a woman to-day to do the same work is a much more remarkable thing for her than for him. And to group separately the work of women, to consider and criticize it as such, is a right and helpful thing—it gives her more assurance and more courage than the unfair comparison with those who have so far occupied the whole field. Moreover—for those who are ahead, either as the leading sex, or as particularly smart members of the other; for those women whose uncommon ability or exceptional opportunity has placed them in equality with men of their profession,—for these to repudiate any measurement save by their standard is manifestly unfair.

So long as the work of most women is inferior to the work of most men, so long should every woman be proud to add her special strength to the growing power of women; to let her gain be theirs and to count in the average—she should not run ahead to join those already ahead, and object to be classed with woman's enormous struggle upward.

3. Charlotte Perkins Gilman, "When Socialism Began," *American Fabian*, vol. 3, no. 2, November 1897, pp. 1–2

One of the commonest misconceptions of Socialism is the belief that it is a new and untried plan, a dangerous experiment—a prospect having certain alluring features, it is true, but full of hidden evils.

This error—as to the novelty of the thing—is quite as common among Socialists as among Individualists. Many most earnest advocates of Socialism speak as if they were pleading for some descent of a new heaven upon a new earth, and spend their strength in the effort to show what Socialism will do—instead of the far safer, sounder, and wider plan of showing what Socialism has done and is doing.

Socialism is coincidental with civilization. In so far as we are civilized, we are socialized.

Civilized—citi-fied—the life of the city is the basis of social progress; and the country is civilized by its contact with the city. A city is not merely a group of houses—a number of people. A city is a group of separate houses arranged along common thoroughfares; it is a number of people living in relation to one another; and to the whole of them, as represented by chosen officials, a city is an organization.

Looked at from above by a sociological student, studied as to its structure merely, a city has certain definite centres of activity; certain main lines of activity, and its citizens flow along these lines, and throb in their centres in ceaseless motion.

The tiniest village, with its one straggling street, is like some primitive worm—a mere thread of life, low in form and function.

The large village or town, with its market-place and public house, shows signs of higher life; and that same market-place begins to bring the country into touch with the city and spread the forces of civilization. From this to London, Paris and New York is but one, long process of social evolution.

The growth in mass, by individual births, is but accretion of particles—as our muscles and component cells grow by fusion; but it is the growth in organization that constitutes social advance.

It is the collectivity of the city that makes its value; the union, the spirit in common and the body in common; without the civic spirit—no city; without the civic body, the ordered streets, the squares and parks and halls where people may meet together—no city. And the principle on which this civic life develops is this:

Moved by the common interests which constitute our human bond, some people draw together live together. Living together, their common interests make to themselves organized methods of expression; from the first simple night-watchman to our elaborate police department; from the first temporary judge elected by acclaim to settle a dispute in the market-place, to our elaborate law department; from the first old woman who had an eye to the babies while the village women worked in the fields, to our elaborate educational department; from the first foul and narrow lane to our miles of level street—all this is nothing but socialization. And how is this done? Who does it? Who pays for it? Whom is it for? How is it distributed?

It is done by the people of the city through their chosen officers. It is paid for by the people of the city by systems of taxation the principle of which, however feloniously evaded, is that the citizens shall contribute according to their ability—their power and possession; it is for the people of the city, all of them.

It is distributed by simply being there for the citizens to take advantage of according to their needs.

This is the organic life of cities. This is civilization. This is Socialism. As this spirit spreads in a faint wide way into the country—giving a common feeling to large sections of country; as this body also is imitated as far as space permits—in better roads and more frequent meeting places; as this organic action spreads, in country schools and country court-houses, and country sheriffs to keep the country peace—so is the country gradually civilized—socialized.

And always it is the same spirit—a recognition of the common interest; the same form—material means of communication and exchange; the same methods—all to unite in paying according to ability for what all may share in according to their needs.

As far as we live on these lines, we are socialized—civilized.

As far as we live on the earlier lines of disconnected individual interests and methods, we are not socialized—civilized.

Every human quality of the animal in which we live stays with us in proportion to our lack of specialization—to our failure to recognize common interests and serve them by common means. The whole evolutionary struggle of humanity is the establishment of our collective life; and its only enemy is the slow-dying beast still seeking to maintain his individual life at any one's or every one's expense. Socialism began when we began to be human. It grows with our humanity. It will never end in its beautiful development till we end the story of human life on earth.

4. Charlotte Perkins Gilman, "Socialism and Patriotism," *American Fabian*, vol. 4, May 1898, pp. 5–6

A Socialist editor in Kansas is reported to have insulted the flag of our country, and the enraged citizens were minded to hang him.

The incident opens a question of deep importance. What is the duty of the Socialist toward the immediate conditions of the hour?

It is the same question that confronts him at the ballot-box; but the imminent call to arms is more imperative than the quiet demand of the polls.

Many conscientious Socialists hold that they have no duty to their country "under the present system;" nothing to vote for but the introduction of Socialism; nothing to fight for but class conquest to the same end. With the one great end in view in which, to their minds, lies all human good, they hold themselves excused from any lesser duties, believing that to stop for halfway measures will only postpone the end we all desire.

Such single-minded devotion to a great cause is fine to see; but heroic enthusiasm is not always the wisest or most direct path to a desired end.

There is still too much of the old religious spirit among our Socialists—a spirit of fierce proselytism, of rampant martyrdom, of blind, deaf, reckless devotion.

This was reasonable enough with a faith whose admitted goal was in another world—in which failure meant success, and death the way to life.

Socialism is of this world, making a new heaven on a new earth; and its processes are the processes of human life. Socialism is a natural growth, too—no new invention or revelation: it is the orderly development of social forces always at work. Every upward step we have made in history is a step toward Socialism: and none is more important in all the endless line than that great burst of human courage, truth, and power which gave us this great land and its democracy. Because our Government is not yet fully socialized, our democracy but part accomplished, is no reason why we should ignore and despise it.

It is true that this Government gives great room and power for the concentration of capital and the rapid intensification of the evils of the wage system; but that very fact proves its advance beyond the older forms of government, under which the same forces lie in wait.

Ours gives fuller room for development, for recognition, for final extinction of these evils under the beneficent power of a higher socialization. We ought never to lose sight of the great work done by those behind us; though we may be burning to achieve far higher things ahead. We stand on ground that our forerunners have built high and firm beneath our feet; and we owe love and duty, honor and allegiance to the country as it is, even while we strive to make it better.

The peace and freedom we enjoy are but a mockery to the peace and freedom of a Socialist century yet to come; but it is heavenly truth compared to the warfare and discord, or the helpless slavery, of older times.

It is true that under a Socialist regime in a later age neither the horrors of Spain's war with Cuba, nor the horrors of our war with

Spain could come to pass.[1] But while the world about us and our home Government "are not perfect, as we are," they are still our world and our government, and we have our duty to the present as well as to the future.

To criticize our industrial system and our political system, and to labor mightily to improve them is a citizen's duty; but all imperfect as they are, it is to these systems that we owe our present existence, our national dignity, our right to interfere in a world-scandal at our doors.

The capacity of the human soul to love humanity, to love justice, to struggle through dark lifetimes, to bring justice to humanity at last, this capacity we owe to the slowly uplifting centuries behind us, with their love of family, love of tribe, love of kingdom, love of country.

This country is ours by birth or adoption; and while we are in it and of it we owe to it our duty and true service.

If it is imperfect—foolish—wrong—all the more we must stand by it and make it right.

Of all emblems that ever sprang from the heart and mind of man, a banner is the highest. The widest, deepest, holiest feelings of humanity are symbolized by that floating piece of cloth. It concentrates and embodies feelings too vast to be otherwise held in the mind. The man who loves and honors the flag, who fights and dies for the flag, has not time to stop to enumerate all the uncounted centuries if advancement, all the millions of human lives, all the record of world progress, that he is really serving.

When the red flag of brotherhood—the flag that means we are all of one blood—waves from every spire and mast on earth, we shall look on it with passionate reverence and love. Until that time the flag of our country is the highest symbol we have; and the Socialist should be no less a patriot, but more because of his Socialism.

5. From Charlotte Perkins Gilman, "Economic Basis of the Woman Question," *Woman's Journal*, vol. 29, 1 October 1898, pp. 313–14

The question before women is how best to do their duty upon earth. To define individual duty is difficult; but the collective duty of a class or sex is clear. It is the duty of women to develop and

---

1 The Cuban War of Independence was fought 1895–98; the Spanish-American War was fought in 1898.

improve themselves; to bring children into the world who are superior to their parents; and to forward the progress of the race.

If we were planted in the world full-grown, clear-brained, unprejudiced, we might grasp its problems more fully and solve them with better judgment. Coming, as we do, to a period of helpless infancy, and, during that period being exposed to the educational forces of the past, a separate struggle is required of each of us, as we reach maturity, to shake off hereditary and educational ideas and influences, and see life for ourselves.

A peculiar condition of women is that their environment has been almost wholly that of the home; and the home is the most ancient of human institutions; the most unalterably settled in its ideals and convictions; the slowest and last to move.

Hereditary impulses and tendencies flow unchecked through unnumbered generations, unless new conditions change them; and this is as true of sociology as in any other department of biological science.

The progressive changes and social evolution accomplish wonders in those fields of life open to their influence; but the motionless, sheltered, inner places remain unchanged among us, like the frozen mastodons, confronting us with their complacent presence, an immense anachronism. So in our social world today, men and women who are familiar with liquefied air and Roentgen rays, who have accepted electric transit and look forward with complacence to air-ships, people who are as liberal and progressive in mechanical lines as need be hoped, remain sodden and buried in their prehistoric sentiment as to the domestic relations. The world of science and invention may change; art, religion, government may change; industry, commerce and manufactures may change; but women and the home are supposed to remain as they are, forever.

The action of natural forces upon man does not wait, fortunately for him, for his recognition and acceptance. While he is shutting his eyes and stoutly maintaining that he will not move, nature, calm and wise mother, move him, willy-nilly. The development of humanity cannot proceed far through one sex only; and in this age it has at least succeeded in stirring the heavy, hidden, centre of our lives, the home, and in rousing woman to face life at last....

The economic position of women in the world heretofore has been that of the domestic servant. Among the wealthier classes she rises to that of housekeeper, or even to that of a sublimated controller of a housekeeper; but her field of economic activity is that of domestic service. Do not confuse with this the sex activities of women as wives and mothers, or their "social" activities in the limited sense of entertainment given and received. Human beings are animals. Animals must eat. Food is produced by labor. Those who do not labor for their food must have it given to them—or steal it. So far as women, taken the world over, throughout history, have labored, it has been mainly in domestic service.

Domestic service is the lowest grade of labor remaining extant. It belongs to an earlier social era. Just behind it is feudal serfdom, and, behind that, slavery. The special relations of individual servant and mistress do not affect the question at all, any more than the ideal relation of slave and master in many Southern homes affected the real status of slavery. As an economic status that of domestic service is the lowest stage of industrial development now in action among us. When a man marries a housemaid, makes a wife of his servant, he alters her social status; but if she continues in the same industry he does not alter her economic status. When he makes a servant of his wife, or she of herself by choice, whatever her social, civil, mental or moral status may be, her economic status is that of domestic service. What she is entitled to receive from society for her labor is the wages of the housemaid. What she gets more than that is given her by her husband without any economic equivalent. She is supported by him on account of her sex. It is a low position in this mighty modern world so complex and stirring, so full of noble activities, to earn no higher place than was open to the slave of countless centuries ago, but it is a far lower position to be fed and clothed as a sex-dependent, as a creature without economic usefulness.

This economic dependence is the underlying ground of the helplessness of women. They have good hands and heads to work with, as every step of their freer education shows; but no human creatures can be free whose bread is in other hands than theirs. No sentiment, no loving feeling, no arbitrary enactment alters the inexorable truth of these economic laws. Husband, father or brother may give wealth to wife, daughter or sister—but that does not make her economically independent in the true sense. As well pile your canary's cage with seed and sugar and say he is independent of your care....

It is not merely a question of training young girls better. The work itself needs to be done better, and done on a different plane. This is the age of organized industry; of specialization; of progressive invention. An exceptional woman in an exceptional house may do wonders, and feel that she has solved the questions; but what really lies before us is the improvement of living conditions for the whole world.

Only in a large, well managed business combination can these matters of heating, lighting, feeding, clothing and cleaning be rightfully carried out; and only in the ample scope of such orderly industry, in its regular hours of labor and free time of rest, and in its well earned, liberal payment for each grade of service, can women fulfil their duties in this line and be free human creatures too. We shall have far cleaner, stiller, healthier, happier homes, when their long outgrown industries are at last cut loose and sent where they belong; and women will enjoy their homes, places of pure rest and loving companionship, far more than is possible to the overworked housewife or idle housemistress of to-day.

Against all this so visible trend of change rises the great cry of frightened motherhood; the protest that women must stay alone at home and do their housework because only so can they do their duty by their children.

How do we know this? How do we know that the care of children by the individual mother in the personally conducted home is the best thing for the world?

There is nothing to reply except that it is "natural"—that it always was so and always will be—the same old deadweight of black feeling without one glimmering flash of thought. Without trying to argue—it is useless to reason against feeling—let it be flatly asserted, first that the vast majority of children are very ill cared for and ill trained by their most loving mothers; that they die in vast proportion, that they are most unnecessarily sick; that they grow up—such of them as survive—to be the kind of tired, timid, selfish, unprogressive people of whom the world is all too full.

Moreover, while women are content with their economic position of house-servant, this cannot be bettered. Only an independent motherhood, working wisely in well-organized businesses, will grow to see that the care of children is a profession in itself—the noblest and most important of all human work, and not to be lightly undertaken and bunglingly struggled through by every female who can bear young. The kind of work, the range of interests, in which women spend their lives, prevent the development of brain which is so desperately needed in the race.

More than any other thing we need better people—much better people. To the women we must look for these, for they are the makers of men; and the hand-made, home-made variety, which we have always had with us, does not seem to improve as fast as it might be hoped. Homes are open to change and improvement as well as kingdoms or churches....

Women need to recognize that they are separate human beings and members of civilized society. As such they have rights, and with the rights, duties. Their struggle, so far, has been for room, freedom, privilege, and right. They have rebelled against the pains and limitations of their dependence, and have striven nobly for liberty. But the basis of their dependence is economic; their freedom must be economic, to be more than a name; and with their economic rights go duties, larger than we know. Life consists of what you do, not what you feel or think or have done to you. These are but conditions. Living is doing. The advance of the world is along lines of ever wider activity; and no part of our vast human network can linger long behind the rest.

While women remain in their present condition of economic dependence, or household labor, the society of which they are a part cannot advance beyond a certain point. Our civilization will break and fall as have all others, unless we consent to move at last and let the world go free. And independent womanhood, clear-headed, strong-hearted, holding social duty so high as to refuse a weak and evil father to their children; happy and busy in their places in the throbbing web of modern industry; doing their share in the maintenance of homes which no longer hide the daylight from them; and at last—at last—seeing that only a united womanhood can give right care to the childhood of the world; only such womanhood as this can fill its place on earth and do full duty here.

And only with full human duty can come full right to human freedom and human power.

Appendix B: Early Reviews of Women and Economics in the United States and Abroad

[In the months following its publication, *Women and Economics* was reviewed in numerous influential newspapers and literary magazines. The passages below are a sample of those reviews. The passages from *The Bookman* (B6), *Book Buyer* (B1), *Literary World* (B2), and the *Independent* (B4) offer an exposition of Gilman's main argument, and they demonstrate that contemporary readers were struck as much by Gilman's persuasive tone and style as by the substance of her work. Advertisements for the book continued to be published months after the book's initial printing, and the notice published in the popular weekly magazine *The Living Age* (B5) highlights for American readers Gilman's growing international appeal.

Mabel Hurd's review for *Political Science Quarterly* (B3), the organ of the Academy of Political Science, interprets Gilman's work to political scientists and members of the professional intellectual class. As noted in the Introduction, Gilman was not formally educated, and while she was a founding member of a professional organization, she never received any advanced training in an academic field. The context in which she wrote helps explain Hurd's justified criticism that *Women and Economics* lacks methodological rigor (similar observations have been made about twentieth-century feminist writing, including Simone de Beauvoir's treatise *The Second Sex* [1949], which also draws on a combination of history, anecdote, and cultural analysis).

The British writer Vernon Lee (1856–1935) was almost a direct contemporary of Gilman (Lee was four years Gilman's senior and they died in the same year), and the two briefly corresponded. In this piece for *North American Review* (B7), Lee credits Gilman with "converting" her to feminism. Lee explains that her earlier hostility to the "woman question" stemmed from her feeling that overzealous activists dehumanize women by reducing them to their sexual identities, but Gilman's argument about women's economic "parasitism" has changed her outlook. Lee had close family and friendship ties to several European countries, and her review was later repurposed for the introduction to the Italian-language translation of *Women and Economics*.]

1. **"Women and Economics, by Charlotte Perkins Stetson,"** *Book Buyer*, vol. 16, no. 2, 1 March 1898, p. 197

In writing this book, it has been Mrs. Stetson's purpose to point out, explain, and justify the changes which are now going on in the relations of women to society. In brief, the position taken is that women have for centuries been economically dependent upon men; that as a result they have become more and more feminine and less and less normal members of the human race. The argument is extended to every branch of social activity with remarkable originality, and in a manner to stimulate the interest of every one. It may safely be said that hardly any book of recent years has treated a confused subject with so much real intelligence and in an attitude so singularly fair and high-minded.

2. **"Women and Economics,"** *Literary World*, vol. 29, no. 26, 24 December 1898, p. 451

Mrs. Charlotte Perkins Stetson, of Beecher descent, has slowly and surely been winning fame by her verses anent[1] Californian life, and by her larger pleas for a wider public justice, but this volume is her first serious effort in book form. It is free from dogmatism and marked with sincerity; and without consideration of woman suffrage in the study of economic social evolution, the author explains and justifies the changes in the relations of women to society. The argument is that women's economic dependence upon man has unduly intensified sex-attraction, and that her sexuo-economic dependence has made her less and less a normal being; partnership in work and economic independence of man will tend to establish a happier and more normal relation. Mrs. Stetson writes with clearness and ease, and her position is that of most thoughtful and loving women, with the addition of courage to speak. There is nothing in the book to offend, and its general argument cannot be gainsaid[2] any more that its vision of better and happier home and state conditions, when a kitchen will not be a necessary equipment of each house, and when women are free to do that for which they are best fitted, independent of, but *not* deprived of, motherhood. There is so much originality and pleasant wit in the book that one reads

---

1 Concerning, about.
2 Denied, contradicted.

along its pages with a sense of enjoyment, without the annoyance which so often nettles a reader who has heard much of the "woman question."

3. Mabel Hurd, "Women and Economics," *Political Science Quarterly*, vol. 14, no. 4, December 1899, p. 712

Students of present social problems who are in no sense disciples of Fabian socialism have none the less learned to look to the Fabians for keen, vigorous and stimulating criticism of modern economics conditions. Mrs. Stetson is typically Fabia, in the suppression of her definite socialistic ideas while discussing a particular subject, in the freshness of her thought and in the interest of her style. As a result, her book will be widely read and discussed, as the cleverest, fairest and most forcible presentation of the views of the rapidly increasing group of people who look with favor upon the extension of the industrial employment of women.

The problem of method, on its formal side, is one that Mrs. Stetson has failed to master, and the whole work suffers in consequence. The main title is ambiguous; a table of contents and headings of chapters are entirely wanting; while the page headings, not grouped in any more general classification, are a mere mass of disconnected phrases, without unity or sequence. In the second edition an index is added, but this is extensive rather than discriminating. The central thought of the book is the advantage to the individual and to society of the economic independence of women. It is claimed that, while formerly the economic dependence of the woman upon the man was racially beneficial, through intensifying his incentives to effort, the need of such pressure is now past, and the relation is productive only of evil, increasing abnormally the difference between the sexes and hampering industrial and social progress. Mrs. Stetson brings a sweeping indictment against the economically dependent woman, as housekeeper, mother, wife, and member of society. She holds that, in the performance of each of these functions, far better physical, intellectual and moral results would be attained by the organization of the primitive home industries of cooking cleaning, and the care of young children, and by the direct employment of all women in some specific form of social service for which they would be personally remunerated, rather than in generalized home work. Women, in thus coming into direct economic relation with society, would, she contends, become more human and less feminine, and the change would react beneficially upon all their specific activities.

The chief value of Mrs. Stetson's book is to be found in her suggestive analysis of the evils of present family and social life, which she traces mainly to the "sexuo-economic relation," rather than in her historical and constructive work. There are no facts, however, more easily juggled with than those of general observation, and one must walk circumspectly when in the realm of a writer's favorite hypothesis. We realize this danger even more fully when we pass from Mrs. Stetson's critical treatment of her subject to her prophetic utterances. In describing the results to be attained through the employment of women in the interests of society, rather than of the family, she has outlined broadly the desirable ends, and has ignored the difficulties which our initial experiments in that direction are making only too evident. The future so glowingly described—the workshops "homelike and beautiful," the disappearance of materialism and selfishness—may come, and come as a result of woman's economic independence; but only a careful analysis of the actual effects of the presence of women in our daily industrial life can be made the basis of confidence in the rosy prophecy; and such a study Mrs. Stetson has failed to give us.

4. "Women and Economics," *Independent*, vol. 51, no. 2617, 26 January 1899, p. 283

This is an attempt to show that our domestic relations are all wrong. The trouble is that women are in a stage of economic development several hundred or thousand years behind men. Women have suffered from too much sex development and too little race development, with the result that human life has been carried on through the male side only. Civilization having been confined to one sex, it inevitably exaggerates sex distinction. "Women have been left behind, outside, below, having no social relation whatever, merely the sex relation whereby they lived." Ties of blood constitute tender relations, "but ties of blood are not those that ring the world with the succeeding waves of progressive religion, art, science, commerce, education—all that makes us human. Man is the human creature—woman has been checked, starved, aborted in human growth; and the swelling forces of race-development have been driven back in each generation to work in her through sex functions alone." It is true that maternity seems to be a responsibility that women cannot well avoid, if the world is to be peopled, but, after all, a woman ought to have twenty-five years before, and as many years after, this responsibility begins. During these periods, at least, she might engage in active outside life. Moreover, it is doubtful if the care of children is best left in the hands of mothers: "the home-cares and industries, still undeveloped, give no play for the increasing specialization of the American woman. She can no longer be an embryonic combination of cook, nurse, laundress, chambermaid, housekeeper, waitress, governess;" she suffers doubly from not being able to do what she wants to do, and from being forced to do what she does not want to do. The care of children should be given over to trained nurses and teachers; "the selection and preparation of food should be in the hands of trained experts." Many families now "put out" their washing; let them also put out their cooking, their sewing, and their children, and women will have leisure to take a more prominent economic position. Doubtless in this way the institution of family life would become much less prominent than it is now; but whether it would continue is questionable. If the children are to be sent out of the home, and if the family is to get its meals in cafes and restaurants, will it really be worth while to marry and beget children, or indeed to maintain a home at all? But while the ideals of this author may not appeal to us, we must admit that there is some force in her criticisms, and some reason in her suggestions.

5. Advertisement for "Women and Economics," *Living Age*, vol. 222, no. 2882, 30 September 1899, p. 2

Mrs. Charlotte Perkins Stetson's brilliant and fascinating "Women and Economics" was published a year ago last June. Few persons realize how steadily the book has grown—and is growing—in public estimation and in consequent sales. This last Summer has seen larger orders, and from more sources, than ever. Indeed, it can almost be said that any given month for the past year has surpassed the record of the month before. During the few months that it has been on sale in England a second edition has been called for, and it is being translated into German, Dutch, and Swedish. In this country interest in the book seems only to have begun, and it is likely that the Fall will see it popular beyond almost any recent book of so serious a kind.

6. From "Women and Economics," *The Bookman* [London], vol. 16, no. 96, September 1899, pp. 163–64

The "woman movement" has travelled far from Mary Wollstonecraft.[1] Even John Stuart Mill[2] is no longer its complete spokesman. Its promoters have been much influenced by the progress of democracy and socialism; and if they still make the old demands, they pioneer on so many new roads, that their friends of twenty years ago would not recognize the cause at all. The later movement has been written on largely; books, newspapers, and articles are devoted to it; but adverse critics have said that they are flabbier, much less able, than the manifestoes of the earlier struggle, and even some of the friends of the cause have owned the criticism to be correct. Here, however, is a book that whether we look on its teaching as wholesome or as dangerous, we are bound to acknowledge to be of exceptional ability. It is the book of a woman of a clear and of trained intellect, and of great courage. As such it demands attention, and very likely will get it, of a hostile kind, from many quarters. It is a revolutionary book; that is, it emphasises the causes and results of a revolution which Mrs. Stetson declares is already practically accomplished, however few persons may realise that it has seriously begun.

In a scientific spirit she acknowledges that the normal condition of women in historic times has been in obedience to a law long useful to the social state and to the care of the race. Sex was emphasised in woman for good social reasons, and man maintained her in return. The sexuo-economical position has been completely outgrown, she asserts; and its recent consequences have been evil for the individual and the race. By woman being over-sexed, the development of the race has been hindered. Further, she declares, we have developed enough for some of us to feel we have got beyond taking for granted that woman's economic profit must come through sex-attraction. A sordid, unnatural state of things has been reached. Women now want to choose their mates, and yet they must not. "When her wealth is made to come though the same channels as her love, she is forbidden to ask for it by her own sex nature and by business honour."

---

1 British philosopher Mary Wollstonecraft (1759–97), whose work *A Vindication of the Rights of Woman* (1792) is sometimes credited with being the first sustained work of feminist philosophy.

2 British philosopher John Stuart Mill (1806–73), whose work *The Subjection of Women* (1869) promoted equality between men and women.

It should be noted that the book is not an attack on men's tyranny over women. If it be an indictment, it is an indictment against women—with an explanation of how they have fallen short in their duties to society. Man's instinct is, she says, to produce, to express himself. Women have been forbidden to produce save in one way. Maintenance is provided irrespective of the quality of their production, and they have therefore become incapable of performing even the functions allotted to them. It is men who have contrived improvements in the clothing and food, in the amusement and the education of the child. Motherhood has been forced on her, but she has been mostly an amateur mother. The woman of the lower classes is a drudge, and in her unskilled way makes her own living and partly that of her household by domestic work. The woman of the upper classes receives without giving anything adequate in return, and women as nonproductive consumers have been an evil influence in society.

Single women by thousands now are economically independent. Mrs. Stetson desires marriage to be no bar to the same condition. The present state of things is unsatisfactory. Whether drudges or drones, women as mothers, for lack of training, amateurs. For nursery education they may have talent. Give them a choice, and see. Also heighten the standard of the care of children enormously by making it a desirable and honourable and specialist career. Give babies a chance of professional care, and of not too much individual attention. (Now we hear the deep matter of revolt.) Economic independence must alter home-life, to some extent break up home life, as we understand it. Oh yes; she wishes it so....

Mrs. Stetson is too wise to describe in detail how economic independence will come about in individual cases. She knows how to choose a career compatible with marriage, ideally conceived, herself; and trusts other women can do the same. They will make experiments and mistakes, and benefit by them.... She has presented her case with admirable clearness and force, and with a wealth of illustration which shows a ready, a vivid mind. If you are in the mood to argue, however, she gives you openings. Surely it would not be so impossible as she thinks to regulate in some fashion the present transition state, whereby the work a woman does in the household, or as a social helper of her husband, should be more openly acknowledged than it is at present, as giving her a claim to economic independence. Then we think that she exaggerates somewhat the present cry for freedom of individuality. Men and women are sheep now only less than they have always been. And such an observation as this, that "it is not so easy now to choose a book that a well-educated family of modern girls and their mother would all enjoy together," does not apply to England, at least. But, in general, she speaks for our young people as well as for young America; and if she does something to make our homes in general a little less sordid, a little less foolishly indulgent, and a little less boring, she will have earned the hearty thanks of youth.

7. From Vernon Lee, "The Economic Dependence of Women," *North American Review*, vol. 175, no. 548, July 1902, pp. 71–91

In recommending Mrs. Stetson's "Women and Economics" ... I am accomplishing the duty of a convert. I believe that "Women and Economics" ought to open the eyes and, I think, also the hearts, of other readers, because it has opened my own to the real importance of what is known as the Woman Question.

I must begin by confessing that the question which goes by that name had never attracted my attention, or, rather, that I had on every occasion evaded and avoided it. Not in the least, however, on account of any ridicule which may attach to it. There is, thank goodness, a spice of absurdity in every one, and in every thing, we care for in this world....

My vague avoidance of the movement was not even due to the perception of some of the less enjoyable peculiarities of its devotees. For a very small knowledge of mankind, and a very slight degree of historical culture, suffice to teach one that it is not the well-balanced, the lucid, the sympathizingly indulgent or the especially gracious and graceful among human beings who are employed by Providence for the attack and possible destruction of long-organized social evils; nay, that the martyrdom in behalf of any new cause begins, one may say, by the constitution of the individual as an inevitable eccentric, unconscious of the diffidence, the skepticism, the sympathy, the sense of fitness and measure which check, divert, or hamper normal human beings.... Feminism, is likely to be taken up by those disconnected and disjointed personalities who are attracted by every other kind of thing in *ism*; whose power consists a little in their very inferiority; and whose abnormal and often morbid "pleasure in saying 'no'" (as Nietzsche puts it[1])

---

1 In his book *Will to Power*, German philosopher Friedrich Wilhelm Nietzsche (1844–1900) posits that art is the opposite of pessimism, which he defined as "saying No to life."

is, after all, alas! alas! so very necessary in this world of quite normally stupid and normally selfish and normally virtuous "pleasure in saying 'yes.'"

All these things I knew, of course, and I did not really think it was any of them which made me thus indifferent, and perhaps even a little hostile, towards that Woman Question. Indeed, when I seek in the depths of my consciousness, I think the real mischief lay in that word "Woman." For, while that movement was, of course, intended to break down the legal, professional, educational, and social barriers which still exist between the sexes, yet, owing to the fact of its necessarily pitting one of these sexes against the other; owing to the inevitable insistence on what *can*, or *cannot*, *must*, or *must not*, be done, said, or thought by women and not men—women—women—women—always women! there naturally arose a certain feeling, pervading, overpowering, intolerable—like that one suffers from in visiting a harem or a convent—the fact of sex, exclusive, aggressive, immodestly out of place, perpetually obtruded on one's consciousness; while the other fact, the universal, chaste, spiritual fact of *humanness*, of *Homo* as distinguished from mere *Vir* and *Femina*, was lost sight of.[1] And somehow—if one is worth one's salt, if one feels normal kinship not only with the talking and (occasionally) thinking creature around one, but also with animals, plants, earth, skies, waters, and all things past and present ... why, then, one feels a little bored, a little outraged, nay, even sickened, by this everlasting question of sex qualifications and sex disqualifications; and (very unjustly, but perhaps therefore very naturally) one gets to shrink from that particular question exactly because it *is* the *Woman* Question.

Very unjustly. Let me repeat that; and remind the reader that what I am describing is my still unregenerate state....

I was converted by Mrs. Stetson's unpretending little book, because in it the rights and wrongs of *Femina, das Weib*, were not merely opposed to the rights and wrongs of *Vir, der Mann*, but subordinated to those of what is, after all, a bigger item of creation: *Homo, der Mensch*.[2]

There was nothing new in connecting the Woman Question with Economics. If I may judge by myself, the majority of people who know anything of Political Economy must be accustomed to regard such questions as marriage, divorce, prostitution, the legal

---

1 Latin: *homo*, human being or mankind; *vir*, man; *femina*, woman.
2 German: *das Weib*, woman; *der Mann*, man; *der Mensch*, mankind.

position of mothers and fathers, and many of the peculiarities of law and custom with respect to the sexes, as hinging upon the facts of wealth production and distribution, tenure of soil, heredity and division of property; upon the whole immense question of the individual's share in the products of nature, of invention, and of industry. Indeed, I much suspect that, as in my case, many thinking persons shelve the question of women's abilities and disabilities exactly because it seems to depend almost completely upon the far more important question of the redistribution of wealth; to represent a minor act of social justice and social practicality (bringing much waste energy under cultivation) inevitably involved in the greater act of social justice and social practicality which, through revolution or evolution, must needs take place some day or other.

The originality, the scientific soundness and moral efficacy of "Women and Economics," appear to me to lie in its partially reversing this fact; and in its substituting a moral and psychological reason for the rather miraculous mechanicalness which mars every form of the "historical materialism" of the Marxian school. In other words, this book shows that the present condition of women—their state of dependence, tutelage, and semi-idleness; their sequestration from the discipline of competition and social selection, in fact their economic parasitism—is in itself a most important factor in the wrongness of all our economic arrangements....

Now the really fine piece of work which Mrs. Stetson has done, has been to demonstrate—to me at least—that, although the exclusion of womankind from the world's active work, and her subordination to man, have been a sociological necessity— the price paid for the lengthened infancy, the increased educability of man, and also for that solid familial organization which alone permitted an accumulation and multiplication of human inventions and traditions; that although the *regression*, or, at all events, the stagnation of one half of the human race has been inevitable and beneficial in the past, it has ceased to be beneficial, and is ceasing to be inevitable, in the present. A particular automatic arrangement of historical evolution has done its work; like slavery, like servage, like feudalism, like centralization (according to socialists), it has grown to be an impediment to progress. For the prolonged infancy and youth of genus *homo* can no longer be endangered; and a large proportion of human education has, since thousands of years, passed from the care of the mother to that of the community as a whole, or of portions—guilds, priesthoods, universities, and so forth—of the community; while, on the other hand, the inventions and traditions have been stored, multiplied, and diffused far beyond the powers of family education. The benefit has long, long ago been obtained beyond all possibility of loss; but the price is still being paid for.

Now, what is that price? The stagnation or regression, answers M. Durkheim,[1] of the female mind. The removal, answers Mrs. Stetson, enlarging the same thought with a different intention, the removal of womankind from the field of action and reaction called "the universe at large" to the field of action and reaction called "the family circle;" the substitution, as a factor of adaptation and selection, of the preference of the husband or possible husband for the preferences, so to speak, of the whole of creation. In other words, the sequestration of the capacities of one half of the human race, and their enclosure inside the habits and powers of the other half of the human race. Briefly, a condition in which the man plays the part of the animal who moves and feeds freely on the earth's surface; and the woman the part of the parasitic creature who lives inside that animal's tissues. The comparison is exact; but we ought not to push the analogy to the point of considering the parasitism of womankind as the parasitism of a destructive microbe. The mischief lies not in the fact of parasitism, but in the fact that this parasitic life has developed in the parasite one set of faculties and atrophied another; atrophied the faculties which the woman had (or might have had, even if in lesser degree) in common with the man, and developed those which were due to the fact of her being a woman....

There is one particular sentence in "Women and Economics" which converted me to the cause of female emancipation: "Women are over-sexed." ...

Women over-sexed! *Over-sexed!* There seems something odious and almost intolerable in that word. In the fact also—but odious and intolerable in a manner more subtle and more serious than mere scandalized modesty can ever understand. Let me try to explain the extreme importance of Mrs. Stetson's thought. *Over-sexed* does not mean over-much addicted to sexual indulgence; very far from it, for that is the case not with women, but with men, of whom we do not say they are *over-sexed*. What we mean by *over-sexed* is that, while men are a great many things besides being males—soldiers and sailors, tinkers and tailors, and all the rest of the nursery rhyme—women are, first and foremost,

---

1 French sociologist David Émile Durkheim (1858–1917).

females, and then again females, and then—still more females.... And here we touch the full mischief. That women are *over-sexed* means that, instead of depending upon their intelligence, their strength, endurance, and honesty, they depend mainly upon their sex; that they appeal to men, dominate men through the fact of their sex; that (if the foregoing seems an exaggeration) they are economically supported by men because they are wanted as wives and mothers of children—that is to say, wanted for their sex. And it means, therefore, by a fearful irony, that the half of humanity which is constitutionally (and by the bare facts of motherhood) more chaste, has unconsciously and inevitably acquired its power, secured its livelihood, by making the other half of humanity less chaste, by appealing through every means, material, aesthetic and imaginative, sensual or sentimental, to those already excessive impulses and thoughts of sex. The woman has appealed to the man, not as other men appeal to him, as a comrade, a competitor, a fellow-citizen, or an open enemy of different nationality, creed, or class; but as a possible wife, as a female. This has been a cause of weakness and degradation to the man; a "fall," like that of Adam; and in those countries where literature is thoroughly outspoken, man, like Adam, has thrown the blame on Eve, as the instrument of the Devil....

How do you propose to remedy it? By what arrangements do you expect to make the wife the economic equal of her husband, and joint citizen of the community?

I propose nothing, because I do not know. All I feel sure of is, that if people only want a change sufficiently strongly and persistently, that change will work out its means in one way or another. Which way? is a question often unanswerable, because the practical detail depends upon other practical details which the continuance of the present state of things is hiding from us, or even forbidding. And because, moreover, we are surrounded on all sides by resources which become available only in connection with other resources, and only under the synthetic power of desire....

One of the very great uses of Mrs. Stetson's most useful book is to accustom those who *can* think, to think in terms of change, of adaptation, of evolution; to free us from the superstition that the present is the type of the eternal, and that our preferences of to-day are what decide the fate of the universe.

Appendix C: Women, Work, and the Home

[Turning a spotlight on the relationship between sexuality and economics, *Women and Economics* upended longstanding sentimental ideas about motherhood and the family, and it provided an intellectual basis for women's claims to economic autonomy and equal access to jobs. Not all Americans were convinced, and antifeminist critics—whom Gilman contemptuously referred to as the "antis"—counterargued that women's claims to economic equality degraded maternity and deprived children of necessary care. In 1913, the New York City Board of Education undertook to fire female, but not male, married teachers who became parents, a move that wasn't wholly unusual for the time, given that numerous American cities already had in place regulations forbidding the employment of married women. The Board's actions led to a heated public debate about whether women had a right to equal employment.

"The Edgell case" referred to throughout this appendix involved the attempted dismissal of the Brooklyn High School teacher Catherine Campbell Edgell. During a pregnancy, Edgell applied for a year's leave from work without pay to give birth to and care for her baby. Edgell's request was initially approved by the Committee on High Schools, but it was ultimately rejected when the Board of Education declined to uphold the Committee's decision. Without parental leave policies in place, women in Edgell's position were obliged to take leave from their posts without permission and thus faced potential suspension or dismissal for failing to perform their duties. The documents below represent the views held by critics on either side of the debate.

The *Independent*'s editorial column, "Penalizing Parenthood" (C1), condemns the Board's decision, comparing its treatment of women teachers to the racialized exclusion of Black people in the nineteenth century and the unjust punishment of accused witches in seventeenth-century Europe. The *Independent* subsequently published letters responding to the editorial (C2). John Martin, a member of the New York Board of Education, writes in defence of the Board's refusal to provide parental leave, expressing his view that women's primary duty is to their children. Martin and his wife, Prestonia Mann Martin, were Fabians and one-time friends of Gilman (Prestonia worked on *The Fabian*

Socialist newspaper, discussed in Appendix A). Read alongside *Women and Economics,* Martin's position on the teacher-mother debacle demonstrates the divergent perspective about gender and power that obtained among socialists at the time. Professor William Pepperell Montague, a professor of philosophy at Columbia University, asserts his support for the women pressing for a change of policy in the schools. The question of the legality of maternity bans for working women was eventually determined by the New York State Supreme Court. "The Case of the Teacher Mothers" (C3) reproduces excerpts from Justice Seabury's findings that dismissing women who become pregnant is "repugnant."]

1. **"Penalizing Parenthood,"** *Independent***, vol. 74, 20 March 1913, p. 1**

The Edgell case bids fair to take rank with the Dred Scott case and the Jane Wenham case as one of those defeats which stand as monuments to measure the onward march of progress. In 1857 the United States Supreme Court declared for the last time that the negro has no rights that the white man is bound to respect [Dred Scott case]. In 1712 an English judge for the last time condemned a woman to death for witchcraft [Jane Wenham case]. In 1913 the New York City Board of Education decide that a woman teacher has no right to have a child. Would that we might write "for the last time" in this case also, but with a vote of 32 to 5 against Mrs. Edgell we fear that we would not be justified in assuming that the force of reactionism is exhausted.

Fortunately, the issue is clear and a plain statement of the case is sufficient to show the enormity of the action. Mrs. Edgell, teacher of physical culture in the Erasmus Hall High School, Brooklyn, and the wife of a teacher in the same school, applied for a leave of absence without pay for one year, stating with unprecedented frankness that she was soon to become a mother. The Committee on High Schools approved the petition, but the Board of Education, on motion of Commissioner Abraham Stern, refused even to allow a discussion of the question. Mrs. Edgell is now liable to dismissal for neglect of duty. If she should later apply for reinstatement she would undoubtedly be refused and if she did manage to enter the school system again she would have to begin at the bottom of the ladder with the lowest salary.

The board is willing enough to grant leave of absence to teachers for recreation, recuperation, travel, and study, yet it is blind to the fact that the experience of maternity is far more important than any of these, considered from the standpoint of educational efficiency. It would have been much more sensible of the board to have granted Mrs. Edgell a leave of absence for a year and a half with salary and a promise of promotion when she came back. In fact, it may be questioned whether any woman except a mother is altogether competent to serve in the responsible position of physical director to girls of the high school age. In France, a woman teacher under such circumstances is allowed a month's pay, and in Great Britain and Australia the Government contributes to the support of working mothers.

But this latest action of the New York Board of Education is what might have been expected from its previous treatment of the thousands of women who are at its mercy. It denied them equal pay for equal work until the women teachers organized in their own defense and by bringing political pressure to bear secured their pecuniary rights. Then the board discharged teachers for marrying—the women, mind you, not the men—but after a long fight in the courts the women teachers secured their right to a marriage. Now they have to make another fight if they are not to be deprived of the most important of all woman's rights, the right to maternity. The Women Lawyers' Club of New York is already preparing to take the Edgell case into the courts.

To readers in our western States this exposure of the treatment of women in New York will seem almost incredible. For their benefit we must explain first that the women in this city have no vote, even on school matters. Second, a large part of the population consists of immigrants from European countries where women are still regarded as inferior beings, having no rights that a man is bound to respect. No one who knows the history of THE INDEPENDENT will accuse it of race prejudice, yet it is necessary to admit that the wave of recent immigration has brought with it the Oriental conception of woman's status. A man whose religion requires him to every morning thank God that he was not born a woman is likely to treat women so that they will wish they had been born men. We must not shut our eyes to the fact that in the future the Christian conception of womanhood is not to be maintained in this country without a struggle.

2. "The Edgell Case: May a Married Woman Be a Teacher?" *Independent*, vol. 74, no. 3362, 8 May 1913, pp. 1030–31

In our editorial on "Penalizing Parenthood," published March 20, 1913, we suggested that the Edgell case might come to have the historic significance of the Dred Scott slavery case and the Jane Wenham witchcraft case as one of those defeats which stand as monuments to measure the progress of the race. In New York City recently a large number of teachers, authors, editors, lawyers, ministers, and sociologists met at the home of one of the leaders of the suffrage movement to organize a Committee on the Civil Service of Women. The question may be taken into the courts in order to reverse the ruling of the Board of Education in this case. After a long legal fight the Board of Education was compelled by the courts to rescind its rule prohibiting women teachers from marrying. It would naturally be supposed that the right to marry, now conceded to the women teachers of New York, includes the right to parenthood, but evidently the Board of Education thinks differently, so another fight will probably have to be made.

The question of the married woman teacher is not peculiar to New York City, but comes up everywhere and involves the wider question of whether women of ability and ambition shall be compelled in all cases to make a choice between marriage and a profession, a choice in which either alternative means a loss to the community. From the many letters and articles which we have received on this subject we select two for publication as they present able arguments on both side of the question. The first is from Mr. John Martin, a member of the New York Board of Education, and one who voted with the majority against allowing Mrs. Edgell a leave of absence. The second is from Prof. W.P. Montague, of Columbia University.—EDITOR.

In Defense of the Board

Your editorial on the refusal of the Board of Education of New York City to grant a year's leave of absence to a teacher in a high school who is about to bear a child, and on the opinion of the board that a teacher, during her childbearing period, should resign school work shows a misconception of vital parts of the case.

You state that the board frowns on maternity and would discourage marriage. On the contrary the board applauds maternity and encourages marriage. But, in addition, the board appreciates, as you do not, the inalienable right of an infant to a mother's care and lays down the general rule that a baby must not be sacrificed that its parents may enjoy superfluous luxury.

The Board of Education accepts the biological fact that the duties of father and mother toward their offspring are not alike, that each has obligations which it is detestable to shirk. Normally and desirably the father is the bread-winner; the mother the nurse and baby-trainer. To convert the woman at the child-bearing age into the bread-winner is to sacrifice the next generation to the cupidity of the present generation. It is one of the indictments against our industrial, capitalistic era that it has drawn women into factory and workshop, there to be exploited for pecuniary profit, while their babies languish for their care and the infant death rate in the factory towns is monstrously high. Humane husbands willingly work to the limits of their strength to save their wives during the exhausting period of pregnancy, lactation and early infancy from the cruel burden of wage earning. Trade unions demand a family living-wage for men. Social reformers compile family budgets as arguments for a minimum wage for fathers. The Board of Education has established salaries in high schools on the assumption that a man teacher should be able to support a family. The teacher-husband of the woman in the case under dispute is receiving $3000 a year—a salary on which the great majority of citizens can live without requiring the mother in her child-bearing period to contribute to the family purse. Employers would be only too glad to substitute the individual living-wage for the family living wage.

Fanatical feminists, while pretending to defend woman's interests, are actually sacrificing the interests of woman and of the race to man's laziness and love of luxury. They would change the condition, still happily normal, in which the mother is exempt from outside labor, into the condition, unhappily found in various mill towns, under which the mother toils at loom and machine almost up to the day of her supreme pangs and returns to the grind a few days later, which her baby's life, never strong, is quickly snuffed out by her enforced neglect. Some actually quote with approval and glee the alleged case of a woman member of the Finnish Parliament who took only a fortnight from her duties for childbirth. "See what a trifling incident motherhood can be made," they exclaim. "Why should motherhood exempt a woman from shouldering half of man's work?"

So horrible is the condition in factory towns that progressive states, for the protection of the next generation, compel the mother to rest for a month or two before and after childbirth. The more progressive the state the longer the compulsory rest. Neither a penurious father nor a misguided mother is allowed to plead that the family needs the mother's earnings. The law compels her to abstain from mill work. Now, the Board of Education says that, normally, the mother should be freed from outside wage-earning for nine months before the birth and at least two years after the birth and that men's wages and salaries should be fixt on that assumption. It views with horror the spectacle of a prospective mother standing for five or six hours before a class at the nerve-wracking work of teaching. It thinks only with grief of the mother deserting the infant whose claims are paramount to all other claims, while she, with mind inevitably reverting every minute to that infant, is pretending to teach a troop of other people's children. And all for what? That the luxury she and her husband enjoy might be softer and more expensive. Where the husband's wages, under our chaotic social system, are not sufficient to provide the rest for the mother and her care for the babe, the remedy is to raise his wages. Where the wages, as in this instance, are ample, the remedy is to teach the parents that no luxury can atone for the loss of a mother's care to a young infant nor of parental affection and delight to a pair of adults.

If the father, being morose, cruel or stingy, refuses to recognize the mother's right, for herself and children, to most of his earnings, the remedy is not to allow his selfishness to prevail, by encouraging the mother to be also a bread-winner; but to give the mother a legal claim, which he cannot escape, to the necessary part of his income.

But, you say, some teachers do not marry and some teacher-mothers can get a cheaper woman to tend their babes as well as they. We are dealing with normal cases. Only in exceptional cases—as yet—do men not marry (tho the general adoption of your assumption that $3000 a year is not enough for parenthood would speedily increase the proportion of bachelors); only in very exceptional cases is some other woman better fitted than the mother to caress, tend and train the infant (as the appalling death record of infant asylums demonstrates). The exceptional woman who is so devoid of maternal instinct that her child can better be handed to a stranger is not the kind we want as a teacher.

The Board of Education assumes that, normally, a mother will have several children. It does not approve the race suicide practised by the very rich, to leave time and money for vainglorious show and debilitating luxury, which is so terrifyingly depicted by Zola in *Fecundity*.[1] Nor does it expect women teachers to emulate that debased example. Therefore it says that a married woman teacher must normally and happily expect to be out of school for maternal duties several times. If the rule were established that twelve months' leave of absence should be granted in each case, the mother, while nominally holding the position which must meanwhile be filled by a procession of transient substitutes, will really be present only for a month or two between successive periods of absence. Thereby the interests of thirty or forty children would be continually sacrificed to the avarice of the teacher.

Can you point out a single case where an employer of women labor has established the rule to grant a year's leave of absence for child-bearing? Have you or any other feminist ever disorganized your business by letting even a stenographer have a year off? Why should the children of New York be made an offering on the altar of feminist perversity?

JOHN MARTIN.

A Criticism of the Board

The recent action of the New York Board of Education in refusing the application of a high school teacher for a year's leave of absence, without pay, for the purpose of becoming a mother, has been justified on the following grounds: (1) That it is for the best interest of women teachers themselves that they be not permitted to add the burden of motherhood to the burden of teaching; (2) that it is to the interest of society at large that women be not permitted to add the burden of motherhood to the burden of teaching; (3) that it is to the interest of children that their mothers devote their whole time to their households; and (4) that it is very emphatically to the interest of the pupils in the schools and of the school system as a whole that the women who teach should be unmarried, or if they marry, that they should at least remain childless. In opposition to these conclusions, however, the following considerations should be taken into account.

1. *The Effect upon the Teachers:* To prove that it is not to the interest of the women teachers to permit them to retain their positions when they wish to bear children, this ruling of the

---

[1] *Fécondité* (1899) is the first novel in French author Émile Zola's four-part series *Les Quatre Évangiles* (1899–1903).

Board of Education has been compared by its defenders to certain beneficent statutes which prohibit manufacturers from employing their women workers directly before and after confinement. This comparison is a strange one, to say the least. Factory work is for the women who engage in it a painful necessity, while teaching, especially when continued by women after marriage, is an art or profession that is freely chosen. Moreover, the intent of the factory laws is to make it easier for women to have children when they wish them, while the intent of this action against the teachers is to make it more difficult for them to have children.

2. *The Effect upon the Race:* Whether or not women *ought* to give up their professions, it is hardly open to dispute that they *will* not, and that for the last twenty years, and for many years to come, more and more women have been seeking and will seek some sort of profession or career outside the home. Recognizing this situation to exist, quite irrespective of its desirability, the question presents itself, Shall we encourage voluntary sterility or shall we do what we can to make it possible for the increasing numbers of professional women to have children? To forbid women to have children on pain of losing their positions obviously tends to weaken the race, for it leaves the function of reproduction to be performed by the less enterprising and ambitious women, in exactly the same way that the great wars of the past left the main burden of reproduction to the less courageous and ambitious men. Professions for women may be as bad as wars for men, but that does not alter the fact that the most courageous men will go to the wars and the most capable women will seek some sort of career.

3. *The Effect upon the Teacher's Children:* A mother who is in a profession cannot, it must be admitted, give her children the same quantity of personal attention as the mother who has no interests outside her home. But in such cases, quality makes up for quantity; for the kind of attention that a mother can give to her children when she has had the broadening influences, the mental and moral discipline and wisdom that come as a result of making a place for herself in the world is infinitely more worth while than the extra hours that she could have given them had she remained in the home. Moreover, the trained woman can enjoy a degree of intellectual comradeship with her children *after they are grown up* which is impossible for the woman who has spent all her best years as her children's nurse. The woman who has no *organized* interest outside her household often hands over

her children to nurses, and spends the leisure so gained in the *unorganized* and relatively profitless activities of "society."

4. *The Effect on the Pupils and on the School System:* it must be conceded that during the two or three years of absence necessitated by motherhood on the part of the teacher the pupils suffer just in proportion to the extent that the substitute teacher is less efficient than the regular teacher who is away on leave. But:

(a) The woman who is a mother is presumably better fitted to instruct and care for children than the spinster who lacks that normal and life-enriching experience. And this compensates also for whatever distraction of interest on the part of the teacher may arise from anxiety to return to her own children at home. As a matter of fact the sense of responsibility for her pupils and the sympathetic understanding of their needs would probably be greater even in the cases in which the teacher-mother had reason to worry about her own children at home than in the case of the average unmarried woman.

(b) Any direct loss to the teacher's pupils due either to the bearing or to the rearing of her children would be more than made up for by the indirect improvement in the status of the teaching profession that would result from freeing it from the indignity and inefficiency of *casual labor*. The Board of Education in its ruling in the Edgell case intimates to the woman who wishes to teach that when she marries she had better resign (for she cannot hope for promotion) and that when she has children she must resign. At the same time the members of the board *feel* that marriage and motherhood are normal and desirable for women. Taking their ruling and their feeling together, the logical result is an acceptance of women teachers with the understanding that they are to be only temporary or "casual" workers. Instead of encouraging celibacy and enforcing sterility for those who are to remain permanently in the profession, how much better it would be to encourage marriage and motherhood and so make it possible for girls to adopt the profession of teaching as a permanent life-work without feeling that by so doing they would have to forego their own natural functions. This whole matter can be summed up in the charge that the Board of Education wrongly and unjustly imposes upon women teachers the following dilemma—either they are to adopt teaching merely as a temporary stopgap, or else they are to forego what is admitted to be their own normal and desirable development. Either the *teaching* must be injured by being made casual labor or the *teachers* must be injured by remaining celibate and childless.

In short, the action of the board in relation to Mrs. Edgell is not justified either (1) by the interests of the teacher; (2) by the interests of posterity and society at large; (3) by the interests of the children of the teachers; or (4) by the interests of the schools and school children.

W. P. MONTAGUE.

3. "The Case of the Teacher Mothers," *Outlook*, 6 December 1913, pp. 729–30

The Outlook has reported the dismissal of a woman from her position as a teacher in the public schools of New York City on the ground that her absence for the purpose of bearing a child constituted "neglect of duty." The teacher appealed to the New York Supreme Court for reinstatement, and her appeal has been granted. Justice Seabury, in handing down the decision, said in part:

> The policy of our law favors marriage and the birth of children, and I know of no provision of our statute law or any principle of common law which justifies the inference that a public policy which concededly sanctions the employment of married women as teachers treats as ground of expulsion the act of a married woman in giving birth to a child.
>
> Whether the legislature should exclude married women from the schools as teachers, assuming that it has the power to do so, is a question upon which there may be differences of opinion, but it is not the province of the court to decide. The fact is that the Legislature had sanctioned the employment of married women as teachers. Married women being lawfully employed as teachers and excusable for absence caused by "personal illness," the idea that because the illness resulting in absence is caused by maternity it therefore becomes "neglect of duty" is repugnant to law and good morals.

With the expression and spirit of Justice Seabury's opinion The Outlook is in hearty sympathy. We have opposed the ruling of the New York City Board of Education from the view-point of both the school and the home. The chief concern of a school system is education. Those who have opposed the employment of married women on the ground that their places are needed for self-supporting single women seem to us to have missed the point entirely. Schools exist not for the teachers but for the taught.

Those who opposed the employment of married women because child-bearing sometimes incapacitates them for their work as teachers have seemed to us equally astray. The spiritual gain more than offsets the temporary loss of time and service. Teaching is not a purely intellectual pursuit. Not how much a teacher knows but how much he or she can impart, is the vital question. This ability to give out knowledge comes not only from experience as a teacher, but from experience with life as well. To sacrifice teachers who have grown into their work for the sake of a dogmatic ruling is the height of folly.

The argument that is sometimes brought forward, that the enforced absence of teacher mothers disorganizes the school system, is hardly creditable to our school system nor credible by any one possessing a moderate amount of information or intelligence. There were, we believe, some fifteen cases of absence for motherhood in New York City during the past year. Surely the New York public school system, employing teachers by the thousands, is robust enough to stand such a relatively insignificant loss!

It has been argued, with greater show of reason, that some young mothers cannot maintain the standard of their school work. If this is true, the question whether a mother should retain her position should be decided not by any hard and fast ruling but upon the merits of each individual case. The solution of this problem, where a particularly capable teacher is concerned, can be found and the interests of both home and school preserved by the granting of a more prolonged leave of absence than is generally deemed necessary.

Individuals and organizations interested in the case of Mrs. Bridget C. Peixotto, the teacher who was dismissed by the Board of Education because she remained away to become a mother, and whose appeal to the Court of Appeals for reinstatement was denied on Tuesday, began a campaign yesterday to amend the rules of the Education Board and the laws of the State to prevent the dismissal of other teacher mothers.

The League for the Civic Service of Women has written to each member of the Board of Education in which six arguments are advanced why teacher mothers should not be dropped. The members of the league have pledged themselves to call upon each member of the board and ask his reasons for his stand. Fifty other cases are still awaiting final action by the board.

The League will also urge the repeal of one of the Board of Education's by-laws, which provides that no married woman shall be appointed to a teaching position unless her husband is incapacitated or has abandoned her for three years. In another by-law, providing for the granting of leaves of absence, the words "or for child bearing" will be added to "purposes of study or restoration of health," which are the reasons for which leaves of absence may now be given. A public hearing on Oct. 27 before the board will be sought.

A bill to be introduced at the next session of the Legislature making it a misdemeanor for an employer to refuse employment on account of marriage or parenthood is being drafted by Mrs. Jean H. Norris of the league's Law Committee and President of the Women's Lawyers' Club. In the passage of this the aid of the labor unions is expected.

"The present conditions are immoral and a moral to the public welfare," said Mrs. Henrietta Rodman de Fremery, Vice President of the league, who married when she was a teacher in Wadleigh High School. "We believe that we are acting in the interest of public opinion when we suggest these changes."

Other members of the league who have pledged themselves to take an active part in the movement are Prof. John Dewey, the Rev. Howard Mellish, the Rev. Anna Howard Shaw, Dr. Stephen S. Wise, Mrs. James Lees Laidlaw, Mrs. John O'Hara Cosgrave, Mrs. Inez Haynes Gilmore, Mrs. Frederick C. Howe, Miss Fola La Follette, and Prof. James T. Shotwell.

The letter addressed to the board asserted that the board's own investigation had proved that married women were most efficient and that their dismissal was at variance with the board's duty to the schools.

Appendix D: Nineteenth-Century Sociological Thought

[In the years following the publication of *Women and Economics*, Gilman became a founding member of the American Sociological Association (ASA). The rise of social science coincided with the popularization of evolutionary theory in the second half of the nineteenth century. Theories about evolution centred on the idea that the conditions of life are not fixed but, rather, undergo perpetual change and growth. The following passages, written by two of Gilman's ASA colleagues, introduce important intellectual context for Gilman's ideas about women, marriage, and the family. Taken together, and read alongside *Women and Economics*, they demonstrate how turn of the century intellectuals used evolutionary theory as a justification for a range of conservative and progressive political positions.

William Graham Sumner (1840–1910) was a social Darwinist and a leading conservative thinker. Sumner believed that human society is an extension of the natural world, and that human beings, like animals, are obliged to engage in an individual struggle for life. In his 1883 political essay *What Social Classes Owe to Each Other*, Sumner argues for the continuation of the *laissez faire* economic system (D1). He satirizes progressive reformers, accusing them of merely producing a "vast number of social ills" through their "tinkering muddling, and blundering." Sumner argues that reformers' attempts to "supervise" society are bound to set things off track; it is impossible to "get a revision of the laws of human life," he insists. *Women and Economics* directly challenges this view, emphasizing, instead, the possibility of progressive improvement for society. For Sumner, the policy of economic redistribution confiscates money from hard working, responsible Americans, and hands it over to the poor, essentially enabling the survival of individuals who would otherwise prove unfit for life—a problematic contravention of natural law, in Sumner's eyes. Sumner's particular brand of free-market, social Darwinian thought has had a lasting impact on conservative politics, and his concept of "the Forgotten Man" is still used today in conservative campaigning.

While conservatives such as Sumner argued that individuals must be allowed to succeed or fail on an individual basis, Lester Frank Ward (1841–1913) drew upon the principles of evolutionary science to make the case for broadening the regulatory powers of the national government. Ward was deeply skeptical of the idea that human society is identical to the natural world, and he rejected outright the idea—espoused by Sumner as well as wealthy industrialists such as Andrew Carnegie—that poor Americans are constitutionally less fit than their wealthy counterparts. In his book *Dynamic Sociology* (D2), Ward argues that evolution has conferred upon human beings the capacity for moral action. Human beings therefore must take responsibility for creating social environments in which all people—irrespective of racial, gender, or class background—might participate and improve together. This excerpt outlines the importance of "organized knowledge." For Ward—and Gilman, too—mass education is a precondition for an enlightened, rational society.

Gilman regarded the sexual subjection of women as a social phenomenon, rather than an essential characteristic of human life, and Ward's work on the sociology of gender influenced her thinking about the social value of female sexual selection. Ward, in turn, was impressed by Gilman, and he initiated correspondence with her after he came across her poetry. In the excerpt below, Ward draws a direct connection between the sexual and economic dimensions of male power, and he expresses his conviction that the "equality of the sexes will be the regeneration of humanity," an optimistic vision that similarly underlies much of Gilman's thinking in *Women and Economics*.]

1. From William Graham Sumner, *What Social Classes Owe to Each Other*, Harper and Brothers, 1883, pp. 13–27

It is commonly asserted that there are in the United States no classes, and any allusion to classes is resented. On the other hand, we constantly read and hear discussions of social topics in which the existence of social classes is assumed as a simple fact. "The poor," "the weak," "the laborers," are expressions which are used as if they had exact and well-understood definition. Discussions are made to bear upon the assumed rights, wrongs, and misfortunes of certain social classes; and all public speaking and writing consists, in a large measure, of the discussion of general plans for meeting the wishes of classes of people who have not been able to satisfy their own desires. These classes are sometimes discontented, and sometimes not. Sometimes they do not know that anything is amiss with them until the "friends of humanity" come to them with offers of aid. Sometimes they are discontented and envious. They do not take their achievements as a fair measure of their rights. They do not blame themselves or their parents for their lot, as compared with that of other people. Sometimes they claim that they have a right to everything of which they feel the need for their happiness on earth. To make such a claim against God or Nature would, of course, be only to say that we claim a right to live on earth if we can. But God and Nature have ordained the chances and conditions of life on earth once for all. The case cannot be reopened. We cannot get a revision of the laws of human life. We are absolutely shut up to the need and duty, if we would learn how to live happily, of investigating the laws of Nature, and deducing the rules of right living in the world as it is. These are very wearisome and commonplace tasks. They consist in labor and self-denial repeated over and over again in learning and doing. When the people whose claims we are considering are told to apply themselves to these tasks they become irritated and feel almost insulted. They formulate their claims as rights against society—that is, against some other men. In their view they have a right, not only to *pursue* happiness, but to *get* it; and if they fail to get it, they think they have a claim to the aid of other men—that is, to the labor and self-denial of other men—to get it for them. They find orators and poets who tell them that they have grievances, so long as they have unsatisfied desires.

Now, if there are groups of people who have a claim to other people's labor and self-denial, and if there are other people whose labor and self-denial are liable to be claimed by the first groups, then there certainly are "classes," and classes of the oldest and most vicious type. For a man who can command another man's labor and self-denial for the support of his own existence is a privileged person of the highest species conceivable on earth. Princes and paupers meet on this plane, and no other men are on it at all. On the other hand, a man whose labor and self-denial may be diverted from his maintenance to that of some other man is not a free man, and approaches more or less toward the position of a slave. Therefore we shall find that, in all the notions which we are to discuss, this elementary contradiction, that there are classes and that there are not classes, will produce repeated confusion and absurdity. We shall find that, in our efforts to eliminate the old vices of class government, we are impeded and defeated by new products of the worst class theory. We shall find that all the schemes for producing equality and obliterating the organization of society produce a new differentiation based on the worst possible distinction—the right to claim and the duty to give one man's effort for another man's satisfaction. We shall find that every effort to realize equality necessitates a sacrifice of liberty.

It is very popular to pose as a "friend of humanity," or a "friend of the working classes." The character, however, is quite exotic in the United States. It is borrowed from England, where some men, otherwise of small account, have assumed it with great success and advantage. Anything which has a charitable sound and a kind-hearted tone generally passes without investigation, because it is disagreeable to assail it. Sermons, essays, and orations assume a conventional standpoint with regard to the poor, the weak etc.; and it is allowed to pass as an unquestioned doctrine in regard to social classes that "the rich" ought to "care for the poor" ... and that clergymen, economists, and social philosophers have a technical and professional duty to devise schemes for "helping the poor." ...

Let us notice some distinctions which are of prime importance to a correct consideration of the subject which we intend to treat.

Certain ills belong to the hardships of human life. They are natural. They are part of the struggle with Nature for existence. We cannot blame our fellow-men for our share of these. My neighbor and I are both struggling to free ourselves from these ills. The fact that my neighbor has succeeded in this struggle better than I constitutes no grievance for me. Certain other ills are due to the malice of men, and to the imperfections or errors of civil institutions. These ills are an object of agitation, and a subject of discussion. The former class of ills is to be met only by manly effort and energy; the latter may be corrected by associated effort.... The distinction here made between the ills which belong to the struggle for existence and those which are due to the faults of human institutions is of prime importance....

Especially we shall need to notice the attempts to apply legislative methods of reform which belong to the order of Nature.

There is no possible definition of "a poor man." A pauper is a person who cannot earn his living; whose producing powers have fallen positively below his necessary consumption; who cannot, therefore, pay his way. A human society needs the active co-operation and productive energy of every person in it. A man who is present as a consumer, yet who does not contribute either by land, labor, or capital to the work of society, is a burden. On no sound political theory ought such a person to share in the political power of the State. He drops out of the ranks of workers and producers. Society must support him. It accepts the burden, but he must be canceled from the ranks of the rulers likewise. So much for the pauper. About him no more need be said. But he is not the "poor man." The "poor man" is an elastic term, under which any number of social fallacies may be hidden.

Neither is there any possible definition of "the weak." Some are weak in one way, and some in another; and those who are weak in one sense are strong in another. In general, however, it may be said that those whom humanitarians and philanthropists call the weak are the ones through whom the productive and conservative forces of society are wasted. They constantly neutralize and destroy the finest efforts of the wise and industrious, and are a dead weight on the society in all its struggles to realize any better things....

Under the names of the poor and the weak, the negligent, shiftless, inefficient, silly, and imprudent are fastened upon the industrious and prudent as a responsibility and a duty. On the one side, the terms are extended to cover the idle, intemperate, and vicious, who, by the combination, gain credit which they do not deserve, and which they could not get if they stood alone. On the other hand, the terms are extended to include wage-receivers of the humblest rank, who are degraded by the combination. The reader who desires to guard himself against fallacies should always scrutinize the terms "poor" and "weak" as used, so as to see which or how many of these classes they are made to cover.

The humanitarians, philanthropists, and reformers, looking at the facts of life as they present themselves, find enough which is sad and unpromising in the condition of many members of society. They see wealth and poverty side by side. They note great inequality of social position and social chances. They eagerly set about the attempt to account for what they see, and to devise schemes for remedying what they do not like. In their eagerness to recommend the less fortunate classes to pity and consideration they forget all about the rights of other classes; they gloss over all the faults of the classes in question, and they exaggerate their misfortunes and their virtues. They invent new theories of property, distorting rights and perpetrating injustice, as any one is sure to do who sets about the re-adjustment of social relations with the interests of one group distinctly before his mind, and the interests of all other groups thrown into the background. When I have read certain of these discussions I have thought it must be quite disreputable to be respectable, quite dishonest to own property, quite unjust to go one's own way and earn one's own living, and that the only really admirable person was the good-for-nothing. The man who by his own effort raises himself above poverty appears, in these discussions, to be of no account. The man who has done nothing to raise himself above poverty finds that social doctors flock about him, bringing the capital which they have collected from the other class, and promising him the aid of the State to give him what the other had to work for. In all these schemes and projects the organized intervention of society through the State is either planned or hoped for, and the State is thus made to become the protector and guardian of certain classes. The agents who are to direct the State action are, of course, the reformers and philanthropists. Their schemes, therefore, may always be reduced to this type—that A and B decide what C shall do for D. It will be interesting to inquire, at a later period of our discussion, who C is, and what the effect is upon him of all these arrangements. In all the discussions attention is concentrated on A and B, the noble social reformers, and on D, the "poor man." I call C the Forgotten Man, because I have never seen that any notice was taken of him in any of the discussions. When we have disposed of A, B, and D we can better appreciate the case of C, and I think that we shall find that he deserves our attention, for the worth of his character and the magnitude of his unmerited burdens. Here it may suffice to observe that, on the theories of the social philosophers to whom I have referred, we should get a new maxim of judicious living: Poverty is the best policy. If you get wealth, you will have to support other people; if you do not get wealth it will be the duty of other people to support you.

No doubt one chief reason for the unclear and contradictory theories of class relations lies in the fact that our society, largely controlled in all its organization by one set of doctrines, still contains survivals of old social theories which are inconsistent with the former. In the Middle Ages men were united by custom and prescription into associations, ranks, guilds, and communities of various kinds. These ties endured as long as life lasted. Consequently society was dependent, throughout all its details, on status, and the tie, or bond, was sentimental. In our modern state, and in the United States more than anywhere else, the social structure is based on contract, and status is of the least importance. Contract, however, is rational—even rationalistic. It is also realistic, cold, and matter-of-fact. A contract relation is based on a sufficient reason, not on custom or prescription. It is not permanent. It endures only so long as the reason for it endures. In a state based on contract sentiment is out of place in any public or common affairs. It is relegated to the sphere of private and personal relations, where it depends not at all on class types, but on personal acquaintance and personal estimates. The sentimentalists among us always seize upon the survivals of the old order. They want to save them and restore them. Much of the loose thinking also which troubles us in our social discussions arises from the fact that men do not distinguish the elements of status and of contract which may be found in our society.

Whether social philosophers think it desirable or not, it is out of the question to go back to status or to the sentimental relations which once united baron and retainer, master and servant, teacher and pupil, comrade and comrade. That we have lost some grace and elegance is undeniable. That life once held more poetry and romance is true enough. But it seems impossible that any one who has studied the matter should doubt that we have gained immeasurably, and that our farther gains lie in going forward, not in going backward. The feudal ties can never be restored. If they could be restored they would bring back personal caprice, favoritism, sycophancy, and intrigue. A society based on contract is a society of free and independent men, who form ties without favor or obligation, and cooperate without cringing or intrigue. A society based on contract, therefore, gives the utmost room and chance for individual development, and for all the self-reliance and dignity of a free man. That a society of free men, co-operating under contract, is by far the strongest society which has ever yet existed; that no such society has ever yet developed the full measure of strength of which it is capable; and that the only social improvements which are now conceivable lie in the direction of more complete realization of a society of free men united by contract, are points which cannot be controverted. It follows, however, that one man, in a free state cannot claim help from, and cannot be charged to give help to, another.

2. From Lester Frank Ward, *Dynamic Sociology of Applied Social Science*, Appleton and Company, 1883, pp. 8–25, 651–57

In the direction of organizing the known science the present epoch is very active. Two important principles of classification are now for the first time recognized and avowed. The one is that of a *causal dependence* in all the phenomena of nature ("monism"). The other is that of the *utilitarian object* of science.

The leading scientists and philosophers now realize and announce that all possible observable phenomena have real antecedents, and that therefore the work of investigating them is no longer a hopeless task, as it certainly would be if the possibility of the absolute independence of any phenomenon were admitted.

The leading thinkers of our time also now concede and declare that the only ultimate object which can be successfully maintained for human effort is the improvement of the human race upon this planet.

Under the healthy stimulus of these two cardinal principles, the work of organizing human knowledge is now progressing with great promise of soon reaching a high state of completeness. Not until the work of classifying the sciences could be undertaken with the clear recognition that they may be arranged in some sort of connected and ascending series, whereby an acquaintance with subordinate stages becomes essential to a complete appreciation of the higher ones, could any satisfactory arrangement of the groups of phenomena be made or expected.

Not until such a clew[1] was discovered and laid hold of, as the purpose of elevating humanity furnishes, could sufficient energy or perseverance be infused into the effort to insure for it a successful issue. The conception of a universal causal dependence of phenomena when transformed into an active working principle takes the shape of a universal theory of development or evolution. The high utilitarian motive, focalizing all considerations in the good of man, can have no other effect than to establish as the ultimate science, for the perfection of which all other sciences exist, the science of human life, which takes the form and name of sociology....

It is impossible ... to overestimate the importance of a well-defined object toward which human effort might be directed.

It is vain to expect men to put forth efforts unless some object is clearly set before them. It is further necessary that this object be a positive or constructive, and not a negative or destructive one. The tendency is to be perpetually building up. Negative objects, whose nature is to tear down, are undertaken with reluctance, and soon relinquished. To insure successful prosecution they must possess the elements of progress, and give earnest of carrying the world forward to a more advanced position. The failure of all religious systems to accomplish this is now apparent to all capable of observing the history of the world from a wholly unbiased stand-point. The influence of imaginary advanced

---

[1] Clue.

states beyond the present life has had no effect in securing such a state in this life. The moral systems that have been more or less mechanically mixed with religious ones have shown themselves incapable of progressing beyond a limit reached in the time of Confucius and Hillel.[1]

The need of some inspiring progressive principle for mankind to lay hold of, for the satisfaction of that fundamental sentiment which aspires to a better condition, is as strongly felt now as it was in the days of Plato or of Paul.[2]

The motive of all action is feeling. All great movements in history are preceded and accompanied by strong feelings. And it is those persons whose feelings have been most violent that have exerted the greatest influence upon the tone and character of society. Purely intellectual feeling is never sufficient directly to sway the multitude.... Throughout all time past, the mass of mankind has been carried along by the power of sentiment. It has never been deeply moved, at least directly, by that of intellect. Hence we see that the psychical agencies that have stirred up mankind have been chiefly of a religious nature. Religion is the embodied and organized state of the emotions. It represents the combined forces of human feeling. The immense success with which religious reformers have met has been due to the almost irresistible power of their emotional nature, and never to their intellectual supremacy.... What I desire to draw especial attention to here is the remarkable fact that not only has the world been thus far ruled by passion and not by intellect, but that the true rulers of the world have had to be, in order to win that distinction, not merely enthusiasts and fanatics, but, in the majority of cases, insane persons, in a certain legitimate acceptation of that term. It is no longer a question among modern medical men that the remarkable actions of those men who have laid claims to divine inspiration and founded religious systems must be referred not only to a pathological but to an actually deranged condition of their minds.

The strange truth thus comes up for our contemplation that, instead of having been guided and impelled by intellect and reason throughout all the years of history, we have been ruled and swayed by the magnetic passions of epileptics and monomaniacs.

---

1 Confucius: Chinese philosopher (c. 551–479 BCE); Hillel: Jewish philosopher (c. 110 BCE–10 CE).
2 Plato: Greek philosopher (c. 429–347 BCE); Paul: St. Paul the apostle (c. 4–64 CE).

But this startling fact only shows us the more forcibly that it is feeling and not intellect which is required to influence human action. Indeed, this proposition is capable not only of a logical and a psychological, but of a truly physical, demonstration. Still, as it is somewhat obscure, it needs the aid of such an illustration as the above to bring it home to the mind. Those persons (and there are some very enlightened ones) who hope one day to see this state of society reversed, and who are looking forward to the time when intellect and reason shall assume control of society, dethroning passion and emotion, are doomed to disappointment, not only in their own time but for ever. Intellect is not an impelling but a directing force. Feeling alone can drive on the social train, whether for weal or woe.

This is one of the great facts which the sociologist, laying aside all personal bias and seeking only the real and the true, must clearly realize and frankly acknowledge, and which, having realized and acknowledged, he must respect by shaping his philosophical system to correspond with fact. Renouncing the hope of an intellectual rule, admitting the right of feeling, or, if he please, of passion, to control the world, it becomes his duty to address himself to the only task remaining, and to inquire candidly how, taking facts as they are, the existing condition of society is to be ameliorated.

All reform which is hoped to bring about by argument, persuasion, or any of the means available to the philosopher, must hold forth moral rather than intellectual inducements.... The condition of society is at all times so bad, the degree of suffering every-where witnessed is so great, and the amount of sympathy thereby excited and constantly experienced in society is so intense, that there has never been an age when there did not exist a deep-seated demand for some improvement of the existing state of things. The great moral systems of the remote past which have sought to accomplish this, owing no doubt to their failure to do so, were gradually transformed in more modern times into religious systems which made no promises for this life, which they perceived could not be fulfilled, but only held out the highest hopes for another life, by which the failure of fulfilment could never be proved. Both classes of systems succeeded because they were adapted each to the degree of credulity of the people to whom they were addressed. As the failure of the first began to be felt, the second were brought forward. Now that in our age the fulfilment of the promises held out by the latter is coming more and more in question, there has been a rapid and increasing amount of dissatisfaction, until the present prevailing systems now fail to respond to the still undiminished demand for better things. But the failure of all previous systems, both moral and religious, to fulfill their promises, makes some despair that any will ever be offered which shall succeed. Others think differently, and still hope that some fundamental movement may yet be set on foot which shall lead to the real improvement of society. The demand is for—1, an increase of enjoyment; and, 2, a diminution of suffering. It is, moreover, of a twofold character—subjective and objective. The motive principle of the former is egoism; that of the latter, altruism.

Egoism is the feeling which demands for self an increase of enjoyment and diminution of discomfort. Altruism is that which demands these results for others. Of course, it can ... be shown ... that ... egoism and altruism are one, that altruism is only an indirect or mediate form of egoism in which the motive is *sympathy*, i.e., a kind of feeling which results from the contemplation of suffering in others, and which is strong in proportion as the organization is delicate and refined. For this reason, and not because it is of a distinct nature, is altruism a far higher and nobler, though thus far a much less powerful, sentiment than egoism....

The problem is to apply the vast emotional forces which are ever striving to improve society, but failing for want of the proper intellectual guidance, to some truly progressive system of machinery that shall succeed in accomplishing the desired end.... [T]he intellect alone cannot do this. It must be joined to facts. In short what is really required is *knowledge*.

Knowledge is simply truth apprehended by the intellect. Intelligent mind, fortified with knowledge, is the only reliable form of the directive force. The only proper knowledge for this purpose is that which can be acquired of the materials and the forces of nature. As it is the utilizing of these which alone can secure the end sought, so the knowledge of these is the prime necessity in the exercise of a directive control over human zeal for the improvement of mankind. Hence the diffusion of this kind of knowledge among the masses of mankind is the only hope we have of securing greater social progress than that which nature itself vouchsafes through its own process of selection. But the knowledge referred to is just that which is embraced in the word *science*, and the diffusion of it is the process which goes by the name of *education*....

It may be asked: "Where can this knowledge be obtained? Must we go to nature for it and dig it out of the bowels of the earth before we can scatter it among men?" This is now happily unnecessary. Unaided nature, operating upon man as upon animals and plants, has impelled him to seek this knowledge for himself, and, obeying this strictly biological law, he has brought to light a vast mass of truth, sufficient, if properly distributed, to place society on the highway to permanent prosperity. But, as the movement, being a purely natural one, has been strictly egoistic, this mass of knowledge has remained locked up in the minds of a few persons, and has only been allowed to exert an indirect influence on the state of society, and scarcely any on the great majority of its individual members. Further, society at large, which has come into the possession of the greater part of this knowledge, has taken no pains to secure its diffusion among its members. The only means of obtaining this knowledge is for each individual to seek it out for himself—an effort which not one in a thousand could afford to make, even should he chance to have a desire. The great majority never even learn the fact that any such fund of knowledge exists in the world. Comparatively few have any idea of its value.

It is customary in our day to recommend in the strongest terms the extension to all our higher institutions of the facilities for increasing knowledge, for independent original research.... This is well, but the fact is that not one-hundredth part of the facts which original research has already brought forth are to-day obtainable by the one-hundredth part of the members of society, so that not one truth in ten thousand is fully utilized. Why go on bringing forth new truth, when in the existing state of society it is impossible to make a proper use of what we already have? It would not be difficult to demonstrate that this constant accumulation of materials for progress so far beyond the capacity of society to utilize them, or even become conscious of their existence, exerts along with some direct benefits a large amount of indirect evil to society itself. It is like gorging the stomach to repletion in the hope that thereby nutrition may be increased.... To this influence, if I mistake not, is to be ascribed the greater part of the evils of which modern society complains. Every cultivated man has often wondered at the extraordinary degree of refinement to which many branches of knowledge have been carried. Considered independently of each other, nearly every so-called science, not to speak of the arts both useful and aesthetic, has been pursued to the most astonishing heights of specialization, and carried out through the most delicate and multiplied ramifications.... Volumes have been written and profusely illustrated with elegant plates to describe the species of certain plants and animals whose practical use to mankind is not appreciable, and is not in the slightest degree increased by such accurate knowledge on the part of a few specialists. Considering the number of important and fundamental problems which every science always presents, and the manner in which these are neglected, while such abstruse and useless niceties are spun out by specialists, I have been led to believe that, except as goaded on by personal want, the human intellect prefers trifles and hairbreadth subtleties to the serious investigation of truth. This tendency, so manifest in science, has, as all know, been still more pronounced in philosophy, and every human effort is constantly in danger of degenerating into a gymnastic.

But not only is all the human knowledge in the world confined to a few, but each different kind of knowledge is in the exclusive possession of a small class of these few; not only is the mass of mankind excluded from knowledge, but those who have any possess only a minute fraction of the useful knowledge extant. It is all chance-work; there is no system, no general scheme for the dissemination of truth. This is of course the worst feature, but second only to it stands the unorganized state of knowledge itself. If knowledge could be diffused, there is probably causality enough in the world to co-ordinate and arrange it. But, unfortunately, those who possess it have obtained it through the mere love of facts, and belong to the class who see only relations of coexistence and not of dependence, and hence, as they hold on to their facts and are incompetent to classify them, they are never generalized and therefore never utilized; or else they come at their knowledge through the force of necessity, like the breeders and gardeners, and have no time or desire to inquire after principles. In either case, their knowledge remains useless, or exerts its beneficial effects only within a very limited circle. Unorganized knowledge cannot be utilized.

The Subjection of Women

The first step toward the subjugation of the female sex was the conquest by the males of her prerogative of selection. This was the surrender of her *virtue* in the primary sense of the term—of her *power* over men, over society, over her own interests. But this crisis was brought on wholly by the force of male passion. It was a victory for male indulgence. Won by the aid of strategy and of superior mental power, it not only secured the result aimed at, but it led to the dominion of man over women. It is one of the few instances where nature seems to have overshot its mark. The very excess of passion with which man (along with the males of all other species) is endowed, and which was apparently designed to prevent the possibility of the failure of reproduction, became, when coupled with this increased mind-force incident to a certain stage of intellectual development, the means of effecting the most extensive and systematic violations of natural laws, and of imposing serious barriers to reproduction itself. Nothing but its very gradual introduction and the slow habituation of woman to the change could have saved the whole race from extinction before the dawn of civilization. Again, the sexual passion in man was one cause of a more rapid intellectual development in him than in woman. Superior cunning, i.e., sharper wits may be regarded as a secondary sexual character as much as the tusks of the boar or the spurs of the cock. Whatever was necessary to insure success in courtship was sure to be developed, and, when cunning became a safe weapon, it rapidly increased in the males until they outstripped the females in vigor of intellect.

It is undoubtedly true that the weaker physical condition of women during the period of gestation and parturition did much to give the advantage to the males. Although we do not perceive any special disposition on the part of other female animals at these times to make themselves dependent upon the males, we can readily understand how, with a higher development of the intellect, and especially of the sensibilities, they might learn to do so. In so far as this has been the case, the present dependent state of women upon men is to be referred to the second great class of results of the operations of the social forces.

But, to follow out the first line of development, we find that woman has already made her first great surrender, and permitted man to become the chooser in the matter of sexual unions instead of herself. He could not stop here.... [T]he various systems of marriage grew up out of this fundamental fact. Woman at once becomes property, since any thing that affords its possessor gratification is property. Woman was capable of affording man the highest of gratifications, and therefore became property of the highest value. Marriage, under the prevailing form, became the symbol of transfer of ownership, in the same manner as the formal seizing of lands. The passage from sexual service to manual service on the part of women was perfectly natural. If woman was man's property for sexual purposes, he would certainly claim that she was so also for all other purposes, and thus we find that the women of most savage tribes perform the manual and servile labor of the camp.

In the earliest ages, when nations were devoted to continual warfare, the duties of men were defined, and, while the women were left behind to care for the children and perform the baser services, the men went forth to war, or took upon them the affairs of the state. This distribution of the labor of the sexes has always been preserved, as nearly as the state of society would permit. No moral or intellectual progress has been sufficient to shake it. The broad recognition of the social equality of the sexes has never been distinctly and practically made. All pretensions to it have been contradicted by the treatment of women, by their exclusion from the most honorable forms of labor, and by withholding from them social, civil, and political rights. To affirm that women are the recognized social equals of men is to betray the prevalent incapacity to see the plainest facts in a rational or abstract light, the inability to see them in any but a conventional light....

If the social equality of the sexes were recognized, we should see men and women performing substantially the same duties.... There would be found very few avenues to wealth or happiness which woman would be incapacitated to enter from purely physical reasons. There are, indeed, very few of them that women have not in some rare cases actually entered and successfully labored in. But if their true equality were recognized, it would not be left for the few who dared to defy the rules of propriety to step forth into fields of usefulness to labor by the side of man. Not only would the duties, labors, and occupations of men be shared by women, but their pastimes, recreations, and pleasures as well.... The present system, both of labor and of recreation, is calculated to bring out the worst side of sexuality. The separate duties and spheres in which the two sexes labor and move tend to render the desire for association a prurient one. The varied restraints of propriety and modesty have the effect of fanning human passions into a flame, and a consequence of this is that both sexes are liable to be whelmed in a vortex of crime, and their character and usefulness ruined. Equality in all respects would prove a certain antidote to all these social evils. It would do far more. It would transfer to the list of productive laborers the legion of women who now deem themselves wholly justified in occupying a position of dependency upon man, and consuming the fruits of his labor without adding the value of a loaf of bread to the wealth of the world. For this non-producing condition of civilized women is an anomaly in the animal world, and even among human races....

The true progress of society must eventually complete the cycle of changes thus begun, and again make both sexes producers, as in the animal and pre-social stages.

If the equality of the sexes were recognized, we should see both sexes educated alike. We should see women admitted along with men, not merely to the common schools, but to all the higher institutions of learning, to the professions and to the technical departments. We should see the principle applied that it is mind which needs instruction, not male mind. Men and women would then stand on an equal intellectual footing, and intellectual superiority, without regard to which sex it appeared in, would receive its just recognition....

The Male Sex not responsible.—In what has been said respecting the dependent and almost servile social condition of the female sex, I should be sorry to be misunderstood upon one point where I fear I may have left room for an unjust inference. Although I have been careful to avoid all allusion to the question of who is responsible for this condition of things, I am aware that the human mind is prone to infer that where matters are bad someone must be to blame, and to assume that, where a state of things is so organized as to discriminate against one class and in favor of another, the class which derives the benefit must somehow be responsible; and I have feared that for these reasons some of my readers might class me in the list of those who see in the male sex only a confederacy of usurpers and tyrants, who do nothing but seek for further means of humiliating and subjecting the female sex for their own gratification and emolument.[1] If any have been inclined to accuse me of this species of *misandry*, they need simply to be reminded that I have been only seeking to study the condition of society, not to criticize the conduct of its members. If there is any responsibility in a sociological phenomenon, it must rest upon society as a whole.... The mere handful of enlightened protesters, who have become aroused within the past few years to a vague sense of their true condition, is but the very embryo of the movement which would be required to accomplish the emancipation of woman. And it is not so much experience as philosophy which is agitating the question. The victims of the system are usually silent, or, if they speak, it is but the bitter language of discontent unsupported by the philosophic analysis of the subject which can alone give weight to their utterances. The greatest champions of social reform are, and will

---

1 For their own profit or reward.

always be, those who possess the capacity to grasp great social truths and an insight into human nature and the causes of social phenomena deep enough to kindle a genuine sympathy, and a sound, rational philanthropy. This phenomenon, like all others, is the result of causes operating through enumerable ages, and for which there is no more responsibility than there is for the physical transformations which species undergo from the operations of similar causes during still more immense periods. And, although the results may be bad and entail evil upon society, though they be irrational, absurd, and pernicious, they are none the less due to causes sufficient in their time to produce them, and their genesis, or true explanation, though perhaps too obscure for man ever to unfold, would still be traceable to their earliest origin if all the circumstances could be known. A state of society, if it be bad for one class, be bad for all. Woman is scarcely a greater sufferer from her condition than man is, and there is, therefore, nothing either improper or inexplicable in man's espousing the cause of woman's emancipation. The freedom of woman will be the ennoblement of man. The equality of the sexes will be the regeneration of humanity. Civilization demands this revolution. It stands in the greatest need of the help which the female sex alone can vouchsafe. Woman is half of mankind.

Works Cited and Select Bibliography

Allen, Judith A. *The Feminism of Charlotte Perkins Gilman: Sexualities, Histories, Progressivism.* U of Chicago P, 2009.

Amigoni, David, and Jeff Wallace, editors. *Charles Darwin's The Origin of Species: New Interdisciplinary Essays.* U of Manchester P, 1995.

Bannister, Robert C. *Social Darwinism: Science and Myth in Anglo-American Social Thought.* Temple UP, 1979.

Barker, Drucilla, and Edith Kuiper. *Toward a Feminist Philosophy of Economics.* Routledge, 2003.

Bederman, Gail. *Manliness and Civilization: A Cultural History of Gender and Race in the United States, 1880–1917.* U of Chicago P, 1995.

Beecher, Lyman. *Autobiography of Lyman Beecher.* Edited by Barbara M. Cross, Belknap Press, 1961.

Blackwell, Antoinette Brown. *The Sexes Throughout Nature.* G.P. Putnam's Sons, 1875.

Bowler, Peter J. *Evolution: The History of an Idea.* U of California P, 1989.

Buhle, Mari Jo. *Women and American Socialism 1870–1920.* U of Illinois P, 1981.

Carnegie, Andrew. "Wealth." *The North American Review*, June 1889, pp. 653–64.

"Charlotte Gilman Dies to Avoid Pain." *New York Times*, 20 Aug. 1935, p. 44.

Darwin, Charles. *Descent of Man, and Selection in Relation to Sex.* J. Murray, 1871.

———. *The Origin of Species.* John Murray, 1859.

Davis, Cynthia J. *Charlotte Perkins Gilman: A Biography.* Stanford UP, 2010.

de Tocqueville, Alexis. "Democracy in America." *Democracy in America and Two Essays on America*, translated by Gerald E. Bevan with an introduction and notes by Isaac Kramnick, Penguin, 2003, pp. 1–862.

Deutscher, Penelope. "The Descent of Man and the Evolution of Woman." *Hypatia*, vol. 19, no. 2, 2004, pp. 35–55.

Drummond, Henry. *The Lowell Lectures on the Ascent of Man.* 1884. James Pott & Co., 1898.

Du Bois, W.E.B. *Darkwater: Voices from Within the Veil.* Harcourt, Brace, and Howe, 1920.

Emerson, Ralph Waldo. "Self-Reliance." *Nature and Selected Essays*, edited by Larzer Ziff, Penguin, 2003, pp. 175–204.

Engels, Friedrich. *The Origin of the Family: Private Property and the State.* 1844. C. H. Kerr & Company, 1902.

Erskine, Fiona. "*The Origin of Species* and the Science of Female Inferiority." Amigoni and Wallace, pp. 95–121.

Finlay, Barbara. "Lester Frank Ward as a Sociologist of Gender: A New Look at his Sociological Work." *Gender & Society*, vol. 13, no. 2, 1999, pp. 251–65.

Geddes, Patrick, and John Arthur Thomson. *Evolution of Sex.* Walter Scott, 1889.

Gilman, Charlotte Perkins. "Comment and Review." *Forerunner*, vol. 5, Jan. 1914, pp. 26–27.

——— [Charlotte Perkins Stetson]. *In This Our World*. McCombs and Vaughn Publishers, 1893.

———. *The Living of Charlotte Perkins Gilman*. Edited by Ann J. Lane, U of Wisconsin P, 1990.

Hamlin, Kimberly A. *From Eve to Evolution: Darwin, Science, and Women's Rights in Gilded Age America*. U of Chicago P, 2014.

Hill, Mary A. *Charlotte Perkins Gilman: The Making of a Radical Feminist, 1860–1896*. Temple UP, 1980.

Kelly, Walter Keating. *Proverbs of All Nations*. W. Kent & Co., 1859.

Kohlstedt, Sally Gregory, and Mark R. Jorgensen. "'The Irrepressible Woman Question': Women's Responses to Evolutionary Ideology." Amigoni and Wallace, pp. 268–93.

Lamarck, Jean-Baptiste. *Zoological Philosophy*. Musée d'Histoire Naturelle, 1809.

Lorde, Audre. *Sister Outsider*. Penguin, 2007.

Madden, Kirsten, and Robert W. Dimand, editors. *Routledge Handbook of the History of Women's Economic Thought*. Routledge, 2018.

McGerr, Michael E. *A Fierce Discontent: The Rise and Fall of the Progressive Movement in America, 1870–1920*. Oxford UP, 2005.

Necker, Anne Louise Germaine [Madame de Staël-Holstein]. *De l'influence des passions sur le bonheur des individus et des nations*. J. Mourer, 1796.

Nelson, Julie A. *Feminism, Objectivity and Economics*. Routledge, 1996.

Nelson, Julie A., and Marianne Ferber. *Feminist Economics Today: Beyond Economic Man*. U of Chicago P, 2003.

Newman, Louise Michele, editor. *Men's Ideas, Women's Realities: Popular Science, 1870–1915*. Pergamon, 1985.

Numbers, Ronald L., and John Stenhouse, editors. *Disseminating Darwinism: The Role of Place, Race, Religion, and Gender*. Cambridge UP, 1999.

Piott, Steven L. *American Reformers, 1870–1920: Progressives in Word and Deed*. Rowman & Littlefield, 2006.

Rafferty, Edward. *Apostle of Human Progress: Lester Frank Ward and American Political Thought, 1841–1913*. Rowman & Littlefield, 2003.

Richards, Evelleen. "Darwin and the Descent of Woman." *The Wider Domain of Evolutionary Thought*, edited by David Oldroyd and Ian Langham, D. Reidel, 1983, pp. 57–111.

Satter, Beryl. *Each Mind a Kingdom: American Women, Sexual Purity, and the New Thought Movement, 1875–1920*. U of California P, 1999.

Scharnhorst, Gary. *Charlotte Perkins Gilman, a Bibliography*. Scarecrow, 1985.

Spencer, Herbert. *First Principles*. 1862. D. Appleton, 1864.

Stetson, Charles Walter. *Endure: The Diaries of Charles Walter Stetson*. Edited by Mary Armfield Hill, Temple UP, 1985.

Sumner, William Graham. *What Social Classes Owe to Each Other*. New York: Harper and Brothers, 1883.

Van Wienen, Mark W. *American Socialist Triptych: The Literary-Political Work of Charlotte Perkins Gilman, Upton Sinclair, and W. E. B. Du Bois*. U of Michigan P, 2014.

Veblen, Thorstein. *The Theory of the Leisure Class; An Economic Study in the Evolution of Institutions*. London: Macmillan, 1899.

Ward, Lester Frank. *Dynamic Sociology*. New York: D. Appleton, 1883.

Washington, Mary Helen. "Anna Julia Cooper: The Black Feminist Voice of the 1890s." *Legacy*, vol. 4, no. 2, 1987, pp. 3–15.

Weinbaum, Alys Eve. "Writing Feminist Genealogy: Charlotte Perkins Gilman, Racial Nationalism, and the Reproduction of Maternalist Feminism." *Feminist Studies*, vol. 27, no. 2, 2001, pp. 271–302.

"Women of Brains as Wives." *The San Francisco Examiner*, 25 Dec. 1892, p. 6.

From the Publisher

A name never says it all, but the word "Broadview" expresses a good deal of the philosophy behind our company. We are open to a broad range of academic approaches and political viewpoints. We pay attention to the broad impact book publishing and book printing has in the wider world; for some years now we have used 100% recycled paper for most titles. Our publishing program is internationally oriented and broad-ranging. Our individual titles often appeal to a broad readership too; many are of interest as much to general readers as to academics and students.

Founded in 1985, Broadview remains a fully independent company owned by its shareholders—not an imprint or subsidiary of a larger multinational.

To order our books or obtain up-to-date information, please visit broadviewpress.com.

broadview press
www.broadviewpress.com